T0099053

"In *Fuck Neoliberalism*, Springer takes aim at more or less everyone (himself included) who continues to reproduce the power of the neoliberal cop in our heads. By thinking and saying the simple phrase 'fuck it,' he argues, we can affirm our rejection, our critique of neoliberalism, but also crucially a desiring energy to create other ways of thinking, being, and doing beyond neoliberal logics. Not even writers of blurbs to be printed on the back of books are exempt from Springer's powerful and provocative call to arms. And on that note, fuck it, I'm outta here."

—Anthony Ince, lecturer in Human
Geography at Cardiff University

Fuck Neoliberalism
Translating Resistance
Simon Springer

Fuck Neoliberalism: Translating Resistance
© Simon Springer
This edition © 2021 PM Press

ISBN: 978-1-62963-789-1 (print)
ISBN: 978-1-62963-813-3 (ebook)
Library of Congress Control Number: 2019946100

Front cover artwork by Ed Repka © 2018
Cover by John Yates / www.stealworks.com
Interior design by briandesign

10 9 8 7 6 5 4 3 2 1

PM Press
PO Box 23912
Oakland, CA 94623
www.pmpress.org

Printed in the USA.

*For all those who have been fucked over by neoliberalism
and suffered as a result of its abhorrent violence.
Fuck it to hell.*

Contents

Introduction

"I wondered if the author Simon Springer really existed. That's the kind of name you'd make up for a comic novel. But, yes, he's real, and he's spectacular."
—*Steven Hayward, Ronald Reagan Professor of Public Policy, Pepperdine University*

Bullying. Defamation. Harassment. Threats of violence. These are the battle scars of having dared to write a paper titled "Fuck Neoliberalism." In defying standard academic convention and its penchant for pompousness, theoretical detachment from reality, and a general stick-up-the-butt protocol, the paper became a lightning rod for the conservative defenders of moral righteousness who descended upon me in legion following its publication. But even before the paper was published, the first sancti-monious guardian of the academic citadel arrived on his high horse. The chair of my former department had less than kind and supportive words for me. I first delivered the paper as a conference talk in San Francisco for the annual American Association of Geographers meeting in April 2016. The week after I returned from that meeting, he cornered me in the hallway and proceeded to berate me in front of a colleague and graduate student. He informed me that I was ruining the reputation of the department, and that my work couldn't be taken seriously. I replied that my paper, like all my work, was deadly serious. He insisted my work was a joke, and that it wasn't up to scientific standards. Well I'm glad to have made him laugh, but otherwise I'm not a scientist. So what? He told me that I should think about how my nonsense impacts upon my colleagues, and that the paper was completely inappropriate. It was the abstract in particular that irked him ("Yep, fuck it. Neoliberalism sucks. We don't need it"). I told him it was my academic freedom to write whatever I wanted. He insisted that academic freedom is one thing, but that it only goes so far and shouldn't extend to cursing in academic forums. Piling on the reactionary bullshit, he claimed that my use of profanity was akin to pornography and an embarrassment for the university. He indicated that senior administrators had been informed and my job was at risk. Amazing! We are off to the races!

Things were relatively calm for a good while thereafter. I didn't get fired, but I did submit a formal complaint to my Faculty Association about threats being made to my academic freedom. The result was ongoing harassment and bullying for the next few years at the hands of various administrators and senior colleagues. In terms of "Fuck Neoliberalism," the response was extremely positive from other scholars but turned sour almost two years later when Powerline, one of the most popular conservative blogs in the United States ran a story about my paper called "Neoliberal Madness."* The blog entry, written by Professor Steven Hayward, included a range of ad hominem attacks and stirred up a hornet's nest of hate in my direction. My email inbox was suddenly flooded with messages telling me what a horrible person

---

* Steven Hayward, "Neoliberal Madness," Powerline, February 27, 2018, accessed September 8, 2020, https://www.powerlineblog.com/archives/2018/02/neoliberal-madness.php.

I was, demanding that I outline an alternative world to capitalism if I was so clever, informing me that I should be ashamed of myself, and otherwise congratulating me on my "efforts in proving doctorates in geography to be even more intellectually specious and idiotic than those in education, neo-Marxist/women's/queer/Latino/Black/Muslim/et al. studies and all other self-indulgent pseudo-intellectual endeavors." Lovely stuff. Powerline is well known for its inflamed comments section, where usually the spewing of hatred and all manner of bigotry and trolling are tolerated, but things got too hot for even them to handle. They eventually closed the discussion on Hayward's entry and deleted all the comments, perhaps recognizing that some of the threats that were being made on their page would place them in legal hot water if they didn't do something about it. But Professor Hayward can hardly be blamed, since he was only living up to his title of "Ronald Reagan Professor of Public Policy" at Pepperdine University. The irony was not lost on me. Unfortunately, irony is not good old Stevie's strong suit. I posted the "fabulous" quote that opens this paper to my website, something he soon discovered and subsequently felt necessary to further blog about.* He insisted to his followers, lest anyone misinterpret his actual intentions, that he was calling me "a boob." I wrote to him personally to thank him again for the glowing, "boobtastic" endorsement.

Endorsed Defamation and Forced Resignation

Not to be outdone, Canada's favorite plagiarist and rape culture denier Margaret Wente wrote a scathing—and

---

* Steven Hayward, "Loose Ends," Powerline, August 24, 2018, accessed September 8, 2020, https://www.powerlineblog.com/archives/2018/08/loose-ends-44.php.

once again ironic—piece on the supposed curbing of free speech on Canadian campuses. The *Globe and Mail*, Canada's national newspaper, gave her a soapbox, publishing a piece that sought to defend the dangerous and hateful right-wing speech of Rick Mehta and Jordan Peterson, while using me and my work as a scapegoat for all that is supposedly wrong with what she calls the "hothouse world of today's universities." She was obviously quite twisted up about my paper, and, stripping the agency of students, she wrote that "students don't need a safe space to protect them from the likes of Prof. Mehta. They need responsible adults to protect them from the likes of Prof. Springer, whose brand of rubbish is depressingly common at our institutions of higher learning."* She concluded with an open invitation for my harassment and the incitement for more hate mail to be sent my way, asserting, "Too bad nobody complains about them. It's about time they did." The comment section there once again had to be closed "for legal reasons or for abuse." Despite running a piece that directly attacked me and was clearly defamatory, the *Globe and Mail* refused to run my response. I asked for a forum of the same space that Wente was afforded to dribble her hatred, and they flatly refused. I was told to write a letter to the editor of 150 words or less. I did just that, and, ultimately, they published it, but not without first editing my words without consultation or permission to do so. They vacated my response of its political content in an effort to protect themselves from having to admit that they willingly published something that called for my targeted harassment. I wrote a longer response published in the

---

* Margaret Wente, "You Can't Say That on Campus," *Globe and Mail*, March 3, 2018, accessed September 8, 2020, https://www.theglobeandmail.com/opinion/you-cant-say-that-on-campus/article38174267.

Conversation that covered some ground in identifying the discourse of "free speech" as a ruse to promote hate speech.[*]

The notorious—while having nothing worthwhile to say—Jordan Peterson shared my response, mocking it on Twitter and his Facebook page, which shook the fragile conservative foundation once more, and a renewed avalanche of hate mail came crashing down on top of me. Good thing I grew up in northern British Columbia, so I'm not really fazed by the snow. Thus, when the small-time internet troll Benjamin Boyce started receiving attention for his pathetic reading of my paper, he received a chilly cease and desist order from YouTube for violating copyright laws. While the original article is published as Creative Commons, that is for noncommercial purposes. Boyce was trying to profit off my work by using it as a platform to beg for money on Patreon. He cried foul and tried to argue that it was ironic for an anarchist to write against neoliberalism and then use copyright law to shut him down. But the only irony is the entitlement that neoliberals feel they have to the commons. He was more than happy to accumulate the fruits of my labor and claim it was his to harvest. Fortunately, his attempts to profit were frozen, but not before a new onslaught of hatred was directed at me.

From all this I learned a few key lessons. First, that irony is not the strong suit of the political right. They appear to be absolutely clueless, which honestly shouldn't surprise anyone. Second, I didn't realize how empty the lives of so many people who were willing to take time out of their day to send me messages attacking my character,

---

[*] Simon Springer, "Anarchist Professor Takes on Hate Speech," Conversation, March 21, 2018, accessed September 8, 2020, https://theconversation.com/anarchist-professor-takes-on-hate-speech-93606.

my personhood, and my family were. I felt sympathy in many ways, because it speaks to the isolation of neoliberalism. These are people who were seeking connection, and, when unable to find it in a positive sense, sought it in negative ways. Finally, my former university, in its cold and callous neoliberal ways, was not only unwilling to offer any support in the face of all the public bullying I was subjected to but were also unprepared to address the harassment I was receiving closer to home. I left that position at the end of 2018 as a result.

Found in Translation

So why translate this article into multiple languages and present it as a book? The answer is twofold. First, neoliberalism is not a phenomenon that is limited to the English language or the English-speaking world. It is a plague upon the whole of the globe. Second, for as much of a shitstorm that this article resulted in on the right, it was equally embraced and celebrated on the left. Never before in my career have I received so much attention, love, and support for an article from other likeminded individuals. Along with the groundswell of hate mail, I was also overwhelmed with the outpouring of support and affirmation from students, activists, and scholars around the world. The idea of translating the paper into multiple languages began very organically, with people approaching me and asking if they could translate it. They communicated their initial surprise and delight with the bluntness of the title, but then found a deeper connection to the message of the article, which they recognized as having emancipatory potential within their own cultural and linguistic frame of reference. The eventual translators of the article repeatedly told me that they would love people in their own countries and cultures to be able to read it in their native tongue. The rationale was quite simply to help spread the message of resistance and solidarity against neoliberalism further afield, beyond the confines of academia, and beyond the limited audience that the English language could offer. In this respect I have come to view translation as a means of countering some of the Anglophonic hegemony that exists within contemporary academia, and since neoliberalism itself is a great homogenizer that results in power asymmetries, there is a need to adopt resistance strategies that help to move us beyond the similar homogenization that occurs within the Anglo-American traditions of academia.

Translation provides a space to work around linguistic hegemonies and toward exploring different interpretive contexts and methods. Given the power of neoliberalism to mutate and articulate within preexisting political economic contexts, the limitations of the English language could never speak to how neoliberalism is experienced in Cambodia or Brazil or Turkey. Since translations can never be viewed as representing a pure transferal of meaning, translating "Fuck Neoliberalism" offered an attempt to enter into the multiple specificities of neoliberalism in different locations where new meaning could be created in response to this powerful form of political, social, and economic violence. As hybrid texts, translations necessitate a shift in meaning that has even greater potential to subvert existing neoliberal logics precisely because "the translator and the translated text are all embedded in their own specific and unique circumstances."[*] This is also why I asked translators to reflect on the article and their translation of it. You will find a brief passage from each translator prior to their translation of the text, as an

---

[*] Shadia Husseini de Arüjo and Mélina Germes, "For a Critical Practice of Translation in Geography," *Acme: An International Journal for Critical Geographies* 15, no. 1 (2016): 1–14.

attempt to shed some light on their goals and motivations and hopefully add even more depth of meaning to their interpretations of the work. Translations inevitably result in a change to the original, and it is my hope that in these shifts in context and meaning, the power of neoliberalism is weakened further still. As we come to a greater understanding of the local and the global as intimately interconnected, my greatest wish is that this book will play a small part in facilitating the translation of local resistance into renewed forms of global action toward a better tomorrow.

Awaiting the Hour of Reprisal

A hoped for better future seems to be well within our reach, something that moments of crisis always bring into sharp relief, precisely because they not only force us to reappraise our priorities both as individuals and as communities, but also because they require us to return to what we know—and have always inherently known—is our best strategy for survival as a species, namely, mutual aid. As we were plunged headlong into the COVID-19 pandemic, a moment in time that has awoken collective human consciousness to the fragility of our systems of organizing (i.e., states and capitalism) in ways that we couldn't have foreseen only a few short months ago, we have seen mutual aid groups spring up all around the world. It would seem that when the shit hits the fan, everyone becomes an anarchist. The flood of community organizing and the expansion of our circles of care beyond our immediate family and friends into our wider communities have prefigured optimism into tangible acts of transformation. As the threatening skies of a virus converge around the insecurities of our health care systems and livelihoods, these rays of sunshine bursting through the otherwise darkened clouds of our despair have been most welcome. But as we seemingly stand on the precipice of systemic change, where some are even heralding of the end of neoliberalism, we should be mindful that the toughest battle is yet to come. Neoliberalism is far more slippery and mutable than most people anticipate, and it's not going to retire without a sustained war of attrition.

While at the time of this writing I am still employed at a university, we know that the higher education sector sits at the frontlines of neoliberal groupthink, and my days could very well be numbered. While a similar situation plays itself out across the planet, here in Australia approximately thirty thousand jobs are at risk as neoliberalism continues to rear its ugly head in the context of university responses. The language of "agility" now stands in for "austerity," presumably because it sounds sharper and doesn't yet have the same negative connotation. But even if the language has changed, the song remains the same, and administrators are banging the neoliberal drum harder than ever. There is seemingly no longer any secret or shame around the idea that universities aren't at all interested in education. They are in the business of selling "job preparedness" and the prospect of career opportunities and must offer the right "products" to meet consumer demand. And so, as Australia's international student market has evaporated overnight, after years of fervently pursuing the seemingly endless growth of this sacred cash cow, it is casual staff and lecturers that are now being scarified on the altar of neoliberalism. Universities are the canary in the neoliberal coalmine. What is happening on campuses around the world is only a snapshot of what is to come across a wide range of sectors where we will see collapse followed by the inevitable consolidation of capital through new rounds of accumulation. As neoliberalism proves once more why it is a living dead nightmare, now is not the time to fall on our swords. With the same vengeance of the death by a thousand cuts it has inflicted upon all of us, the fight against neoliberalism must continue.

Simon Springer
May 2020

CHAPTER 1

English

Fuck Neoliberalism

Simon Springer

Fuck Neoliberalism. That's my blunt message. I could probably end my discussion at this point, and it wouldn't really matter. My position is clear, and you likely already get the gist of what I want to say. I have nothing positive to add to the discussion about neoliberalism, and, to be perfectly honest, I'm quite sick of having to think about it. I've simply had enough. For a time, I had considered calling this paper "Forget Neoliberalism" instead, as in some ways that's exactly what I wanted to do. I've been writing on the subject for many years,[1] and I came to a point where I just didn't want to commit any more energy to this endeavor for fear that continuing to work around this idea was functioning to perpetuate its hold. On further reflection I also recognize that as a political maneuver it is potentially quite dangerous to simply stick our heads in the sand and collectively ignore a phenomenon that has had such devastating and debilitating effects on our shared world. There is an ongoing power to neoliberalism that is difficult to deny, and I'm not convinced that a strategy of ignorance is actually the right approach.[2] So my exact thoughts were, "well, fuck it then," and while a quieter and gentler name for this paper could tone down the potential offence that might come with the title I've chosen, I subsequently reconsidered. Why should we be more worried about using profanity than we are about the actual vile discourse of neoliberalism itself? I decided that I wanted to transgress, to upset, and to offend, precisely because we *ought* to be offended by neoliberalism. It *is* entirely upsetting, and, therefore, we *should* ultimately be seeking to transgress it. Wouldn't softening the title be making yet another concession to the power of neoliberalism? I initially worried what such a title might mean in terms of my reputation. Would it hinder future promotion or job offers should I want to maintain my mobility as an academic, either upwardly or to a new location? This felt like conceding personal defeat to neoliberal disciplining. Fuck that.

It also felt as though I was making an admission that there is no colloquial response that could appropriately be offered to counter the discourse of neoliberalism. As though we can only respond in an academic format using complex geographical theories of variegation, hybridity, and mutation to weaken its edifice. This seemed disempowering, and although I have myself contributed to the articulation of some of these theories,[3] I often feel that this sort of framing works against the type of argument I actually want to make. It is precisely in the everyday, the ordinary, the unremarkable, and the mundane that I think a politics of refusal must be located. And so I settled on "Fuck Neoliberalism," because I think it conveys most of what I actually want to say. The argument I want to make is slightly more nuanced than that, which had me thinking more about the term "fuck" than I probably have at any other time in my life. What a fantastically colorful word! It works as a noun or a verb, and as an adjective it is perhaps the most used point of exclamation in the English language. It can be employed to express anger, contempt, annoyance, indifference, surprise, impatience, or even as a meaningless emphasis because it just rolls off the tongue. You can "fuck something up," "fuck someone over," "fuck around," "not give a fuck," and there is a decidedly geographical point of reference to the word, insofar as you can be instructed to "go fuck yourself." At this point you might even be thinking "okay, but who gives a fuck?" Well, I do, and if you're interested in ending neoliberalism so should you. The powerful capacities that come with the word offer a potential challenge to neoliberalism. To dig down and unpack these abilities we need to appreciate the nuances of what could be meant by the phrase "fuck neoliberalism." Yet, at the same time, fuck nuance. As Kieran Healy has recently argued, it "typically obstructs the development of theory that is intellectually interesting, empirically generative, or practically successful."[4] So, without fetishizing nuance, let's quickly work through what I think we should be prioritizing in fucking up neoliberalism.

The first sense is perhaps the most obvious. By saying "fuck neoliberalism" we can express our rage against the neoliberal machine. It is an indication of our anger, our desire to shout our resentment, to spew venom back in the face of the noxious malice that has been shown to all of us. This can come in the form of mobilizing more protests against neoliberalism or in writing more papers and books critiquing its influence. The latter preaches to the converted, and the former hopes that the already perverted will be willing to change their ways. I don't discount that these methods are important tactics in our resistance, but I'm also quite sure that they'll never actually be enough to turn the tide against neoliberalism and in our favor. In making grand public gestures of defiance, we attempt to draw powerful actors into a conversation, mistakenly believing that they might listen and begin to accommodate the popular voice of refusal.[5] Shouldn't we instead be done talking? Here is the second sense of "fuck neoliberalism," which is found in the notion of rejection.

This would be to advocate for the end of neoliberalism (as we knew it) in a fashion advanced by J.K. Gibson-Graham, where we simply stop talking about it.[6] Scholars in particular would discontinue prioritizing it as the focus of their studies. Maybe not completely forgetting about or ignoring neoliberalism, which I've already identified as problematic, but to instead get on with writing about other things. Once again, this is a crucially important point of contact for us as we work beyond the neoliberal worldview, but here too I'm not entirely convinced that this is enough. As Mark Purcell argues, "We need to turn away from neoliberalism and toward ourselves, to begin the difficult—but also joyous—work of managing our affairs for ourselves."[7] While negation, protest, and critique are necessary, we also need to think about actively fucking up neoliberalism by doing things outside of its reach.

Direct action beyond neoliberalism speaks to a prefigurative politics,[8] which is the third and most important sense I think we should be focusing on when we invoke the idea "fuck neoliberalism." To prefigure is to reject the centrism, hierarchy, and authority that come with representative politics by emphasizing the embodied practice of enacting horizontal relationships and forms of organization that strive to reflect the future society being sought.[9] Beyond being "done talking," prefiguration and direct action contend that there was never a conversation to be had anyway, recognizing that whatever it is we want to do, we can just do it ourselves. Nonetheless, there has been significant attention to the ways in which neoliberalism is able to capture and appropriate all manner of political discourse and imperatives.[10] For critics like David Harvey, only another dose of the state can solve the neoliberal question, and they are, therefore, quick to dismiss nonhierarchical organization and horizontal politics in particular as greasing the rails for an assured neoliberal future.[11] Yet in his pessimism he entirely misunderstands prefigurative politics, which are a means not to an end but only to future means.[12] In other words, there is a constant and continual vigilance already built into prefigurative politics, so that the actual practice of prefiguration cannot be coopted. It is reflexive and attentive, but always with a view toward production, invention, and creation to satisfy the desire for community. In this way prefigurative politics are explicitly anti-neoliberal. They are a seizing of the means as *our* means, a means without end. To prefigure is to embrace the conviviality and joy that comes with being together as radical equals, not as vanguards and proletariat on the path toward the transcendental empty promise of utopia or "*no place,*" but as the grounded immanence of the *here* and *now* of actually making a new world "in the shell of the old" and the perpetual hard work and reaffirmation that this requires.[13]

There is nothing about neoliberalism that is deserving of our respect, and so in concert with a prefigurative politics of creation, my message is quite simply "fuck it." Fuck the hold that it has on our political imaginations. Fuck the violence it engenders. Fuck the inequality it extols as a virtue. Fuck the way it has ravaged the environment. Fuck the endless cycle of accumulation and the cult of growth. Fuck the Mont Pelerin Society and all the think tanks that continue to prop it up and promote it. Fuck Friedrich Hayek and Milton Friedman for saddling us with their ideas. Fuck the Thatchers, the Reagans, and all the cowardly, self-interested politicians who seek only to scratch the back of avarice. Fuck the fear-mongering exclusion that sees "others" as worthy of cleaning our toilets and mopping our floors, but not as members of our communities. Fuck the ever-intensifying move toward metrics and the failure to appreciate that not everything that counts can be counted. Fuck the desire for profit over the needs of community. Fuck absolutely everything neoliberalism stands for, and fuck the Trojan Horse that it rode in on! For far too long, we've been told that "there is no alternative," that "a rising tide lifts all boats," that we live in a Darwinian nightmare world of all against all "survival of the fittest." We've swallowed the idea of the "tragedy of the commons" hook, line, and sinker; when in reality this is a ruse that actually reflects the "tragedy of capitalism" and its endless wars of plunder.[14] Garrett Hardin's Achilles heel was that he never stopped to think about how grazing cattle were already privately owned.[15] What might happen when we reconvene an actual commons as a *commons* without presuppositions of private ownership?[16] What might happen when we start to pay closer attention to the prefiguration of alternatives that are already happening and privileging these experiences as the most important forms of organization?[17] What might happen when instead of swallowing the bitter pills of competition and merit we focus our energies not on medicating ourselves with neoliberal prescriptions but on the deeper healing that comes with cooperation and mutual aid?[18]

Jamie Peck once called neoliberalism a "radical political slogan,"[19] but it is no longer enough to dwell within the realm of critique. Many years have passed since we first identified the enemy, and from that time we have come to know it well through our writing and protests. But even when we are certain of its defeat, as in the aftermath of the 2008 financial crisis and the subsequent Occupy movement, it continues to gasp for air and reanimate itself in a more powerful zombified form.[20] Japhy Wilson calls this ongoing power the "neoliberal gothic,"[21] and I'm convinced that to overcome this horror show we must move our politics into the realm of the enactive.[22] What if "fuck neoliberalism" were to become a mantra for a new kind of politics? An enabling phrase that spoke not only to action but to the reclamation of our lives in the spaces and moments in which we actively live them? What if every time we used this phrase we recognized that it meant a call for enactive agency that went beyond mere words, combining theory and practice into the beautiful praxis of prefiguration? We must take a multipronged approach in our rejection of neoliberalism. While we can't entirely ignore or forget it, we can actively work against it in ways that extend beyond the performance of rhetoric and the rhetoric of performance. By all means, let's advance a new radical political slogan. Use a hashtag (#fuckneoliberalism) and make our contempt go viral! But we have to do more than express our indignation. We have to enact our resolve and realize our hope as the immanence of our embodied experiences in the *here* and *now*.[23] We need to remake the world ourselves, a process that cannot be postponed.

We've willfully deluded and disempowered ourselves by continuing to appeal to the existing political arrangement of representation. Our blind faith has us waiting endlessly for a savior to drop from the sky. The system has proven itself to be thoroughly corrupt, with our next great political candidate proving to be a failure time and again. In this neoliberal moment it's not a case of mere problematic individuals being in power. Instead, it is our very belief in the system itself that epitomizes the core of the problem. We produce and enable the institutional conditions for "the Lucifer effect" to play itself out.[24] "The banality of evil" is such that these politicians are just doing their jobs in a system that rewards perversions of power, because it is designed to serve the laws of capitalism.[25] But we don't have to obey. We're not beholden to this order. Through our direct action and the organization of alternatives we can indict the entire structure and break this vicious cycle of abuse. When the political system is defined by, conditioned for, enmeshed within, and derived from capitalism, it can never represent our ways of knowing and being in the world, and so we need to take charge of these lifeways and reclaim our collective agency. We must start to become enactive in our politics and begin embracing a more relational sense of solidarity that recognizes that the subjugation and suffering of one is in fact indicative of the oppression of all.[26] We can start living into other possible worlds through a renewed commitment to the practices of mutual aid, fellowship, reciprocity, and nonhierarchical forms of organization that reconvene democracy in its etymological sense of *power* to the *people*. Ultimately neoliberalism is a particularly foul idea that comes with a whole host of vulgar outcomes and crass assumptions. In response, it deserves to be met with equally offensive language and action. Our community, our cooperation, and our care for one another are all loathsome to neoliberalism. It hates that which we celebrate. So when we say "fuck neoliberalism" let it be more than just words, let it be an enactment of our commitment to each other. Say it loud, say it with me, and say it to anyone who will listen, but most of all mean it as a clarion call to action and as the embodiment of our prefigurative power to change the fucking world. *Fuck Neoliberalism!*

CHAPTER 2

বাংলা – Bengali

নব্য উদারবাদ নপিাত যাক

Translated by কুনালজিৎ রায় – Kunaljeet Roy

Translator's Commentary

Translating "Fuck Neoliberalism" to Bengali was a a challenging task, as it was my first formal translation, and initially I was not confident in my ability to accurately convey the tone and content. But there's a zeal, I suppose, to create a linguistic bridge between the original piece and the translation through my vernacular. So I accepted the challenge but was aware that there would be difficulties in translating particular phrases into Bengali.

As a citizen of a developing nation, the evils of neoliberalism are known to me, and some of my everyday observations helped me to figure out exactly what the author wanted to express through his writing. To me, political and social corruption, exaggeration of power, mass illiteracy, unemployment, and ethnic and communal tensions in any form are the adverse impacts of neoliberalism, which is the disguised demon behind every imbalance. I agree that there's always a risk of coming under surveillance when you attempt such an academic task to portray it, but I turned down the option to remain anonymous, as I admire the principled stand taken by the author against the beast. I am not sure exactly how the target audience will react to reading my translation, but I am fairly confident that they might relate to the argument. If my little contribution is fruitful, it may unleash a new chapter of translating original pieces to various global languages from English. This translation will certainly help the author's strong critical views to reach a larger audience in academia. So, leaving aside all the limitations of hybrid forms aroused by my translation, let us all stand with the spirit of the academic movement against all forms of oppression. That's what Professor Springer intended with this text.

নব্য উদারবাদ নিপাত যাক

নব্য উদারবাদ নিপাত যাক। এটাই আমার সুস্পষ্ট বার্তা। আমি হয়ত এখানেই আলোচনা শেষ করে ফেলতে পারতাম এবং তাতে কিছুই যেত- আসত না। আমার অবস্থান আপনাদের কাছে এই ব্যাপারে খুব পরিষ্কার এবং ইতিমধ্যেই আপনারা আশা করি আমার বক্তব্যের অভিপ্রায় সম্পর্কে অবগত হতে পেরেছেন। নব্য উদারবাদ সম্পর্কিত এই আলোচনা প্রসঙ্গে নতুন করে আমার কিছুই যোগ করার নেই এবং সত্যি করে বলতে গেলে আমি এই প্রসঙ্গে আলোচনা করতে গেলেই বিতৃষ্ণা অনুভব করি। যথেষ্ট হয়েছে। একটা সময় আমি এই প্রবন্ধটির শিরোনাম দেব ভেবেছিলাম ' নব্য উদারবাদ বিস্মৃত হোক', এবং কিছুমাত্রায় এটি আমার প্রকৃত উদ্দ্যেশের সাথে সাযুজ্যপূর্ণ হত। আমি এই বিষয়ের উপর বহু বছর ধরেই লিখছি[1] এবং এই সিদ্ধান্তে উপনীত হয়েছি যে আমি এর পিছনে আর কোন সময় অপচয় করব না কারন আমার ভয় হয় যে এই বিষয়টির চারিদিকে যত বিচরন করব ততই হয়ত এর কার্যকারিতা আমার মনজগতের দখল নেবে। আমি এও বলব যে আমি এর আরও একটি বিশেষ রূপ শনাক্ত করেছি এবং তা হল একটি রাজনৈতিক রণকৌশল যা ততটাই ভয়ানক যে সরাসরি আমাদের প্রবলভাবে আচ্ছন্ন করে রাখে, ফলে আমরা নব্য উদারবাদের ক্ষতিকারক এবং বিধ্বংসী প্রভাবগুলিকে নিজেদের অজান্তেই অবহেলা করি, অথচ আমাদের পারস্পরিক জগতে এর কুপ্রভাব সুদূরপ্রসারী। নব্য উদারবাদের একপ্রকার প্রবহমান শক্তি রয়েছে যাকে অস্বীকার করা সম্ভব নয় এবং আমি নিশ্চিত নই যে একে উপেক্ষা করাটাই একে প্রতিরোধ করার সঠিক পদ্ধতি কি না[2]। সুতরাং আমার স্পষ্ট অভিমত

হল – 'বেশ তবে নিপাত যাক' এবং যদিও এই নিবন্ধের ক্ষেত্রে একটি তুলনামূলক নমনীয় নামকরন হয়ত আমার নির্বাচিত শিরোনামের মাধ্যমে তৈরি হওয়া সম্ভাব্য অপরাধকে কিছুটা লঘু করতে সক্ষম হত। কিন্তু কেনই বা আমরা অপবিত্রতা বিষয়ে অযথা এতটা ভাবিত হচ্ছি বরং আমাদের কি উচিৎ নয় নব্য উদারবাদ কৃত প্রকৃত নিম্নগামী বক্তব্যের বিরুদ্ধে সোচ্চার হওয়া? আমার লেখার মধ্য দিয়ে আমি হয়ত কিছু সীমা অতিক্রম করব, অনেককে বিক্ষুব্ধ করব, হয়ত অনেকে আঘাতও পেতে পারেন কিন্তু আমাদের একথা ভুলে গেলে হবে না যে নব্য উদারবাদ আমাদের যেভাবে ক্ষতি করছে তা চরম অপমানজনক এবং এর বিরুদ্ধে গর্জে ওঠা ছাড়া আর কিছুই আমি ভাবতে পারছি না। এই নিবন্ধের শিরোনামটিকে নমনীয় করার অর্থ নব্য উদারবাদকে কিছুটা সুযোগ করে দেওয়া নয় কি? প্রাথমিক পর্বে আমার মনে আশঙ্কা তৈরি হয়েছিল যে এই শিরোনাম আমার নিজের সম্মানহানি ঘটাতে পারে কিংবা আমার ভবিষ্যৎ সমৃদ্ধি বা জীবিকা পরিসরকে সংকুচিত করতে পারে এবং একজন শিক্ষাবিদ রূপে আমার উত্তরন বা নতুন সুযোগ তৈরির ক্ষেত্রে বাধা হয়ে দাঁড়াতে পারে। কিন্তু এই ধরনের ভাবনা পোষণ করার অর্থ ব্যক্তিগত ভাবে নব্য উদারবাদের কাছে পরাজয় স্বীকার করে নেওয়া। সুতরাং এইসব ভাবনা স্রেফ অবান্তর।

এরকম ধারনা হওয়া স্বাভাবিক যে আমি একপ্রকার স্বীকার করছি যে নব্য উদারবাদের মূল ভিত্তিকে প্রতিরোধ করার আর কোন কথ্য বা চলতি ভাষা আমার কাছে নেই। আসলে ভূগোলচিন্তার নির্দিষ্ট তথা জটিল পরিসরের মধ্যে থেকে যদি আমাদের এই প্রতিরোধ গড়ে তুলতে হয় তবে কর্বুরতা, বর্ণসংকরতা এবং পরিব্যক্তি সংক্রান্ত তত্ত্বগুলিকে আশ্রয় করেই একে দুর্বল করতে হবে। নব্য উদারবাদকে পরাজিত করার জন্য এগুলির প্রয়োজন এবং আমি ইতিমধ্যেই স্পষ্টভাবে আমার লেখার মাধ্যমে এই তত্ত্বগুলির কয়েকটিকে আশ্রয় করে আমার বক্তব্য তুলে ধরেছি,[৩] আমার প্রায়শই মনে হয় যে এই ধরনের কাঠামোবদ্ধ কাজ হয়ত আমার প্রকৃত বক্তব্যকে সম্পূর্ণভাবে প্রকাশ করতে সক্ষম হবে না। খুব প্রাঞ্জলভাবে বলতে গেলে দৈনন্দিন চিন্তাভাবনা ও জাগতিক ধারনার প্রেক্ষাপটে

একপ্রকার নস্যাৎধর্মী রাজনৈতিক পন্থা দিয়েই আমি এর
মোকাবিলা করার কথা ভেবেছি। এই জন্যই শিরোনাম হিসেবে
'নব্য উদারবাদ নিপাত যাক' এটাই ভাবলাম, কারন আমি ঠিক
যা বলতে চাই তা এর মধ্যে দিয়েই প্রকাশিত হচ্ছে। যদিও
আমার প্রকৃত বক্তব্য আরও কিছুটা সূক্ষ্ম এবং বোধ করি
এই জন্যই আমি 'fuck' শব্দটি নিয়ে জীবনে প্রথমবার এত
গভীরভাবে ভেবেছি। কি অসাধারন একটি বর্ণময় শব্দ! একে
বিশেষ্য, বিশেষণ, ক্রিয়াপদ যেকোনো প্রকারে ব্যবহার
করা যায়, এমনকি এটাই সম্ভবত ইংরাজি ভাষায় সর্বাধিক
ব্যবহৃত বিস্ময়সূচক শব্দ। একে একই সাথে ক্রোধ, অবজ্ঞা,
বিরক্তি, বিস্ময় বা যেকোনো তথাকথিত উদ্দেশ্যহীন কথা
রূপে ব্যবহার করা যায়, যা মুখ থেকে স্বাভাবিক ভাবে বেরিয়ে
আসতে পারে। এই একটি শব্দ (fuck) কে আপনি বৈচিত্র্যপূর্ণ
ভাবে ব্যবহার করতে পারেন। যেমন কোনোকিছুকে অবজ্ঞা
করতে পারেন (fuck something up), কাউকে অবজ্ঞা করতে
পারেন (fuck someone over), নিজের সামনে থেকে দূর করে
দিতে পারেন (fuck around) বা কিছুই বরাদ্দ না করতে পারেন
(not give a fuck) এবং এই শব্দটির একটি বিশেষ ভৌগলিক
দিক রয়েছে যে আপনাকেই নির্দেশ দেওয়া হতে পারে নিজিকে
নিপাত দাও (go fuck yourself)। এই মুহূর্তেই হয়ত আপনি
ভাবছেন ঠিক আছে, কিন্তু এতে কার কি যায় আসে? আসলে
আমার যায় আসে বৈকি এবং যদি আপনিও নব্য উদারবাদকে
চিরতরে নির্মূল করতে চান তবে আপনারও যায় আসে। এই
সবিশেষ শব্দটির সাথে যে আপাতনিহিত ক্ষমতা রয়েছে তা নব্য
উদারবাদের কাছে একটা বড় বাধা হয়ে দাঁড়াবে নিশ্চয়। আরও
তলিয়ে ভাবতে গেলে আমাদের এই 'নব্য উদারবাদ নিপাত যাক'
শব্দবন্ধটির সংলগ্ন সূক্ষ্ম ভাষাগত তারতম্য মাথায় রাখা
দরকার। আবার একই সঙ্গে যে কোন ধরনের তারতম্যকেও
স্রেফ নিপাত দিতে পারেন। যেমন Kieran Healy[4] সাম্প্রতিক
অতীতে মতপ্রকাশ করেছেন যে, কোন তথাকথিত তত্ত্ব যখন
বুদ্ধিমত্তার দিক থেকে অসাধারন, ভয়ানক মাত্রায় অভি-
জ্ঞতালব্ধ এবং প্রায়োগিক দিক থেকে ফলপ্রসূ হয় তখন
দুর্ভাগ্যজনক ভাবে সেই তত্ত্বটির অগ্রগতি হওয়া প্রায়
অসম্ভব। সুতরাং সুক্ষ প্রভেদ নিয়ে অযথা বাক্যব্যয় না
করে খুব দ্রুত আমাদের সেই বিশেষ লক্ষ্যে কাজ শুরু করে দিতে

হবে যার একমাত্র অগ্রাধিকার হল নব্য উদারবাদকে নরকে নিক্ষেপ করা।

প্রাথমিক ধারনাটি এক্ষেত্রে বিশিষ্ট তাৎপর্যপূর্ণ। যখন আমরা বলছি 'নব্য উদারবাদ নিপাত যাক' তখন এর মাধ্যমে আমরা নব্য উদারবাদ যে যান্ত্রিকতার জন্ম দেয় তার বিরুদ্ধে নিজিদের ক্রোধ ব্যক্ত করছি। এটা একপ্রকার আমাদের ক্রোধের বহিঃপ্রকাশ, আমাদের বিরক্তি ব্যক্ত করার উপায়, এমনকি চরম আক্রোশে এই বিনাশকারী ধারনাটির উপর সেই বিষ বমন করার প্রয়াশ যা এতদিন আমাদের মধ্যে সচেতন ভাবে প্রবেশ করানো হয়েছে। এর বাস্তব প্রয়োগ আরও সংঘবদ্ধ প্রতিবাদ সংগঠনের মধ্যে দিয়ে আসতে পারে অথবা নব্য উদারবাদ বিরোধী নিবন্ধ বা বই লেখার মধ্যে দিয়ে এর প্রভাবকে সরাসরি সমালোচনা করা যেতে পারে। শেষোক্তটি অনেক বেশি উপদেশ ধর্মী যা সতত পরিবর্তনশীল এবং পূর্বোক্তটি আজও আশাবাদী যে এইসব বিকৃত মানসিকতা একদিন নিজেকে শুধরে নেবার কথা ভাববে। আমি অস্বীকার করছি না যে এইসব উপকরণগুলি আমাদের প্রতিরোধ কর্মসূচীর অন্যতম রণকৌশল, কিন্তু আমি পুরোপুরি নিশ্চিত যে এগুলি নব্য উদারবাদের বিরুদ্ধে আমাদের পালে হাওয়া তৈরি করার জন্য যথেষ্ট নয়। খুব বড় মাপের গনজমায়েতের মধ্যে দিয়ে আমরা যে দ্বন্দ্ব-মূলক পরিসর সৃষ্টি করি তার দ্বারা শক্তিশালী প্রতিবাদী বক্তব্য উপস্থাপন করা যায় হয়ত কিন্তু এক্ষেত্রে এক ভ্রান্তি জন্ম নেয় যে এই বক্তব্য তথা গনপ্রত্যাখ্যান নব্য উদারবাদীদের শ্রুতিগোচর হবে এবং তারা তাতে গুরুত্ব দিতে শুরু করবে[5]। আমাদের কি উচিত নয় কথা বলার পরিবর্তে করে দেখানো? এখানেই নিহিত রয়েছে নব্য উদারবাদকে নিক্ষেপে করার দ্বিতীয় পন্থা, যা হল একে সরাসরি বাতিল করা। এটি হয়ত কার্যকরী ভাবে নব্য উদারবাদের বিদায় ঘণ্টা বাজাতে সক্ষম হবে (যেমন আমরা জানি) এমন একটা পদ্ধতিতে যা J.K. Gibson-Graham[6] উপস্থাপন এবং বিশ্লেষণ করেছেন যেখানে আমরা এর ব্যপারে কোনোপ্রকার আলোচনাই বন্ধ করে দেব। গবেষকেরা বিশিষত তাদের গবেষণার ক্ষেত্রে একে যেন কোনোভাবেই গুরুত্ব না দেন। হয়ত সম্পূর্ণ ভাবে নব্য উদারবাদকে ভুলে যাওয়া বা উপেক্ষা করা সম্ভব

নয় যা আমি ইতিমধ্যে একটি সমস্যা বলে উল্লেখ করেছি কিন্তু আমাদের উচিত অন্য গুরুত্বপূর্ণ বিষয়গুলিকে আমাদের লেখনীর মাধ্যমে তুলে ধরা। এটি অন্যতম একটি পারস্পরিক যোগাযোগের মাধ্যম হতে পারে যা হয়ত আমাদের নব্য উদারবাদের চলতি বিশ্বজনীন ধারনার বাইরে গিয়ে কাজ করতে সাহায্য করবে, কিন্তু এক্ষেত্রেও আমি পুরোপুরি নিশ্চিত হতে পারছি না যে এটাই যথেষ্ট কি না। যেমন Mark Purcell[7] বলেছেন " আমাদের উচিত নব্য উদারবাদী চিন্তাধারা থেকে নিজেদের সম্পূর্ণ সরিয়ে নিয়ে নিজেদের অভিমুখে নিয়ে আসা, এই কঠিন তথা আনন্দদায়ক কাজটি আমাদের করতেই হবে যাতে নিজেদের ব্যাপারে আমরা নিজেরাই সিদ্ধান্ত নিতে সক্ষম হই"। একদিকে যেমন অস্বীকৃতি, প্রতিবাদ এবং সমালোচনা প্রয়োজন তেমনই আমাদের কার্যকরী ভাবে নব্য উদারবাদের ব্যপ্তি বহির্ভূত কাজকর্ম চালিয়ে যেতে হবে যাতে একে সম্পূর্ণ নিপাত দেওয়া যায়।

নব্য উদারবাদের ব্যপ্তি বহির্ভূত প্রত্যক্ষ কার্যকারিতা নিহিত রয়েছে একপ্রকার পূর্ব কল্পিত রাজনৈতিক (prefigurative politics) ধারনার মধ্যে,[8] যা তৃতীয় তথা সর্বাধিক গুরুত্বপূর্ণ পন্থা এবং আমার মতে নব্য উদারবাদকে সমূলে উৎপাটিত করার জন্য এর উপর বিশেষ গুরুত্ব আরোপ করতে হবে। পূর্ব পরিকল্পনা করার নিমিত্তে আমাদের মধ্যপন্থা, স্তরায়ন ধর্মিতা এবং ক্ষমতাকে নস্যাৎ করতে হবে যা প্রতিনিধিত্বমূলক রাজনীতি থেকে উৎপন্ন এমন এক ব্যবস্থা যেটি কতৃত্ববাদী অনুভূমিক সম্পর্ক এবং কিছু বিশিষ্ট সংগঠনের মাধ্যমে কার্যকরী হয় যাদের ভবিষ্যৎ সমাজের রূপরেখা নির্বাচনের তথাকথিত গুরুদায়িত্ব অর্পণ করা হয়েছে[9]। আলোচনার গণ্ডী অতিক্রম করে, পূর্ব পরিকল্পনা এবং প্রত্যক্ষ কার্যকারিতার মধ্যে কোন তথাকথিত কথোপকথনের সুযোগই নেই বরং যা আমাদের কর্তব্য তা আমরা সচ্ছন্দে নিজেরাই নির্বাহ করতে পারি। যাই হোক, নব্য উদারবাদ সব ধরনের রাজনৈতিক বক্তব্য ও মতাদর্শের উপর কতখানি প্রভাব বিস্তার করতে সক্ষম হয়েছে তা নিয়ে অনেক আলোচনার সময় অতিবাহিত হয়েছে[10]। David Harvey[11] – এর মত সমালোচকদের মতে রাষ্ট্র প্রদত্ত রাজনৈতিক ঔষধের মাত্রা আরও কিছুটা বৃদ্ধি করলেই এই নব্য উদারবাদজাত

সমস্যাগুলির সমাধান সম্ভব ,খুব নির্দিষ্টভাবে বলতে গেলে তিনি অতিদ্রুত অ-স্তরায়নবাদী সংগঠন এবং অনুভূমিক রাজনীতির প্রভাবকে নস্যাৎ করেছেন যা নিশ্চিত ভাবে নব্য উদারবাদী ভবিষ্যতের শংকটের চাকায় গতিবৃদ্ধির প্রয়াসে নিয়ত। আসলে তিনি তার এই নৈরাশ্যবাদী চিন্তাধারার মধ্যে দিয়ে উক্ত পূর্ব পরিকল্পিত রাজনৈতিক ধারনার বিষয়টিকে সম্পূর্ণ ভুল বুঝেছেন, যা প্রকৃতপক্ষে ভবিষ্যতের লড়াইয়ের মাধ্যম হয়ে উঠতে পারে[12]। অন্য ভাবে বলতে হলে, এক্ষেত্রে একটি স্থিতিশীল এবং ধারাবাহিক নজরদারীর সুযোগ পূর্ব পরিকল্পিত রাজনীতির মধ্যে নিহিত রয়েছে যার জন্য পূর্ব পরিকল্পনার একে সহজে রোধ করা সম্ভব নয়। ইহা এমন এক প্রকার সচেতন ব্যবস্থা যা সর্বদা এমন ভাবনা লালন করে যেটি উৎপাদন, উদ্ভাবন ও সৃষ্টিশীলতাকে সমর্থন তথা সর্বসাধারণের চাহিদার প্রতিফলন ঘটায়। এই যুক্তিতে পূর্বকল্পিত রাজনৈতিক চেতনা স্পষ্টভাবেই নব্য উদারবাদ বিরোধী। আসলে নব্য উদারবাদী চিন্তাধারা আমাদের উপকরন গুলিকে করায়ত্ত করার চেষ্টায় রত যার কোন শেষ নেই। একে পূর্ব নির্ধারণ করে ফেলার অর্থ একপ্রকার অনির্বচনীয় উৎসবের আনন্দে সামিল হওয়া যা আমাদের প্রতিবাদী একতাকে উদ্যাপনের মধ্যে দিয়ে আসে, সর্বহারার অগ্রদূত সাজার তুরীয় আনন্দের ফাঁকা প্রতিশ্রুতি দেবার মাধ্যমে নয় অথবা বাস্তবের রুক্ষ জমিতে উক্ত বিশ্বাস এই সর্বশিষ্ট মুহূর্তেই পুরনো ধ্যানধারণার গর্ভে এক নতুন পৃথিবী সৃষ্টির কথা বলে এবং তা অর্জনের পশ্চাতে নিহিত এক শাশ্বত পরিশ্রমী কর্মযজ্ঞের কাহিনী ব্যক্ত করে[13]।

নব্য উদারবাদের মধ্যে এমন কিছুই নেই যা আমাদের ন্যুনতম সম্মান অর্জন করতে পারে এবং এই মর্মে ইতিমধ্যে আলোচিত পূর্ব পরিকল্পিত সৃষ্টিশীল রাজনৈতিক চেতনার সাথে সহমত পোষণ করে আমার স্পষ্ট বার্তা 'নিপাত যাক'। নিপাত যাক সেই হিংসার বাতাবরণ যা এর মাধ্যমে উৎপন্ন হয়েছে। নিপাত যাক সকল প্রকার বৈষম্য যা এর প্রত্যক্ষ মদতের অভিশাপে উৎপন্ন হয়েছে। নিপাত যাক সেই সকল পন্থা যার মাধ্যমে এটি আমাদের পারিপার্শ্বিক পরিবেশকে ধ্বংস করে চলেছে। নিপাত যাক সেই স্বার্থান্বেষণ ও তথাকথিত উন্নয়নের মিথ্যা ভজনাকারী যতিহীন চক্র। নিপাত যাক

Mont Pelerin Society তথা তাদের মত সেই সব বুদ্ধিজীবীদের গোষ্ঠী যারা ক্রমাগত নব্য উদারবাদকে নির্লজ্জ ভাবে সমর্থন জুগিয়ে চলেছেন। নিপাত যান Friedrich Hayek এবং Milton Friedman, যারা তাদের চিন্তাভাবনা আমাদের উপর চাপিয়ে দেবার চেষ্টা করেছেন। নিপাত যান Thatchers, Reagans বা তাদের মত আরও দুর্বল, ভীরু, স্বার্থান্বেষী রাজনৈতিকের দল যারা শুধুমাত্র অর্থলিপ্সার জন্য সময় ব্যয় করেছেন। নিপাত যাক সেই ভীতি উদ্রেককারী বিচ্ছিন্নতা যা সেইসব তথাকথিত 'অন্য' মানুষদের প্রয়োজনীয় রূপে বিবেচনা করেন নিজিদের শৌচাগার পরিষ্কার রাখার জন্য অথবা মেঝে সাফসুতরো রাখার জন্য, কিন্তু তাদের কখনই নিজিদের সম্প্রদায়ের অংশ রূপে মেনে নিতি সম্মত নন। নিপাত যাক সেই সদাজাগ্রত পরিমাপবাচক চিন্তা যা কখনই হৃদয়ঙ্গম করতে পারে না যে সবকিছুই যা হয়ত মাপা যায় তা আসলে মাপা উচিত নয়। নিপাত যাক সেই মুনাফাবাদী চিন্তাধারা যা জনগনের সামগ্রিক প্রয়োজনের কথা কখনই ভবে দেখে না। নিপাত যাক সেই সব চিন্তাভাবনা যা নব্য উদারবাদের সাথে কোন না কোন ভাবে সম্পর্কিত এবং বিশিষত সেই ট্রয়ের ঘোড়াকে নিক্ষেপ করা প্রয়োজন যার গতিতে নব্য উদারবাদীরা সওয়ার। বহুদিন আগে থেকেই আমাদের শোনানো হয়েছে ' এর কোন বিকল্প নেই', ' একটি শক্তিশালী জোয়ারের ধাক্কাই যথেষ্ট সব নৌকোগুলি এগিয়ে নিয়ে যাবার জন্য', আমরা এমন এক ডারউইনবাদী দুঃস্বপ্নের জগতে বাস করি যেখানে তথাকথিত 'যোগ্যতমের উদ্বর্তনের' নিয়মে সকলেই সকলের প্রতিদ্বন্দ্বী। আমরা আত্মস্থ করেছি 'সাধারনের দুর্দশা' (tragedy of the commons) সূচক আপ্তবাক্যটি যার মধ্যে আসলে আমাদের ডুবিয়ে রাখা হয়েছে বা আমাদের সামনে ঝুলিয়ে দেওয়া হয়েছে; কিন্তু প্রকৃতপক্ষে এটি একপ্রকার ছলনা যা ' ধনতন্ত্রের দুর্দশা' (tragedy of capitalism) এবং তার সাথে সম্পর্কিত লুণ্ঠনের সেই যুদ্ধের প্রতিরূপ যা কোনোদিন শেষ হয় না[14]। Garett Hardin[15] –এর দ্বারা বর্ণিত একিলিসের গোড়ালি (Achilles' heel) এই ধারনাই ব্যক্ত করে যে কোন যুক্তিতে চারণভূমিতে থাকা গবাদিপশুরা কারোর ব্যক্তিগত সম্পত্তি হতে পারে? কি ঘটবে যদি আমরা সাধারনের (commons) ধারনার সাথে প্রকৃত সাধারনের (actual commons) ধারনার মেলবন্ধন ঘটাই পূর্বোক্ত ব্যক্তিগত সম্পত্তির ধারনা দূরে সরিয়ে দিয়ে[16]? কি হবে যদি আমরা মেধা আর প্রতিযোগিতার লড়াইয়ের তিক্ত ঔষধ গলাধঃকরণ না করে নিজেদের প্রকৃত শক্তির উপর বিশ্বাস রাখি যা স্বাভা- বিকিভাবেই নব্য উদারবাদ প্রদত্ত ঔষধের তালিকার পরিপন্থী বরং এর মধ্যে দিয়ে পারস্পরিক সহযোগিতার এক দীর্ঘস্থায়ী উপশম লাভ করা[17] সম্ভব নয় কি?[18]

Jamie Peck[19] একদা নব্য উদারবাদকে ' বৈপ্লবিক রাজনৈতিক জিগির' (radical political slogan) বলে অভিহিত করেছিলেন, কিন্তু তা কোনোমতেই আর সমালোচনার গণ্ডীর মধ্যে যথেষ্ট গুরুত্ব পাচ্ছে না। নব্য উদারবাদ নামক এই শত্রু কে সনাক্ত করার পর বহুবছর কেটে গেছে এবং সেই দিন থেকেই আমাদের লেখা ও প্রতিবাদের ভাষায় এর স্বরূপ উপলব্ধি করতে পেরেছি। কিন্তু ঠিক যেই মুহূর্ত থেকে আমরা এর পরাজয়ের ব্যাপারে নিশ্চিত হয়েছিলাম, অর্থাৎ ২০০৮ (2008) এর সেই ভয়ানক অর্থনৈতিক সংকটের সময় বা তৎপরবর্তী দখল আন্দোলনের বাতাবরণে ইহা সমকালীন মননশীলতার প্রেক্ষাপটে নব্য উদারবাদ নিজেকে আরও শক্তিশালী এক ভয়াবহ জীবিত মৃতবৎ (zombified) রূপে পুনর্জীবিত করেছে[20]। Japhy Wilson[21] এই ক্রমান্বয়িক ক্ষমতার আস্ফালনকেই 'neoliberal gothic' বা 'নব্য উদারবাদের মর্মর স্তম্ভ' বলে উল্লেখ করেছেন এবং আমি এই বিষয়ে নিশ্চিত যে এই ভয়াবহ পর্যায় অতিক্রম করতে হলে আমাদের রাজনৈতিক চিন্তাধারাকে বিধিবদ্ধ বাস্তবের এক্তিয়ারের মধ্যে এনে আরও ক্ষুরধার করতে হবে[22]। কি হবে যদি 'নব্য উদারবাদ নিপাত যাক' (fuck neoliberalism) একটি বীজমন্ত্রে পরিনত হয় যা এক নতুন প্রকারের রাজনৈতিক ধারনার জন্ম দেবে? এটি এমন একটি সক্রিয় শব্দবন্ধ যা শুধু প্রতিক্রিয়ার কথাই বলে না বরং একান্ত কাঙ্ক্ষিত পরিসরের এবং মুহূর্তের মধ্যে আমাদের জীবন পুনরুদ্ধারে রত থাকে। কি হবে যদি প্রতি মুহূর্তে আমরা সেই শব্দবন্ধটি ব্যবহার করতে শুরু করি যা আমাদের বিধিবদ্ধ সাংগঠনিক সত্ত্বা আহ্বান করে এবং কথার সীমা পেরিয়ে তত্ত্ব ও প্রায়োগিক কৌশলকে মিলিয়ে দিতে পারে পূর্বকল্পিত প্রথার সৌন্দর্যের বহিঃপ্রকাশের সঙ্গে সঙ্গতি বজায় রেখে? আমাদের নব্য উদারবাদ বর্জনকারী প্রচেষ্টার ক্ষেত্রে আরও

বহুমুখী পদ্ধতি অবলম্বন করতে হবে। যেহেতু একে আমরা সম্পূর্ণ উপেক্ষা করতে পারব না তাই এর বিপক্ষে পদক্ষেপের তীব্রতা আমাদের সেই পথে চালিত করতে হবে যা সক্রিয়তার আলঙ্কারিক প্রয়োগ বা আলঙ্কারিক সক্রিয়তার বাধা অতিক্রম করতে সক্ষম হয়। সব ক্ষেত্রে সবাই মিলে একটি নতুন বৈপ্লবিক রাজনৈতিক জিগির উত্থাপন করতে হবে। একটি হ্যাশট্যাগ (#fuckneoliberalism) ব্যবহার করতে শুরু করি এবং আমাদের মন্তব্য গুলি যতটা সম্ভব দ্রুত ছড়িয়ে দিতে সচেষ্ট হই। আসলে আমাদের ঘৃণামিশ্রিত ক্রোধের বহিঃপ্রকাশের বাইরেও আরও বেশি কিছু করতে হবে। আমাদের সক্রিয় ভাবে বোধগম্যতা এবং সমাধানের আশায় অগ্রসর হতে হবে যা আমাদের বাস্তবিক অভিজ্ঞতার নিরিখে এখন এবং এই মুহূর্তেই কার্যকরী হয়[23]। নিজেদের পৃথিবী আমাদের নিজেদের মত করেই সাজাতে হবে, এটি এমন এক প্রক্রিয়া যা কোনোভাবেই থেমে থাকা চলবে না। আমরা

আসলে সচেচ্ছায় নিজেদের নিজেরাই ক্রমাগত প্রবঞ্চনা ও দুর্বল করেছি এই প্রতিনিধিত্বমূলক রাজনৈতিক ব্যবস্থার উপর আস্থা রেখে। আমাদের অন্ধ বিশ্বাস আমাদের অনন্তকাল ধরে অপেক্ষা করিয়ে রেখেছে এই ভ্রান্ত ধারনায় যে কবে আকাশ থেকে একজন দেবদূত প্রকট হবেন এবং আমাদের সব দুর্দশা দূর হবে। উক্ত কাঠামোটি যারপরনাই দুর্নীতিতে নিমজ্জিত, যেখানে দিনের পর দিন ধরে আমাদের আকাঙ্ক্ষিত ভবিষ্যতের রাষ্ট্রনায়ক শুধু ব্যর্থ হয়েই এসেছেন। এই চলতি নব্য অর্থনৈতিক ধারনায় ক্ষমতাসীন ব্যক্তিরাই শুধু আমাদের একমাত্র চিন্তার বিষয় নন। আরও গভীরভাবে ভাবলে আমরা অনুধাবন করব যে এই নব্য উদারবাদী ধারনার উপর আস্থা রাখাটাই আমাদের সমস্যার কেন্দ্রে চুম্বকের মত আকর্ষণ করে রেখেছে। আমরা সেই প্রাতিস্থানিক পরিস্থিতি উৎপন্ন তথা প্রয়োগে সক্ষম হয়েছি যা 'the Lucifer effect' কে কার্যকরী হবার পর্যাপ্ত সুযোগ করে দিয়েছে[24]। 'The banality of evil' বা শয়তানি মস্তষ্কের প্রভাব এইসব তথাকথিত রাজনৈতিকের ক্ষেত্রে এতটাই যে তারা আসলে তাদের সাধারন কর্তব্যটুকু নির্বাহ করছেন এমন এক প্রক্রিয়ার অংশ হিসাবে যেটি বিকৃত ক্ষমতার আস্ফালনকেই সমর্থন করে এবং তা আদপে এমনভাবেই সাজানো হয়েছে যাতে ধনতন্ত্রের রক্ষাকবচ রূপে

কাজ করে[25]। কিন্তু আমাদের একে মান্য করার কোন দায় নেই। আমরা এই অন্যায্য প্রক্রিয়ার সামনে কখনই নতজানু নই। আমরা আমাদের প্রত্যক্ষ কার্যাবলী তথা বিকল্প সংগঠনের মাধ্যমে এই চলমান অপপ্রয়োগের দুষ্টচক্রের হাত থেকে নিষ্কৃতি পেতে পারি। যখন চলতি রাজনৈতিক কর্মকাণ্ড ধনতন্ত্রের সাথে সাযুজ্য রেখে উৎপন্ন তথা লালিত হয় তখন তা কোনোভাবেই আমাদের ধ্যানধারণা বা বিশ্বভাবনাকে প্রতিফলিত করতে সক্ষম নয়। সুতরাং আমাদের উচিৎ নিজেদের কাম্য জীবনযাত্রার ভবিতব্য নিজেদেরই নির্ধারণ করা এবং আমাদের সম্মিলিত প্রচেষ্টাকে আবার পুনরাবিস্কার করার চেষ্টা করতেই হবে। আমাদের নিজেদের রাজনৈতিক মতাদর্শকে একতাবাদী পারস্পরিক সম্মিলনের পথেই চালিত করতে হবে যাতে আমরা সবাই মিলে এই সত্যটা অনুধাবন করতে সক্ষম হই যে একজনের উপর হওয়া অত্যাচার ও বঞ্চনা আসলে সকলের উপর দমনপীড়নের সমকক্ষ[26]। আমাদের পারস্পরিক আদান-প্রদানের মাধ্যমে এমন এক নতুন বিশ্বব্যবস্থা গড়ে তুলতে হবে যেখানে পারস্পরিক সহায়তা, গবেষণাবৃত্তি, সহযোগিতা ও অ-স্তরায়িত সাংগঠনিক ব্যবস্থার জন্ম হয় যা গনতন্ত্রকে তার প্রকৃত ভিত্তিমূলে প্রতিষ্ঠা করবে অর্থাৎ জনগনের ক্ষমতায়ন কে নিশ্চিত করবে। পরিশিষে বলা চলে নব্য উদারবাদ নিঃসন্দেহে একটি ভ্রান্ত মতাদর্শ যা পুরোপুরি কয়েকটি সম্পূর্ণ বিকৃত, সংবেদনহীন ধারনাবলীর সমষ্টি। সুতরাং প্রতিক্রিয়াস্বরূপ আমাদের তরফ থেকে এর প্রাপ্য হল আক্রমণাত্মক ভাষা এবং কড়া প্রতিক্রিয়া। আমাদের সম্প্রদায়গত একতা তথা আমাদের পারস্পরিক সহযোগিতা এবং একে অপরের প্রতি যত্নবান হওয়া প্রয়োজন যা আবার নব্য উদারবাদের কাছে কখনই কাম্য নয় বরং তার চোখে ঘৃণিত ও বর্জনীয়। ইহা সেই সব কিছুকেই ঘৃণা করে যা আমরা সবিশিষ্ঠ উদযাপন করি। সুতরাং যখন আমরা বলব ' নব্য উদারবাদ নিপাত যাক' সেটা যেন শুধু কথার থেকে বেশি কিছু হয়, যেন আমাদের মিলিত শপথের নতুন ধারার সূচনা করে। উদাত্ত কণ্ঠে সকলে বলুন, আমার সঙ্গে একসুরে বলুন, এবং এমন যে কোন ব্যক্তিকে বলুন যিনি মনোযোগ সহকারে শুনবেন, কিন্তু সবিশিষ্ঠ গুরুত্বপূর্ণ হল যে এটি যেন আমাদের প্রতিক্রিয়া ও পূর্বকল্পিত শক্তিশালী মতাদর্শের সাথে একীভূত হয় যা এই

চলতি বিশ্বজনীন ব্যবস্থাকে চিরতরে বদলাতে সক্ষম হয়।
নব্য উদারবাদ নিপাত যাক।

CHAPTER 3

简体中文 – Simplified Chinese

操新自由主义

The translator of both the simplified and traditional Chinese versions chose to remain anonymous (ed.)

Translator's Commentary

It has been a quandary to translate "Fuck Neoliberalism" into traditional and simplified Chinese. As the economic sphere becomes more liberal, the political sphere becomes more conservative. As the mainland government challenges the autonomy of the internet through the development of its Great Firewall, it would be naive to assume that the simplified translation of "Fuck Neoliberalism" would reach a wide audience within mainland China, as, needless to say, the concept of *neoliberalism* is itself still very much confined to the academic realm. Moreover, I was told that in academic writing in mainland China "neo-liberal" is no longer permitted as a description of China, as the country has never given up its socialism. Indeed, while the Chinese Dream for an individual is nothing more than neoliberalism in its high patriotic and nation-alist form, the deregulations that define neoliberalism have never been the case for the Leninist state. For now, the situation is brighter in Hong Kong, Taiwan, and Macao, where at least academic and internet freedom prevails. In recent years, Hong Kong and Taiwan wit-nessed backlashes against and resistance to neoliberalism, particularly as a reaction to the state-directed injection of mainland Chinese capital and technology, suspected of carrying political agendas. However, such resistance is aligned with either xenophobic localism against mainland Chinese or "authentic" neoliberalism from the West, particularly the US. Chinese denials of being a "Western" neoliberal state are accompanied by the rise of a neoliberal techno-authoritarian socialist state with Chinese characteristics. Is that a way out of "Western" neoliberalism or a deeper abyss with less of a way out? Is anarchism the only way out?

操新自由主义

操新自由主义！就是这么直接。文章到这里可以停了，因为信息就这么简单。我的立场简单明了，我想你已经理解了。我根本不想加入什么新自由主义的正面因素。说实话，连去想我都觉得恶心。真心够了。有段时间，我在想要不要把文章称作《忘了新自由主义》，因为这就是我想做的。这么多年我写了12篇新自由主义的学术文章[1]，我已经不想再用多一丝一毫的精力去写更多文章了。我怕写出来的东西反而给新自由主义新的生机。进一步讲，在政治策略层面上，把头埋在沙里，然后集体忽略这样一个具有毁灭性、伤害性的现象是十分危险的。新自由主义已经愈演愈烈，而忽略真的不是办法。[2] 所以慎重考虑后，我决定不采用更温和的说法，而是直截了当的"操它吧！"凭什么在邪恶的新自由主义面前我们还要更在意语言的礼貌性？我就是要造反、惹怒、攻击新自由主义，因为我们有一万个理由被它伤害。新自由主义就是让人心不安的臭东西，我们要永远的反抗。要是题目软了，岂不是又是对新自由主义

的变相承认？我的确一开始担心过我的声誉是不是会受到影响。会不会升不了职，或者去不了其他地方工作？但这不就是承认自己被新自由主义打败了吗？操！

感觉以前的我认为日常生活的语言是无法抨击新自由主义的。似乎用了复杂枯燥的学术语言，特别是地理的多元、杂糅和变异理论后，我们才能削弱新自由主义这个庞大的建筑。虽然我自己曾经也是写这些理论的其中一人[3]，但我总觉得这样的框架和我想要的背道而驰。我想要的反抗，正正要发生在日常生活中最平凡，最不被注意，最经常发生的事务中。所以，"操新自由主义"才是我想要的。其实这个观点是非常复杂多元的，至少在写文章以后，我对"操"的理解可谓是进入了新高度。这是个多么优秀多彩复杂有深度的词啊！它又是名词，又是动词，还是在英语中最经常用的表示感叹的形容此。它可以用来表达愤怒、鄙视、恼怒、冷漠、惊讶、焦躁、甚至不带意思的说只因为舌头想说。你可以"搞砸了件事""毁了个人""吊儿郎当""关我屁事"，你也可以轻松的想起在一个情境中你被喝令到"滚回家打飞机"（译者按：以上引号短语英文中都用到操）。这时候你可能会想"关'谁'屁事"？好吧，关我事，其实也关想要终结新自由主义的你事。"操"这个词的力量给了新自由主义一个挑战。它可以让我们思考"操新自由主义"深沉多元的含义。但是同时。我们也操"深层多元"。Kieran Healy[4] 说了，"深沉多元的思维通常给有趣、有实践意义、和实战的理论以打击。"所以别多想了，赶快看看操新自由主义里最重要的因素。

　　首先，最为了当的是，说"操新自由主义"的时候我们可以表达我们内心的愤怒和不满。我们可以把这个恶毒的机械给我们的毒液吐回在它脸上。"操"的方法可以是游行或者写更多的书和文章去批判它。后者是为了给被新自由主义荼毒的人说教，前者是为了给被荼毒者一个希望改变。这些方法不是不重要，但是远远不足以让大潮和我们一起对抗新自由主义。抗争让我们可以和社会权贵对话，误以为他们真的会听取群众的意见改进[5]。难道我们自己不可以做说话的人吗？第二个"操新自由主义"的含义是拒绝这个概念。它首先由J.K. Gibson-Graham[6] 提出，号召大家以不谈的方法来结束新自由主义。渐渐的，学者都不把这个概念放在重点的位置了。或许这不是我前文中批判的"掩耳盗铃"的心态，而是用另一种方法来谈论同样的问题。或许这对把论述扩展到别的领域来说是一个好的策略，但是我仍然觉得这样不足以消灭新自由主义。Mark Purcell[7] 说到："我们需要把注意力从新自由主义转移到我们自己身上，去调理我们和自己的复杂和有趣的关系。"虽然这些批判和忽略政治是有用的，但是我们仍然要积极的去从新自由主义都触及不到的方面去操新自由主义。

　　其中一个直截了当的方法是参与前瞻性的政策制定，[8] 这是我的"操新自由主义"的第三个层面。前瞻政治否定了代表政治的阶级性、中心性和权威性。前瞻政治强调的是未来社会需要的一种水平民主的关系和组织模式[9]。我们不需要和权贵交谈，我们要的是清楚的知道自己想要的，去做——前瞻性和行动力。但是，需要注意的是，新自由主义似乎有囊括一些政治想法和行动

的能力[10]。对于像 David Harvey[11] 这个批判者，政府的一剂改革就可以解决他们说的新自由主义的问题，然后他便会放弃追求水平民主，眼看新自由主义走向更猖狂的明天。他完全误解把前瞻政治误解成未来了，但是我说前瞻政治是手段而不是结论[12]。换句话来说，前瞻政治必须具有恒久持续的敏锐度，所以绝不会出现指派的现象。它敏锐而有自我反省能力，并且永恒的为了社会的更好、发展和创新而存在。这样的前瞻政治才是反新自由主义的。这是一个没有结论的手段，并且它永远都是我们的手段。前瞻政治让我们拥抱极端平等的快乐。我们无需成为去那空虚的乌托邦承诺的先锋或者无产者，而是永远站在当时当下，不断的努力反抗[13]。

　　新自由主义没有什么值得我们尊重的，所以让我们拥抱前瞻政治，"操新自由主义"。操它给我们制造的幻想；操它带来的破坏；操它把不平等说成是一种美德；操它破坏环境；操无休止的资本积累和盲目追求资本；操朝圣山学社和各自试图粉饰它的智库；操给我们洗脑的Friedrich Hayek 和Milton Friedman；操撒切尔夫人、里根和所有给权贵折腰的政客；操那些一面制造排外言论一面用"外人"来打扫自己厕所的伪善之人；操越来越数字化的潮流也操那些不懂不是所有东西东可以衡量的人；操那些把金钱放在社区之上的人；操新自由主义的一起也操它带来的特洛伊木马!这么多年我们听到的借口都是"没有别的办法"，"蛋糕大了自然分的多"，"物竟天择"没用就要被淘汰的噩梦。这么多年我们听到的平凡人的惨案其实都是资本家无尽的诡计[14]。Garrett Hardin's[15] 从未停止想这些牧场上的牛是怎么被人

占为己有的。当我们把没有私有权概念的人召集起来的时候会是什么样子的呢[16]？当我们把更多的关注力放在前瞻性政治的先驱上并仔细学习总结他们的经验组织模式的时候会发生什么呢[17]？当我们不再用新自由主义给我的药丸，而用互助和合作来治愈我们在无尽的竞争中受到的伤痛时会发生什么呢[18]？

　　Jamie Peck[19] 曾把新自由主义称作"极端政治口号"，但是这个称谓以及承载不了它该受到的批判了。从我们第一次认清敌人到现在已经有些年份了，而在这些岁月里我们也从我们的反抗和写作中对他认识越来越深。虽然我们很清楚的知道什么时候我们曾经打赢某个战役 – 如 2008 年金融海啸后的占领华尔街的胜利 – 但是新自由主义总能死灰复燃、如僵尸如野鬼[20]。Japhy Wilson把其称作"哥特式新自由主义"，[21] 而我很相信消灭这个鬼魂的方法是我们更加积极的行动[22]。让我们把"操新自由主义"变成新的魔咒怎么样？一个不仅让我们行动起来反抗，也让我们从新生活在真正属于我们自己的空间的魔咒。当我们每次使用这个魔咒的时候，我们都感觉到语言之外的力量，把理论和行动都放在前瞻政治的魔幻里。我们要椒炒多角度抗拒新自由主义。虽然我们不能忘记它，但是我们可以从语言里外反抗它。总之，我们要迎来新的政治口号。开始用 #fuckneoliberalism 标签让我们的口号猖狂起来吧！当然，比起表达愤怒，我们要做更多。我们要下定决心，认识到我们行动的当下当时性[23]。我们要夺回我们的世界，刻不容缓！

　　我们要在代表政治面前不断的出现。天上不会掉下个救世主。这个系统已经腐烂透了，我们

每每选择的下个领袖都是另一次的失败。其实领袖不是问题核心，问题核心是选出领袖作为代表的系统。我们都参与了让系统继续的路西法效应[24]。这些政客只是在做他们的工作，因为本来他们就是要为资本家的法律服务的[25]。但是，我们无需服从，也没有义务服从。通过我们的直接行动和另类的组织模式去摧毁这个系统和这个压迫的循环。当一个政治系统由资本定义、操控、结合、甚至赋予生命，它永远不可能代表我们的想法和存在。所以我们要重新掌握我们的生命，掌握我们的主权。我们要更加积极更加团结，并且理性的意识到对一个个体的压迫就是对我们所有人的伤害[26]。我们要创造另一个空间，一个以互助、友情、互利、没有等级的组织模式的空间。在这里，把权力赋予人民的民主哲学被最认真的对待。绝对的新自由主义是最粗鲁、最有破坏力的。为了对抗它，我们也要用同样力度的语言和行动。我们的社区、我们的合作、我们的互相关怀都是新自由主义最不想见到的。我们一庆祝，它就愤怒。当我们说"操新自由主义"时，说的不仅仅是几个字，而是我们对对方的承诺。大声说吧，和我一起，说给会听的人！吹响行动和前瞻政治的号角，改变这个不可理喻的世界！操新自由主义！

CHAPTER 4

繁體中文 – Traditional Chinese

干新自由主義

The translator of both the simplified and traditional Chinese versions chose to remain anonymous (ed.)

Translator's Commentary
See Chapter 3.

干新自由主義

干新自由主義！就是這麼直接。文章到這裡可以停了，因為信息就這麼簡單。我的立場簡單明了，我想你已經理解了。我根本不想加入什麼新自由主義的正面因素。說實話，連去想我都覺得噁心。真心夠了。有段時間，我在想要不要把文章稱作《忘了新自由主義》，因為這就是我想做的 。這麼多年我寫了12篇新自由主義的學術文章[1]，我已經不想再用多一絲一毫的精力去寫更多文章了。我怕寫出來的東西反而給新自由主義新的生機。進一步講，在政治策略層面上，把頭埋在沙裡，然後集體忽略這樣一個具有毀滅性、傷害性的現像是十分危險的。新自由主義已經愈演愈烈，而忽略真的不是辦法。[2]所以慎重考慮後，我決定不採用更溫和的說法，而是直截了當的"干它吧！"憑什麼在邪惡的新自由主義面前我們還要更在意語言的禮貌性？我就是要造反、惹怒、攻擊新自

由主義，因為我們有一萬個理由被它傷害。新自由主義就是讓人心不安的臭東西，我們要永遠的反抗。要是題目軟了，豈不是又是對新自由主義的變相承認？我的確一開始擔心過我的聲譽是不是會受到影響。會不會升不了職，或者去不了其他地方工作？但這不就是承認自己被新自由主義打敗了嗎？干！

感覺以前的我認為日常生活的語言是無法抨擊新自由主義的。似乎用了複雜枯燥的學術語言，特別是地理的多元、雜糅和變異理論後，我們才能削弱新自由主義這個龐大的建築。雖然我自己曾經也是寫這些理論的其中一人[3]，但我總覺得這樣的框架和我想要的背道而馳。我想要的反抗，正正要發生在日常生活中最平凡，最不被注意，最經常發生的事務中。所以，"干新自由主義"才是我想要的。其實這個觀點是非常複雜多元的，至少在寫文章以後，我對"干"的理解可謂是進入了新高度。這是個多麼優秀多彩複雜有深度的詞啊！它又是名詞，又是動詞，還是在英語中最經常用的表示感嘆的形容此。它可以用來表達憤怒、鄙視、惱怒、冷漠、驚訝、焦躁、甚至不帶意思的說只因為舌頭想說。你可以"搞砸了件事""毀了個人""吊兒郎當""關我屁事"，你也可以輕鬆的想起在一個情境中你被喝令到"滾回家打飛機"（譯者按：以上引號短語英文中都用到干）。這時候你可能會想"'關'誰'屁事"？好吧，關我事，其實也關想要終結新自由主義的你事。"干"這個詞的力量給了新自由主義一個挑戰。它可以讓我們思考"干新自由主義"深沉多元的含義。但是同時。我們也干"深層多元"。 Kieran Healy[4] 說了，"深沉多元的思

維通常給有趣、有實踐意義、和實戰的理論以打擊。"所以別多想了,趕快看看干新自由主義裡最重要的因素。

首先,最為了當的是,說 "干新自由主義" 的時候我們可以表達我們內心的憤怒和不滿。我們可以把這個惡毒的機械給我們的毒液吐回在它臉上。 "干" 的方法可以是遊行或者寫更多的書和文章去批判它。後者是為了給被新自由主義荼毒的人說教,前者是為了給被荼毒者一個希望改變。這些方法不是不重要,但是遠遠不足以讓大潮和我們一起對抗新自由主義。抗爭讓我們可以和社會權貴對話,誤以為他們真的會聽取群眾的意見改進[5]。難道我們自己不可以做說話的人嗎?第二個 "干新自由主義" 的含義是拒絕這個概念。它首先由 J.K. Gibson-Graham[6] 提出,號召大家以不談的方法來結束新自由主義。漸漸的,學者都不把這個概念放在重點的位置了。或許這不是我前文中批判的 "掩耳盜鈴" 的心態,而是用另一種方法來談論同樣的問題。或許這對把論述擴展到別的領域來說是一個好的策略,但是我仍然覺得這樣不足以消滅新自由主義。 Mark Purcell[7] 說到: "我們需要把注意力從新自由主義轉移到我們自己身上,去調理我們和自己的複雜和有趣的關係。" 雖然這些批判和忽略政治是有用的,但是我們仍然要積極的去從新自由主義都觸及不到的方面去干新自由主義。

其中一個直截了當的方法是參與前瞻性的政策制定,[8] 這是我的 "干新自由主義" 的第三個層面。前瞻政治否定了代表政治的階級性、中心性和權威性。前瞻政治強調的是未來社會需要的一種水平民主的關係和組織模式[9]。我們不需要和

權貴交談，我們要的是清楚的知道自己想要的，去做——前瞻性和行動力。但是，需要注意的是，新自由主義似乎有囊括一些政治想法和行動的能力[10]。對於像 David Harvey[11] 這個批判者，政府的一劑改革就可以解決他們說的新自由主義的問題，然後他便會放棄追求水平民主，眼看新自由主義走向更猖狂的明天。他完全誤解把前瞻政治誤解成未來了，但是我說前瞻政治是手段而不是結論[12]。換句話來說，前瞻政治必須具有恆久持續的敏銳度，所以絕不會出現指派的現象。它敏銳而有自我反省能力，並且永恆的為了社會的更好、發展和創新而存在。這樣的前瞻政治才是反新自由主義的。這是一個沒有結論的手段，並且它永遠都是我們的手段。前瞻政治讓我們擁抱極端平等的快樂。我們無需成為去那空虛的烏托邦承諾的先鋒或者無產者，而是永遠站在當時當下，不斷的努力反抗[13]。

　　新自由主義沒有什麼值得我們尊重的，所以讓我們擁抱前瞻政治，"干新自由主義"。干它給我們製造的幻想；干它帶來的破壞；干它把不平等說成是一種美德；干它破壞環境；干無休止的資本積累和盲目追求資本；干朝聖山學社和各自試圖粉飾它的智庫；干給我們洗腦的 Friedrich Hayek 和 Milton Friedman；干撒切爾夫人、裡根和所有給權貴折腰的政客；干那些一面製造排外言論一面用"外人"來打掃自己廁所的偽善之人；干越來越數字化的潮流也干那些不懂不是所有東西東可以衡量的人；干那些把金錢放在社區之上的人；干新自由主義的一起也干它帶來的特洛伊木馬!這麼多年我們聽到的藉口都是"沒有別的辦法"，"蛋糕大了自然分的多"，"物竟天擇"

沒用就要被淘汰的噩夢。這麼多年我們聽到的平凡人的慘案其實都是資本家無盡的詭計[14]。 Garrett Hardin's[15] 從未停止想這些牧場上的牛是怎麼被人佔為己有的。當我們把沒有私有權概念的人召集起來的時候會是什麼樣子的呢[16]？？當我們把更多的關注力放在前瞻性政治的先驅上並仔細學習總結他們的經驗組織模式的時候會發生什麼呢[17]？當我們不再用新自由主義給我的藥丸，而用互助和合作來治愈我們在無盡的競爭中受到的傷痛時會發生什麼呢[18]？

   Jamie Peck[19] 曾把新自由主義稱作 "極端政治口號" ，但是這個稱謂以及承載不了它該受到的批判了。從我們第一次認清敵人到現在已經有些年份了，而在這些歲月裡我們也從我們的反抗和寫作中對他認識越來越深。雖然我們很清楚的知道什麼時候我們曾經打贏某個戰役 – 如2008年金融海嘯後的佔領華爾街的勝利 – 但是新自由主義總能死灰復燃、如殭屍如野鬼[20]。 Japhy Wilson 把其稱作 "哥特式新自由主義" [21]，而我很相信消滅這個鬼魂的方法是我們更加積極的行動[22]。讓我們把 "干新自由主義" 變成新的魔咒怎麼樣？一個不僅讓我們行動起來反抗，也讓我們從新生活在真正屬於我們自己的空間的魔咒。當我們每次使用這個魔咒的時候，我們都感覺到語言之外的力量，把理論和行動都放在前瞻政治的魔幻裡。我們要椒炒多角度抗拒新自由主義。雖然我們不能忘記它，但是我們可以從語言里外反抗它。總之，我們要迎來新的政治口號。開始用 #fuckneoliberalism 標籤讓我們的口號猖狂起來吧！當然，比起表達憤怒，我們要做更多。我們要下定決心，認識到我們行動的當下當時性[23]。我們要

奪回我們的世界，刻不容緩！

　　我們要在代表政治面前不斷的出現。天上不會掉下個救世主。這個系統已經腐爛透了，我們每每選擇的下個領袖都是另一次的失敗。其實領袖不是問題核心，問題核心是選出領袖作為代表的系統。我們都參與了讓系統繼續的路西法效應[24]。這些政客只是在做他們的工作，因為本來他們就是要為資本家的法律服務的[25]。但是，我們無需服從，也沒有義務服從。通過我們的直接行動和另類的組織模式去摧毀這個系統和這個壓迫的循環。當一個政治系統由資本定義、干控、結合、甚至賦予生命，它永遠不可能代表我們的想法和存在。所以我們要重新掌握我們的生命，掌握我們的主權。我們要更加積極更加團結，並且理性的意識到對一個個體的壓迫就是對我們所有人的傷害[26]。我們要創造另一個空間，一個以互助、友情、互利、沒有等級的組織模式的空間。在這裡，把權力賦予人民的民主哲學被最認真的對待。絕對的新自由主義是最粗魯、最有破壞力的。為了對抗它，我們也要用同樣力度的語言和行動。我們的社區、我們的合作、我們的互相關懷都是新自由主義最不想見到的。我們一慶祝，它就憤怒。當我們說"干新自由主義"時，說的不僅僅是幾個字，而是我們對對方的承諾。大聲說吧，和我一起，說給會聽的人！吹響行動和前瞻政治的號角，改變這個不可理喻的世界！干新自由主義！

نئولیبرالیزم لعنتی

Translated by مرتضی غلامزاده – Morteza Gholamzadeh

Translator's Commentary

Throughout the centuries, translations have played a substantial role in the processing and exchange of ideologies among people. The complexity of language systems and cultural perspective created specific norms among researchers interested in translating books and articles from another language. The present article employed deconstruction as an approach to interpreting our political world more explicitly than has previously been the case. As we know, translating political articles that use offensive language is not an easy decision for a translator who lives in an Islamic country like Iran. Luckily, Persian literature is one with fruitful language, which, by using poetry in polemical articles, makes the process of translating these words and sentiments less controversial for readers. For instance, I translated the term "well, fuck it then" by using a verse from Saadi Shirazi who is one of the major Persian poets in Iran, often called the Master of Speech. Moreover, my perception is that translation is the social phenomenon of transferring cultural elements from one language into another. To achieve that, I have preferred to use and find some similar idioms and terms in Farsi, which people use in their daily life. Moreover, I was committed to transferring the author's message more transparently and attractively for the Iranians and Persian languages speakers, given that "neoliberalism" is not a delusionary belief or ideology but is truly against all of humanity in our common world.

شیطانی به حدی است که سیاستمداران در حال انجام وظایفشان در سیستمی هستند که فساد منحرف را تشویق و قوانینی را که کاپیتالیسم برای آنها طراحی کرده است را اجرا کنند[25].اما ما مجبور به اطاعت نیستیم!ما مدیون و زیربار منت این نظم نیستیم.ما از طریق مستقیم و گزینه‌های سازمانی میتوانیم کلیه ساختار را متهم به کیفرخواست کنیم و این چرخه زشت سوء استفاده را از بین ببریم و بشکنیم.زمانیکه سیستم سیاسی به‌وسیله کسی تعریف،برای کسانی مشروط ،و به مخمصه‌ای دچار میشود که مشتق از کاپیتالیسم است.لذا این امر به‌هیچ‌وجه بیانگر و بازنمایی از شیوه‌های ما در شناختن و بودن در جهان نیست.ازینرو ما نیازمند این مهم هستیم که طرز زندگی مان را خودمان بر عهده بگیریم و مرام اشتراکی خودمان را پس بگیریم و احیا کنیم.ما باید در سیاست‌هایمان فعالانه باشیم و درک انسانی و همبستگی بیشتری را در آغوش بگیریم که انقیاد و اطاعت یک نفر میتواند نشاندهنده ظلم به همه ما باشد[26].

ما میتوانیم زندگی را در جهان های ممکن دیگری از سر بگیریم این امر از طریق تعهد تازه مان به شیوه های کمک متقابل،رفاقت،عمل متقابل و اشکال غیر سلسله مراتبی سازمانی است که دموکراسی را به خواستگاه اصلی قدرت یعنی مردم باز میگرداند. در نهایت نئولیبرالیزم یک ایده نامطبوع است که منتج شده از پیامدهای مبتذل و مفروضات فراوان است.در پاسخ،سزاوار این است که به‌تناسب زبان و عمل به همان اندازه توهین‌آمیز با آن برخورد شود.جامعه ما،همکاری ما و مراقبت از یکدیگر برای نئولیبرالیزم نفرت‌انگیز است.نئولیبرالیزم متنفر از جشن و سرور ماست.زمانیکه ما میگوییم لعنت بر نئولیبرالیزم این فراتر از لغات است.این به معنای تعهد ما به یکدیگر در عمل است.این را با صدای بلند بگو،با من بگو.این را به کسانی که دوست دارند بشنوند بگو.اما بیشتر از همه به معنای همنوایی به عمل و تجسم قدرت پیشنمایانه به تغییر جهان لعنتی است!نئولیبرالیزم لعنتی!

جنبش،نئولیبرالیزم حرکت اش را با استنشاق هوای جدید و با شکلی از مرده متحرک تجدید حیات بخشید[20]. جفی ویلسون[21] این قدرت در حال پیشرفت را (گوتیک نئولیبرال) نامید و من معتقدم که برای غلبه بر این نمایش وحشت ما باید سیاست‌هایمان را به حوزه وضع‌کننده قانونی سوق دهیم[22]. چه حالتی پیش می‌آمد اگر نئولیبرالیزم لعنتی به نوع جدیدی از سیاست‌ها تبدیل به قرائتی از رهایی(مانترا) میشد؟ عبارت توانمندی که نه‌تنها در عمل سخن می‌گفت بلکه احیاسازی زندگی‌مان در فضاها و لحظاتی که ما فعالانه در آن زندگی می‌کنیم را نیز میسر می‌ساخت ؟چه می‌شد اگر زمانی که ما از این عبارت استفاده می‌کردیم این به معنای فراخوانی برای عاملیت وضع قانونی باشد که فراتر ازصرفا کلمات می‌بود و ترکیبی از تئوری و عمل برای پراکسیس زیبایی از پش نمایان جلوه می‌داشت؟ما باید رویکرد چندوجهی برای عدم پذیرش نئولیبرالیزم را اتخاذ کنیم.در حالیکه ما نمی‌توانیم تماماً چشم‌پوشی و یا فراموش کنیم.ما می‌توانیم فعالانه در مقابلش بیاستیم و به شیوه‌هایی که فراتر از عملکرد لفاظی و لفاظی در عملکرد است و با به کارگیری تمامی ابزارهای ممکنه،شعار سیاسی رادیکال را گسترش دهیم.با استفاده از هشتگ# نئولیبرالیزم لعنتی اهانت مان را گسترش دهیم.اما ما باید خشم مان را بیشتر نشان دهیم.ما باید تصمیم خود را به وضع قانونی تبدیل کنیم و امیدمان را به عنوان (وجود در همه‌جا حاضر) از تجربه تجسم بخش مان از (اینجا) و (اکنون) درک کنیم[23].ما نیازمند ساختن مجدد از جهان هستیم.رویه ای که نمی‌تواند به تأخیر بی افتد.

ما تعمداً خودمان را فریب‌خورده و ناتوان میدانیم و با آرایش سیاسی از بازنمایی وضعیت فعلی در حال پیشرو را جذاب میدانیم. اعتقاد کور ما می‌گوید که برای ناجی بی‌وقفه صبر کنید که قطره‌ای از آسمان خواهد چکید!این سیستم ثابت کرده است که کاملاً فاسد است.در زمانهای مختلف کاندیدای عالی سیاسی ما شکست را ثابت کرده است.در عوض ایده قطعی ما خود نئولیبرالیزم است که نمونه بارزی از هسته وجود مشکل است.ما شرایط سازمانی را قادر ساختیم که (اثر شیطانی)را تولید و به خودمان عرضه کند[24]. ابتذال

ای که به آن تعلق دارند و آنها را صرفا برای تمییز کردن توالت‌ها و رفت‌وروب‌ها مفید می‌دانند.لعنت بر حرکات تشدید شده به‌سوی معیارها و شکست‌ها، به خاطر اینکه هر چیز باارزشی لزوماً ارزشمند نیست!لعنت به میل برای سود از طریق نیازهای اجتماع!لعنت به هر چیزی که نئولیبرالیزم مطلقاً بر آن حکومت میکند.لعنت بر اسب تروایی که بر آن سوار است.برای مدت های طولانی به ما این‌طور گفته می‌شد که (گزینه دیگری وجود ندارد) و با مد دریا همه قایق‌ها به حرکت درخواهند آمد یعنی همه در بازار آزاد منتفع خواهند شد.ما در کابوس داروینی جهانی، همه در مقابل هم زندگی می‌کنیم که شعارش (بقاء اصلح) است. ایده (تراژدی مشترکات)ما را بلعیده، به دام انداخته و غرق کرده است.در حالیکه در واقعیت این نیرنگی است که منعکس کننده تراژدی کاپیتالیسم و جنگ بی پایان چپاول و غارت می باشد[14]. نظریه گریت هاردین[15] مبنی بر پاشنه آشیل این بود که او هرگز فکر و تمرکزش را بر روی این مسئله که چگونه احشام در حال چرا پیش‌ازاین مالکیت داشته‌اند را کنار نگذاشت.چه اتفاقی می‌افتاد اگر اشتراکات واقعی با مشترکینی بدون فرض پیشین از مالکیت خصوصی گرد هم جمع می‌شدند[16] ؟اصلاً چه چیزی ممکن است اتفاق بیافتد زمانیکه ما در مورد گزینه‌های متصور شده غور و تعمق کنیم که پیش‌ازاین هم اتفاق افتاده‌اند و رجحان و امتیاز این تجارب به‌عنوان مهم‌ترین اشکال سازمانی باشد[17] ؟.اصلاً چه چیزی ممکن است اتفاق بیافتد زمانیکه به جای قرص‌های تلخ رقابت و شایستگی ما در عوض تمرکزمان بر روی انرژی‌مان نه به‌عنوان مداوا کردن خودمان با تجویزهای نئولیبرال بلکه گزینه‌های شفابخش از همکاری متقابل و تعاون باشد[18] ؟

جمی پک[19]زمانی نئولیبرالیزم را شعار سیاسی رادیکال نامید.اما این امر برای پرداختن به قلمرو نقد آن کافی نیست. سالیان زیادی گذشته است که از زمانیکه ما دشمن را شناسایی کردیم و بعدازآن زمان ما با نوشته‌ها و اعتراض‌هایمان آن را به‌خوبی دریافتیم.اما حتی وقتی‌که به‌یقین به شکست آن پی بردیم مخصوصاً در زمان بحران مالی ۲۰۰۸ و متعاقباً تسخیر

می‌تواند راه حل نئولیبرال را پاسخ دهد.در حالیکه او به طور جدی
در رد سازمان های غیر سلسله مراتبی و سیاست‌های افقی به‌عنوان
جاده‌ای هموار برای آینده نئولیبرالیزم یقین حاصل میکند.در عین
بدبینی او تماماً سیاست‌های پیش نمایانه را بد درک میکند که آنها
روش هایی برای پایان نیستند بلکه تنها روش های برای آینده
هستند[12].به عبارت دیگر،یک گوش‌به‌زنگی دائمی به سیاست‌های
پیش نمایانه پیش از این ساخته شده است.تا اینکه عمل واقعی این
سیاست نتوانسته تطبیق داده شود.این انعکاس و توجه ویژه است
اما دیدی به سوی تولید،خلق و ابتکار به عنوان رضایت و تمایل
به اجتماع هم هست.به این ترتیب،سیاست های پیش نمایانه به
صراحت ضد نئولیبرالیزم است.آنها روش هایی از روش های قبض
شده ماست .روش هایی که پایانی برای آنها متصور نیست. پیش
نمایان به معنای در آغوش گرفتن و خوش گذراندن و خوشحالی
کردن به معنای با هم بودن تساوی های رادیکال است نه نه به
معنای پش قراولان و پرولتاریا به سوی جاده متعالی تهی شده از
اتوپیای وعده داده‌شده در(ناکجا آباد) می باشد.بلکه به‌عنوان
وجود در همه‌جا حاضر زمینی(اینجا) و (اکنون) برای ساختن جهانی
دیگر(در پوسته قدیمی اش) و تلاش همیشگی و تائید مجددانه ای
که بایسته اش است[13].

هیچ چیزی در مورد نئولیبرالیزم که مستحق احترام باشد
وجود ندارد.بنابراین در تطابق به سیاست پیش نمایانه تکوین پیام
من ساده است:لعنت بهش!لعنت بر استمرارطلبی که بر رؤیاهای
سیاسی ما دارد.لعنت بر خشونتی که بوجود می آورد.لعنت بر
نابرابری که حمل بر اخلاق میکند.لعنت بر غارت و ویرانی که بر
طبیعت میکند.لعنت بر چرخه بی پایان انباشت و اندیشه رشد.
لعنت بر مکتب مونت پله رن و تمامی متخصصان و حامیانش
که برای ترویج آن میکنند.لعنت بر فردریش فن هایک و میلتون
فریدن برای ایدهایی که ما را مجبور به واکنش کردند.لعنت بر
تاچر ها و ریگان ها و تمامی بزدلان و سیاستمداران منتفعی که
در جستجوی زیادی خواهی و طمع به یکدیگر نون قرض میدهند.
لعنت بر پراکندگان ترس برای جلوگیری از (دیگران) در جامعه

قلمداد کرد که ما اینجا وارد بحث اش نمی‌شویم.پژوهشگران نئولیبرالیزم را معمولاً به عنوان مرکز مطالعاتشان اولویت بندی نمی‌کنند.ممکن است به طور کامل فراموش نکنند و یا روی‌هم‌رفته از نئولیبرالیزم چشم پوشی کنند. کما اینکه من بیش از این آن را مسئله ای مشکل دار و بغرنج میدانستم، اما در عوض باعث شروع نوشتن درباره موضوعات دیگر میشود.به این نکته توجه داشته باشیم که این نقطه تماس مهمی برای ارتباط ماست از آنجائیکه ما ورای چشم انداز جهانی نئولیبرالیزم مطالعه میکنیم.اما من در اینجا هم به طور کامل قانع نشده ام که این امر کافی باشد.مارک پرسل[7] میگوید:ما باید از نئولیبرالیزم روی برگردانیم و به خودمان برگردیم. از مشکلات شروع کنیم،مسرور باشیم،امور را خودمان حل و فصل کنیم در حالیکه نفی می‌کنیم.اعتراض و انتقاد لازم و ضروری است. ما همچنین نیازمند این هستیم که فعالانه به نئولیبرالیزم آسیب وارد کنیم مخصوصاً .به کارهایی که خارج از حیطه آن است است.

اقدام مستقیم فراتر از نئولیبرالیزم به سیاست های پش نمایانه[*] می پردازد[8].این میتواند سومین و مهمترین عاملی باشد که من فکر میکنم ما باید تمرکز بیشتری بر روی آن بگذاریم علی‌الخصوص زمانیکه ما ایده نئولیبرالیزم لعنتی را فرا میخوانیم.پیش نمایان مقارن با عدم پذیرش مرکزیت،سلسله مراتب و اقتدارگرایی است که از سیاست‌های نمایندگی منتج می‌شود با تأکید بر عمل تجسم‌بخشی که روابط افقی را به وضع قانونی تبدیل میکند و اشکال سازمانی که تلاش می‌کنند جامعه آینده را به دنبال داشته باشد را به صحنه عمل تبدیل میکند[9].فراتر از صحبت انجام‌شده،پیش نمایان و عمل مستقیم مدعی این هستند که هیچ‌وقت صحبتی وجود نداشته است.با به رسمیت شناختن این مطلب که هر کاری که ما می‌خواهم انجام دهیم باید خودمان آنرا انجام دهیم.بااین‌همه، توجه زیادی به شیوه‌های که نئولیبرالیزم قادر به پذیرش تمامی شیوه های گفتمان سیاسی و لازم‌الاجرا و ضرورت است وجود دارد.[10].برای منتقدانی چون دیوید هاروی[11] کمیتی از یک دولت

---

[*]   اهدفی را که برای آن مبارزه می‌کنیم، از هم اکنون زندگی‌اش کنیم و اینگونه حال را تبدیل به آینده کنیم

به این فکر کنید که باشه.اما برای چه کسی این موضوع اهمیت
ندارد؟خوب،برای من!و اگر شما هم علاقه‌مند به پایان نئولیبرالیزم
هستید باید با من همراه شوید!گنجایش‌های قدرتمندی که با این
کلمه همراه میشود چالش بالقوه‌ای را برای نئولیبرالیزم به همراه
آورده است.برای بررسی و بروز این توانایی ها ما باید قدردان این
اختلافات جزئی باشیم که در اصطلاح میتواند به معنی (نئولیبرالیزم
لعنتی) باشد.به طور همزمان،کران هلی[4] در مقاله‌ای (ظرافت
لعنتی) را مطرح و در مورد آن بحث‌وجدل کرده است.این معمولاً
مانع بسط تئوری میشود که به‌صورت عقلانی جذاب،به‌صورت
تجربی مولد، و به‌صورت عملی موفق آمیز است.بنابراین بدون
شی گرایی این تفاوت‌های ظریف اجازه بدهید فوراً به سراغ آنچه
که من فکر میکنم باید درباره الویت بندی نئولیبرالیزم منزجرکننده
مطرح است بپردازیم.

اولین استنباط به نظر واضح‌ترین است اینکه بگوییم
نئولیبرالیزم لعنتی.ما می‌توانیم غضب مان را به ماشین نئولیبرالیزم
این‌طوری بیان کنیم.این نشان‌دهنده خشم ماست.این میل به
فریاد انزجار ماست.این فوران کینه در مواجهه به بدخواه مهلکی
است که به چهره کریه اش را به ما نشان داده است.این می‌تواند
به شکل بسیج اعتراضات بیشتر در مقابل نئولیبرالیزم و با نوشتن
مقالات و کتب بیشتر در انتقاد از اثرات آن باشد.دست‌آخر این
موعظه‌ها می‌توانید تغییر داده شوند و امیدهای پیشین که منحرف
شده بودند را مایل خواهند کرد که مسیرشان را تغییر دهند.من
نمی‌خواهم منکر این روش‌ها بشوم که این روش‌ها تکنیک های
مهمی در مقاومت مدنی هستند.اما مطمئن هستم که این‌ها برای
تغییر رویدادها در مقابل نئولیبرالیزم هرگز کافی نیستند.برای عرض
و اندام کردن و اعتراض عمومی ما تلاش خواهیم کرد که بازیگران
قدرت را فرا بخوانیم.با این اعتقاد اشتباه که آنها ممکن است
صدای امتناع مردمی ما را بشنوند و شروع به پذیرش کنند.[5]آیا نباید
صحبتی مطرح شود؟این دومین استنباط نئولیبرالیزم لعنتی است
که در مفهوم عدم پذیرش متجلی می‌شود.این را میتوان حمایتی از
کتاب پایان نئولیبرالیزم(آنطور که ما میشناسیم) گیبسون و گراهام[6]

پیشنهادات شغلی ام مانعی ایجاد کند.آیا من باید پویایی و تحرک دانشگاهی خودم را حفظ کنم و به فکر ارتقاء جایگاه و موقعیت‌های جدیدتر باشم؟ این حس به معنای تصدیق شکست من از نظم و انضباط نئولیبرالیزم است.پس لعنت بهش!

این‌طور احساس می‌شود که گویی من در حال تصدیق امری هستم که هیچ واکنش محاوره‌ای به‌طور مناسب به آن داده نشده که گفتمان نئولیبرالیزم را نقد و کم اثر کند.اگرچه ما می‌توانیم فقط پاسخ مناسبی در قالب آکادمیک بدهیم و از تئوری‌های پیچیده و متنوع جغرافیایی نظیر هایبردی،جهش ژنتیکی برای تضعیف بنیان‌ها و شالوده عمارت نئولیبرالیزم استفاده کنیم.این‌ها به نظر میرسد در به تحلیل رفتن قدرت کارآمد باشد.اگرچه من خودم هم برای پیکربندی چهارچوب‌های نظری از این‌ها استفاده کرده‌ام[3].بعضی مواقع احساس می‌کردم که این قالب‌بندی‌ها در تقابل بحث جدلی بود که من می‌خواستم واقعاً مطرح کنم. این دقیقاً در زندگی روزمره،معمولی،بی‌هیاهو و حیات دنیوی ما سرچشمه می‌گیرد جائیکه من فکر می‌کنم باید سیاست امتناع آنجا قرار گیرد.بنابراین من (نئولیبرالیزم لعنتی) را انتخاب کردم.بدین دلیل که فکر میکنم این دقیقاً همان چیزی که من می‌خواهم بگویم را به‌درستی منتقل میکند.بحثی را که من میخواهم به آن بپردازم دارای یک سری اختلافات جزئی‌تری است از آن چیزی که من در باب اصطلاح(لعنتی)در طول زندگی‌ام با آن روبرو شده‌ام.چه واژه فوق‌العاده رنگارنگی است!این واژه می‌تواند به‌عنوان اسم و فعل و همچنین صفت به کار رود.این شاید بیشترین استفاده را در بانگ‌ها و نداهای شورانگیز در زبان انگلیسی داشته است.این واژه می‌تواند دربرگیرنده خشم،تحقیر،ایذا،بی‌تفاوتی،بی‌طاقتی و همچنین حالتی تأکیدی داشته باشد دلیلش این است که سر زبان است!شما می‌توانید کاری را مفتضحانه انجام دهید.شما می‌توانید باکسی رفتار تحقیرآمیز داشته باشید و یا می‌توانید زمان را به بطالت سپری کنید.اما نمی‌توانید بی تفاوت باشید.همچنین به طور دقیق،نقطه جغرافیایی مرجع کلمه به شما آموزش داده می‌شود مثل(ازاینجا گم شو.یا برو به جهنم!)در اینجا شما ممکن است

نئولیبرالیزم لعنتی

این پیام بی پرده من است.من میتوانستم مخلص کلام را همین
جا به پایان برسانم و اصلا چیز مهمی نیست.جایگاه آکادمیک
من مشخص است و شما میتوانید لب مطلب را بگیرید که من
چه چیزی را میخواهم بگویم.هیچ چیز مثبتی راجع به نئولیبرالیزم
نیست که من بخواهم به آن بیافزایم،واگر خواسته باشم صادقانه
بگویم،من از فکر کردن در باره این موضوع کلا بیزارام.بس است.
مدتی بود که به این موضوع فکر میکردم که اسم مقاله را (نسیان
نئولیبرالیزم) نام گذاری کنم درعوض، و به شیوه های دیگر این
همان کاری است که من میخواهم انجام دهم.چندین سال است
که در این باب مطلب مینویسم[1]..واقعیت این است که به نقطه
ای رسیدم که از این بیشتر نمی خواستم انرژی و وقت ام را صرف
این مطلب کنم.ترس من از این بود که چرخیدن حول این موضوع
میتواند جایگاه آن را استحکام ببخشد.با ملاحظاتی دیگر تشخیص
دادم که به عنوان یک مانور سیاسی این امری بالقوه خطرناک
است که به آسانی خودمان را به بیخیالی بزنیم و همگی به پدیده
ای چشم بپوشیم که اثرات فاجعه بار و منحطی را بر جهان مشترک
ما گذاشته است.این قدرت در حال پیشرفت نئولیبرالیزم است که
نمیتوان آن را انکار کرد و من هنوز قانع نشدم که استراتژی انکار
رویکرد درست و صحیحی باشد[2].افکار دقیق من خلاصه این مطلب
بود،خواه از سخنم پند گیر و خواه ملال. ازینرو نامگذاری بهتر و
بامسماتر برای این مقاله میتوانست ذات زشت و کریه این مسئله
را کمتر جلوه دهد و دوباره ملاحظاتی کردم.چرا ما باید بیشتر
نگران به‌کارگیری لحن فحش آلود نئولیبرالیزم در مقایسه با گفتمان
شنیع و ناخوشایندش باشیم؟من تصمیم ام را گرفتم و می‌خواهم
سرپیچی کنم،واژگون کنم،توهین کنم.به خاطر اینکه ما باید به
خاطر نئولیبرالیزم مجازات شویم.این امر به‌طور کل توهین‌کننده
است و ما باید راهی را برای تحقیر آن پیدا کنیم. آیا انتخاب عنوانی
مناسب انحصار دیگری را برای قدرت نئولیبرالیزم ایجاد نمی‌کند؟من
در ابتدا نگران بودم که عنوان مقاله چه شهرتی را ممکن است
برای من ایجاد کند.آیا ممکن است برای ارتقاء شغلی‌ام و یا

Fuck le néolibéralisme

Translated by Anonyme – Anonymous

The translator of the French version did so anonymously and we were unable to make contact with them to request a commentary (ed.)

Fuck le néolibéralisme

Fuck le néolibéralisme. Ni plus, ni moins. Je pourrais probablement terminer mon argumentation ici et ça n'aurait pas beaucoup d'importance. Ma position est claire et vous saisissez probablement l'essentiel de ce que je veux dire. Je n'ai rien de positif à ajouter à la conversation sur le néolibéralisme, et pour être tout à fait honnête, j'en ai même assez d'avoir à y penser. J'en ai simplement ma claque. J'ai d'abord envisagé d'appeler ce papier « Oublions le néolibéralisme », car d'une certaine manière, c'était exactement ce que j'avais envie de faire. Cela fait de nombreuses années que j'écris sur ce sujet[1] et j'en étais arrivé à un point où je n'avais plus envie de dédier aucune énergie à cette entreprise, craignant que de continuer à travailler sur cette idée ne permette de perpétuer son emprise. Après plus ample réflexion, il me semble que la manœuvre politique qui consiste à faire l'autruche et ignorer collectivement un phénomène qui a eu des effets dévastateurs et débilitants sur le monde que nous partageons puisse être dangereux. Le néolibéralisme jouit d'un pouvoir continu qu'il est difficile de nier, et je ne suis pas convaincu qu'une stratégie d'ignorance soit la bonne approche à adopter[2]. Alors, ma pensée exacte a été la suivante : « bon, et bien qu'il aille se faire foutre, *fuck* le néolibéralisme » ; et bien qu'un terme moins vulgaire eut sans doute atténué l'outrage potentiel que pourrait susciter le titre que j'ai choisi, j'ai changé d'avis selon la logique qui suit. Pourquoi devrions-nous nous préoccuper davantage de notre usage de grossièretés que de l'infamie du discours néolibéral ? J'ai pris la décision de transgresser, de déranger, d'outrager, précisément parce que nous nous *devons* d'être outragés par le néolibéralisme ; il *est* entièrement dérangeant, et c'est pourquoi nous *devrions* chercher à le transgresser. Trouver un titre plus acceptable ne serait-il pas une concession de plus au pouvoir néolibéral ? J'ai d'abord pensé à ce que ce titre pourrait signifier pour ma réputation. Freinerait-il une future promotion ou offre de travail, dans le cas où je souhaiterais poursuivre ma carrière académique ? Cette logique me donnait l'impression de concéder une défaite personnelle à la discipline néolibérale. « *Fuck that* ».

J'avais également l'impression d'admettre que le langage courant ne pouvait offrir aucune réponse appropriée, aucun contre-discours à celui du néolibéralisme. Comme si nous ne pouvions qu'y répondre dans un format académique, en utilisant des théories géographiques complexes de bigarrure, hybridité et mutation, pour affaiblir son édifice. Ceci me semblait déresponsabilisant, et bien que j'aie moi-même contribué à articuler certaines de ces théories[3], j'ai souvent le sentiment que ce type d'approche va à l'encontre de l'argument que je souhaite réellement défendre. C'est précisément dans le quotidien, l'ordinaire, l'invisible et la banalité, me semble t-il, qu'une politique du refus doit se situer. Et c'est ainsi que j'ai fini par choisir « *Fuck le néolibéralisme* ». J'estime qu'il transmet en grande partie ce que je veux vraiment dire. L'argument que je souhaite défendre est légèrement plus nuancé que cela, ce qui m'a fait réfléchir davantage au terme « *fuck* » que je ne l'ai jamais fait dans ma vie. Quel mot fantastique et riche en couleurs ! Il fonctionne comme nom ou verbe, et comme adjectif, il est peut-être l'exclamation la plus employée de la langue anglaise. On l'utilise pour exprimer la colère, le mépris, le mécontentement, l'indifférence, la surprise, l'impatience, et même comme une interjection sans sens particulier simplement parce que « *fuck* » (comme « foutre » en français), se dit si facilement. On peut foutre quelque chose en l'air (« *fuck something up* »), se foutre de quelqu'un (« *fuck someone over* »), dire des foutaises (« *fuck around* »), n'en avoir rien à foutre (« *not give a fuck* »), et ce mot a décidément un point de référence géographique intrinsèque dans la mesure où l'on peut vous inviter à aller vous faire foutre (« *go fuck yourself* »). Au point où on en est, vous pourriez même vous dire, okay, mais qu'est-ce qu'on en a à foutre ? (« *okay, who gives a fuck ?* »). Et bien moi j'en ai quelque chose à foutre, et si en finir avec le néolibéralisme vous intéresse, vous devriez aussi. Le choc provoqué par ce mot peut mettre au défi le néolibéralisme. Pour creuser et libérer ce potentiel, nous devons apprécier les nuances de ce que pourrait signifier la phrase « *Fuck le néolibéralisme* ». Et en même temps, « *fuck* » la nuance. Comme l'a récemment soutenu Kieran Healy, elle « fait typiquement obstacle au développement d'une théorie intéressante d'un point de vue intellectuel, générative d'un point de vue empirique, ou brillante d'un point de vue pragmatique ».[4] Alors, sans fétichiser la nuance, examinons rapidement quelles sont à mon sens nos priorités pour foutre en l'air le néolibéralisme.

Le premier sens est probablement le plus évident. En proclamant « *fuck le néolibéralisme* », nous pouvons exprimer notre colère contre la machine néolibérale. C'est une indication de notre exaspération, de notre désir de dire haut et fort notre ressentiment, de cracher le venin du mal à sa propre figure. Cela peut prendre la forme d'une plus grande mobilisation autour des manifestations contre le néolibéralisme ou en écrivant des articles et des livres critiquant son influence. La dernière action prêche aux convertis, la première espère que ceux déjà pervertis changeront leurs manières de faire. Je ne néglige pas l'importance de ces méthodes dans notre résistance, mais je suis aussi assez certain qu'elles ne seront pas suffisantes pour changer le sens du courant contre le néolibéralisme et en notre faveur. En manifestant publiquement notre défiance, nous tentons d'attirer l'attention et l'implication d'acteurs puissants dans la conversation, et nous nous méprenons en croyant qu'ils pourraient commencer à écouter l'opposition et s'accorder à la voix du peuple[5]. Ne devrions-nous pas plutôt arrêter de parler ? Voici le deuxième sens de « *fuck le néolibéralisme* » : il repose sur la notion de rejet. Cela consisterait en plaider la fin du néolibéralisme (tel que nous le connaissons) selon le moyen proposé par J.K. Gibson-Graham[6] : arrêter tout simplement d'en parler. Les intellectuels en particulier arrêteraient de traiter ce thème en priorité dans leurs recherches. Peut-être ne pourrions-nous pas oublier ni ignorer complètement le néolibéralisme, ce que j'ai déjà identifié comme problématique, mais nous entreprendrions de continuer à écrire sur d'autres choses. Il s'agit là d'un point de contact tout aussi crucial pour nous qui travaillons au-delà d'une vision du monde néolibérale, mais là encore, je ne suis pas entièrement convaincu que ce soit suffisant. Comme le soutient Mark Purcell[7], « Il nous faut tourner le dos au néolibéralisme et nous recentrer sur nous-mêmes, pour commencer le travail difficile—mais néanmoins joyeux—de gérer nos affaires par nous-mêmes ». Bien que la négation, la protestation et la critique soient nécessaires, nous devons aussi penser à foutre le néolibéralisme en l'air activement, en prenant des mesures qui dépassent sa portée.

L'action directe au-delà du néolibéralisme relève d'une politique préfigurative[8], qui constitue la troisième et plus importante signification de ce sur quoi nous devrions nous concentrer lorsque nous invoquons l'idée de « *fuck le néolibéralisme* ». Préfigurer, c'est rejeter le centrisme, la hiérarchie et l'autorité associés à la politique représentative, en soulignant la pratique incarnée des relations horizontales et des formes organisationnelles qui s'efforcent de refléter la société future que nous recherchons[9]. Par delà la fin des discours, la préfiguration et l'action directe affirment qu'aucune conversation n'aurait jamais dû avoir lieu, car indépendamment de ce que nous souhaitons faire, nous pouvons simplement le faire nous-mêmes. Cependant, suffisamment d'attention a été portée sur les manières dont le néolibéralisme peut capturer et s'approprier toutes les formes de discours et d'impératifs politiques[10]. Pour certains critiques tels que David Harvey[11], seule une nouvelle dose d'état peut résoudre la question néolibérale, écartant là rapidement l'idée de l'organisation non hiérarchique et de la politique horizontale qui nous conduiraient tout droit vers un avenir néolibéral assuré. Pourtant, dans son pessimisme, il se méprend complètement sur la politique préfigurative, qui est un moyen non pas vers une fin mais uniquement vers d'autres moyens futurs[12]. En d'autres termes, la politique préfigurative repose sur une vigilance constante et continue, c'est pourquoi sa pratique ne peut être récupérée. Elle est réflexive et attentive, toujours tournée vers la production, l'invention et la création comme satisfaction du désir de la communauté. Entendue de cette manière, la politique préfigurative est explicitement anti-néolibérale. Elle se réapproprie les moyens pour en faire *nos* moyens, des moyens sans fin. Préfigurer c'est embrasser la convivialité et la joie qui émanent d'être rassemblés comme égaux radicaux ; non pas comme des soldats au front ni comme le prolétariat sur la voie de la promesse transcendantale et vide de l'utopie ou du « *non lieu* », mais comme l'immanence enracinée de l'*ici* et *maintenant*, de la fabrique d'un nouveau monde « dans la coquille du vieux », du travail constant et de la réaffirmation que tout cela implique[13].

Rien du néolibéralisme ne mérite notre respect, c'est pourquoi de concert avec une politique préfigurative de création, mon message est tout bonnement : « *fuck it* ». Fuck l'emprise qu'il a sur nos imaginations politiques. Fuck la violence qu'il engendre. Fuck l'inégalité qu'il vante comme une vertu. Fuck la manière dont il a ravagé l'environnement. Fuck le cycle sans fin d'accumulation et le culte de la croissance. Fuck la société du Mont-Pèlerin et tous les *think tanks* qui continent de la soutenir et la promouvoir. Fuck Friedrich Hayek et Milton Friedman pour nous avoir refourgué leurs idées. Fuck les Thatcher, les Reagan, et tous les politiciens lâches et intéressés qui ne cherchent qu'à satisfaire leur avarice. Fuck l'exclusion basée sur la peur qui perçoit les « autres » comme méritant de laver nos toilettes et d'éponger nos carrelages, mais pas comme des membres de nos communautés à part entière. Fuck l'attrait grandissant des chiffres et l'incapacité d'apprécier que tout ce qui compte ne peut être compté. Fuck le désir du profit qui prime sur les besoins de la communauté. Fuck absolument tout ce que le néolibéralisme représente, et fuck le cheval de Troie dans lequel il est arrive ! Depuis bien trop longtemps, on nous a répété qu' « il n'y a pas d'alternative », qu' « une marée montante fait avancer tous les bateaux », que nous vivons dans un monde darwinien cauchemardesque régi par la loi du plus fort. Nous avons mordu à l'hameçon et tout avalé de la « tragédie des communs » ; alors qu'en réalité, ceci est une ruse qui reflète la « tragédie du capitalism » et ses pillages sans fin[14]. Le talon d'Achille de Garrett Hardin[15] était qu'il n'a jamais arrêté de penser au bétail comme appartenant à un propriétaire privé. Que se passera t-il lorsque nous invoquerons l'idée des communs comme le *bien commun* sans présupposition de propriété privée[16] ? Que se passera t-il lorsque nous commencerons à porter plus d'attention à la préfiguration des alternatives qui existent déjà et privilégient ces expériences comme les formes les plus importantes d'organisation[17] ? Que se passera t-il lorsque au lieu d'avaler l'amère pilule de la concurrence et du mérite, nous concentrerons nos énergies non pas sur les remèdes que nous prescrit le néolibéralisme, mais sur la guérison plus profonde qui résulte de l'entraide et la coopération[18] ?

Jamie Peck[19] a appelé le néolibéralisme un « slogan politique radical », mais camper dans le domaine de la critique ne suffit plus. De nombreuses années ont passé depuis que nous avons identifié pour la première fois l'ennemi, et depuis lors, nous avons appris à le connaître à travers nos écrits et nos protestations. Mais même lorsque nous sommes certains de sa défaite, comme ce fut le cas au lendemain de la crise financière de 2008 et avec le mouvement Occupy qui en est résulté, il continue d'haleter et de se réanimer tel un zombie plus puissant que jamais[20]. Japhy Wilson[21] appelle ce pouvoir perpétuel le « gothique neoliberal », et je suis convaincu que pour dépasser ce film d'horreur nous devons resituer notre politique dans le domaine de l'action[22]. Et si « *fuck le néolibéralisme* » devait devenir un mantra pour une nouvelle forme de politique ? Une phrase stimulante qui inviterait non seulement à l'action, mais aussi à la réappropriation de nos vies dans les espaces et les instants où nous les vivons activement ? Et si chaque fois que nous utilisions cette phrase, nous reconnaissions qu'elle est un appel au pouvoir d'agir au-delà des simples mots, combinant la théorie et la pratique dans la sublime expérience de la prefiguration ? Nous devons adopter une approche combinant plusieurs fronts lorsque nous rejetons le néolibéralisme. Bien que nous ne puissions l'ignorer ni l'oublier complètement, nous pouvons l'affronter activement en utilisant des méthodes dont la portée dépasse la performance de la rhétorique et de la rhétorique de la performance. Par tous les moyens, faisons avancer un nouveau slogan politique radical. Utilisons un hashtag (#fuckneoliberalism) et rendons notre mépris viral ! Mais nous devons faire plus qu'exprimer notre indignation. Il nous faut matérialiser notre détermination et réaliser notre espoir comme l'immanence de nos expériences incarnées dans l'*ici* et *maintenant*[23]. Nous devons refaire le monde nous-mêmes, sans plus attendre.

Nous nous sommes délibérément leurrés et affaiblis en continuant à avoir recours à l'aménagement politique existant de la représentation. Notre foi aveugle nous condamne à attendre à perpétuité le sauveur qui tombera du ciel. Le système s'est montré entièrement corrompu, et le temps n'y fait rien : notre prochain grand candidat politique bientôt échouera lui aussi comme tous ses prédécesseurs. À l'âge du néolibéralisme, il ne s'agit pas simplement d'individus problématiques au pouvoir. C'est plutôt notre propre croyance dans ce système qui est le cœur du problème. Nous produisons et permettons les conditions institutionnelles propices à l' « effet Lucifer »[24]. « La banalité du mal » est telle que ces politiciens ne font que leur travail dans un système qui récompense les perversions du pouvoir car il est conçu pour servir les lois du capitalisme[25]. Mais nous ne sommes pas obligés d'obéir. Nous ne devons rien à cet ordre établi. À travers notre action directe et l'organisation d'alternatives, nous pouvons mettre en accusation la structure entière et rompre ce cercle vicieux d'abus. Quand le système politique est défini, conditionné, empêtré et dérivé du capitalisme, il ne peut en aucun cas représenter nos manières de connaître et d'être au monde, c'est pourquoi nous devons prendre ces modes de vie en main et nous réapproprier notre pouvoir collectif. Nous devons commencer à établir un nouvel ordre politique et à redonner un sens plus relationnel à la solidarité, en reconnaissant que la soumission et la souffrance des un-e-s indique l'oppression de tous[26]. Nous pouvons commencer à vivre dans d'autres mondes possibles à travers un engagement renouvelé des pratiques de l'entraide, de la fraternité, de la réciprocité, et des formes organisationnelles non hiérarchiques qui ravivent la démocratie dans son sens étymologique du *pouvoir* au *peuple*. Au final, le néolibéralisme est une idée particulièrement nauséabonde qui vient avec son lot d'obscénités et de vils postulats. En réponse, il mérite d'être opposé par un langage et une action tout aussi offensive. Notre communauté, notre coopération et notre attention aux autres sont toutes détestables pour le néolibéralisme. Il hait ce que nous célébrons. Alors, quand nous disons « *fuck le néolibéralisme* », que ce soit plus que des mots, que ce soit la preuve de notre engagement les un-e-s pour les autres. Dîtes-le haut et fort, dîtes-le avec moi, et dîtes-le à quiconque écoutera, mais surtout, que cela vous vienne du cœur et claironne comme un appel à l'action, et comme l'incarnation de notre pouvoir préfiguratif de changer ce putain de monde. *Fuck le néolibéralisme!*

Fick den Neoliberalismus!

Translated by Ursula Brandt

Translator's Commentary

Translating Simon's text was a lot of fun. I particularly enjoyed the ranting style. One thing turned out to be quite challenging for me, though: the translation of the slogan "fuck neoliberalism" itself. Although the phrase "Fick (something)" exists in German, it's an anglicism that has not been around here for more than a few decades and is not quite as frequently used in German as its counterpart in English. Therefore, its connotations are not completely identical with those of the English "Fuck (something)." In my ears, "fick", or its plural "fickt," sound slightly more aggressive than "fuck." Maybe that's because the English "fuck (something)" has, due to its frequent and varying use, lost some of its edge and some of its literal meaning—which is, if you consider it, nothing less than a call to have sex with someone or something, regardless of the consent of the object. I first went for the more common "Scheiß auf (Shit on). . ." instead. This decision was supported by the fact that all the other English idioms containing "fuck" also have German equivalents that contain forms of "Scheiße" or "scheiß. . ." (whatever you want to conclude from that. . .). For example, you can translate "don't give a fuck" with "einen Scheiß drauf geben," etc. Still, I was not totally satisfied with this solution. "Scheiß auf. . ." has more of a resigned, "I don't care" vibe to it. To shit on something, you turn your back on it. This is also part of what Simon says—the mentioned "notion of rejection" that is also in the word "fuck." But the English "fuck," in its literal sense, seems to be more active—and action is what this text basically calls for. What ultimately tipped the balance for me was when I saw the future cover of this book. I decided that it had to be "Fick den Neoliberalismus," and that I will have to live with the friction that comes with translating the other more "shit-loaded" German idioms differently.

Fick den Neoliberalismus!

Fick den Neoliberalismus. Das ist, in aller Kürze, meine Botschaft—und damit wäre eigentlich auch schon alles gesagt. Mein Standpunkt ist klar, und ihr habt sicher schon eine Ahnung davon gekriegt, worum es mir geht. Der Diskussion zum Neoliberalismus habe ich nichts Positives hinzuzufügen. Es widert mich ehrlich gesagt geradezu an, überhaupt weiter darüber nachzudenken. Es steht mir schlicht bis hier oben. Eine Zeitlang hatte ich überlegt, diesen Artikel „Vergiss den Neoliberalismus" zu nennen— weil ich eigentlich genau das wollte. Ich schreibe schon viele Jahre über das Thema.[1] Irgendwann kam ich an einen Punkt, wo ich einfach nicht noch mehr Energie in dieses Thema stecken wollte. Meine Befürchtung war, dass ich dieses Konzept durch meine fortgesetzte Arbeit daran nur bestätige. Bei längerer Betrachtung wurde mir aber natürlich klar, welche Gefahr darin liegt, kollektiv den Kopf in den Sand zu stecken und ein solch global verheerendes und lähmendes Phänomen einfach zu ignorieren. Der Neoliberalismus übt eine fortwährende Macht aus, die wir nur schwer verleugnen können. Deswegen glaube ich auch nicht, dass eine Strategie des Ignorierens der richtige Weg ist[2]. „OK, dann fick ihn eben"—genau das waren meine Gedanken. Sicher hätte ich statt eines vulgären auch einen sanften, freundlichen Titel wählen können. Letztendlich habe ich mich aber dagegen entschieden. Warum sollte ich mir mehr Gedanken über den Gebrauch von Schimpfwörtern machen als über den tatsächlich stattfindenden und widerlichen Neoliberalismusdiskurs? Ich beschloss, dass ich Grenzen überschreiten, verärgern und verletzen wollte, genau weil wir durch den Neoliberalismus gekränkt sein *sollten*, weil er ganz und gar verletzend *ist*. Darum müssen wir endgültig versuchen, gegen seine Regeln zu verstoßen. Wäre eine Abmilderung des Titels nicht ein weiteres Zugeständnis an die Macht des Neoliberalismus? Zu Beginn war ich unsicher, welche Auswirkungen eine solche Überschrift auf meinen akademischen Ruf haben würde. Würde das meine künftige Karriere beeinträchtigen und verhindern, dass ich meine Mobilität als Akademiker beibehalten kann—Beweglichkeit nach oben oder an einen anderen Ort? Aber hieße das nicht, sich der disziplinierenden Macht des Neoliberalismus zu beugen? *Fuck it!*

Außerdem kam mir das wie ein Eingeständnis vor— als gäbe es keine angemessene umgangssprachliche Erwiderung auf den Neoliberalismusdiskurs. Als könnten wir nur in einem akademischen Format und mithilfe komplexer geografischer Theorien von Hybridität, Variation und Mutation reagieren, um dieses Gedankengebäude anzugreifen. Das kam mir vor wie eine Selbstentmachtung. Auch wenn ich selbst zur Formulierung mancher dieser Gedanken beigetragen habe[3], glaube ich, dass ein solcher Rahmen im Grunde meiner eigentlichen These zuwiderläuft. Meiner Ansicht nach sollte eine Politik der Verweigerung gerade im Alltäglichen, Gewöhnlichen, Unauffälligen und Banalen angesiedelt sein. Und so bin ich bei „Fick den Neoliberalismus" geblieben—weil ich glaube, es vermittelt die Essenz dessen, was ich sagen will. Dass meine These dann doch etwas nuancierter ist, hat dazu geführt, dass ich in der Folge so viel über den Begriff „Fuck" nachgedacht habe wie nie zuvor in meinem Leben. Was für ein unglaublich vielseitiges und farbenfrohes Wort! Es kann sowohl als Substantiv als auch als Verb eingesetzt werden. Als Adjektiv ist es vielleicht der am häufigsten benutzte Ausruf der englischen Sprache. „Fuck" kann zum Ausdruck von Wut, Verachtung, Ärger, Gleichgültigkeit, Überraschung und Ungeduld dienen oder schlicht als inhaltslose Akzentuierung—einfach, weil es so leicht von der Zunge geht. Man kann etwas versauen („fuck something up"), Scheiße bauen („fuck around"), jemand bescheißen („fuck someone over"), sich einen Scheiß scheren („don't give a fuck"). Und es gibt sogar einen speziell geografischen Bezugspunkt des Wortes, indem man dazu aufgefordert werden kann, „sich selbst zu ficken" („go fuck yourself"). Spätestens jetzt fragt ihr euch vielleicht, „OK, was soll der Scheiß—wen interessiert das?" („Who gives a fuck")? *Mich* interessiert es— und wenn euch etwas daran liegt, den Neoliberalismus zu beenden, sollte es euch auch interessieren. Das kraftvolle Potenzial des Wortes stellt eine mögliche Gefahr für den Neoliberalismus dar. Um dieses Potenzial offenzulegen und sichtbar zu machen, muss man die verschiedenen Nuancen betrachten, die durch die Phrase „Fick den Neoliberalismus" ausgedrückt werden können. Allerdings, wenn ichs mir recht überlege: Fick die Nuancen. Wie Kieran Healy es kürzlich ausgedrückt hat, „behindern sie gewöhnlich den Aufbau intellektuell interessanter, empirisch generativer oder praktisch erfolgreicher Theorien".[4] Also lasst uns zügig und ohne weitere Fetischisierung der Nuancen dazu kommen, was für uns meiner Ansicht nach beim Zerstören des Neoliberalismus an oberster Stelle stehen sollte.

Die erste Bedeutung ist vielleicht die offenichtlichste. Wir können durch die Formulierung „Fick den

Neoliberalismus" unserer Wut auf die neoliberale Maschinerie Ausdruck geben. Der Satz steht für unseren Zorn und unsere Sehnsucht, den Hass hinauszuschreien, Gift zurückzuspucken in die garstige Fresse des offensichtlichen Übels—indem wir zum Beispiel noch mehr Proteste gegen den Neoliberalismus organisieren. Ein anderer Weg ist das Schreiben von Artikeln und Büchern, die den Einfluss des Neoliberalismus kritisieren. Mit dem ersten Ansatz richten wir uns nur an Menschen, die bereits bekehrt sind. Beim zweiten Ansatz hoffen wir darauf, dass die Pervertierten sich vielleicht doch noch ändern mögen.

Beide Methoden sind zweifellos wichtig für den Widerstand. Trotzdem reichen sie sicher nicht dazu aus, das Blatt zu wenden: gegen den Neoliberalismus und für unsere Sache. Wir versuchen so, durch ein öffentliches Zurschautragen unserer Missachtung mächtige Akteure in die Diskussion einzubeziehen. Fälschlicherweise hoffen wir, dass sie zuhören und die populäre Stimme der Verweigerung in sich aufnehmen könnten[5]. Aber sollten wir nicht eher sagen: Schluss! Genug geredet! Die Diskussion ist beendet!? Hier kommen wir zur zweiten Bedeutung von „Fick den Neoliberalismus", die im Begriff der Ablehnung steckt—das Eintreten für das Ende des (uns bekannten) Neoliberalismus, wie es von J. K. Gibson-Graham[6] vertreten wird: indem einfach nicht mehr darüber gesprochen wird. Danach sollten speziell wir Wissenschaftler damit aufhören, den Neoliberalismus in den Fokus unserer Forschung zu stellen. Wir sollten ihn zwar vielleicht nicht völlig zu den Akten legen oder ignorieren (dass das problematisch ist, habe ich weiter oben bereits dargelegt), aber uns stattdessen daran machen, über andere Dinge zu schreiben. Auch dies ist ein wichtiger Anknüpfungspunkt für die Arbeit jenseits der neoliberalen Weltsicht. Aber es reicht meiner Ansicht nach ebenfalls nicht aus. Um es mit Mark Purcell[7] zu sagen:

„Wir müssen dem Neoliberalismus den Rücken zukehren und uns uns selbst zuwenden, um eine so lustvolle wie schwierige Arbeit in Angriff zu nehmen: das Regeln unserer eigenen Angelegenheiten." Verneinung, Protest und Kritik sind zwar ganz sicher notwendig. Darüber hinaus müssen wir aber auch Formen finden, durch die der Neoliberalismus aktiv zerstört wird, indem wir außerhalb seines Zugriffs agieren.

Direkte Aktion jenseits des Neoliberalismus bedeutet eine präfigurative, vorwegnehmende Politik[8]. Dies ist meiner Ansicht nach die dritte und wichtigste Bedeutung von „Fick den Neoliberalismus". Präfiguratives Handeln bedeutet die Zurückweisung vom Zentrismus, der Hierarchie und Autorität einer repräsentativen Politik. Stattdessen wird die verkörperte Praxis betont, horizontale Beziehungen und Organisationsformen zu leben, die die angestrebte zukünftige Gesellschaftsform widerspiegeln sollen[9]. Präfiguration und Direkte Aktion stehen nicht nur am „Ende der Diskussion": Sie behaupten vielmehr, dass es ohnehin nie eine relevante Diskussion gegeben hat. Sie begreifen, dass wir alles, was wir tun wollen, selbst tun können. Es wurde schon viel darüber geschrieben, wie es dem Neoliberalismus immer wieder gelingt, alle möglichen politischen Diskurse und Imperative zu schnappen und sich einzuverleiben[10]. Für Kritiker wie David Harvey[11] kann nur eine weitere Dosis Staat die neoliberale Frage lösen. Besonders nichthierarchische Organisationen und horizontale Politik tut er schnell mit dem Argument ab, sie würden angeblich nur den Weg in eine neoliberale Zukunft ebnen. In seinem Pessimismus versteht er dabei die präfigurative Politik völlig falsch: Sie ist nicht Mittel zum Zweck, sondern nur für zukünftige Mittel[12]. Anders gesagt, zeichnet sich präfigurative Politik schon ihrer Natur nach durch eine konstante und stetige Wachsamkeit aus. Daher ist es nicht möglich, sich der eigentlichen Präfigurationspraxis für andere Zwecke zu bedienen. Sie ist reflexiv und aufmerksam, hat aber dabei immer die Produktion, Erfindung und Neuschöpfung zur Befriedigung der gemeinschaftlichen Wünsche im Blick. Dadurch ist präfigurative Politik explizit antineoliberal. Sie ist eine Bemächtigung der Mittel als *unserer* Mittel: als Mittel ohne Zweck. Präfiguratives Handeln bedeutet, sich für die Geselligkeit und die Freude zu öffnen, als kritische, gleichberechtigte Menschen zusammenzukommen. Und das nicht als Avantgarde und Proletariat auf dem Weg zum traszendentalen leeren Versprechen von Utopia—einem „Nicht-Ort"—, sondern als bodenständige Immanenz im Hier und Jetzt, als tatsächliche Erschaffung einer neuen Welt „in der Schale der alten", mitsamt der fortwährenden schwierigen Arbeit und Reaffirmation, die das bedeutet[13].

Nichts am Neoliberalismus verdient unseren Respekt. Im Sinne einer präfigurativen Politik der Schöpfung ist meine Botschaft daher schlicht: Fickt ihn! Fickt die Macht, die der Neoliberalismus über unsere politischen Vorstellungen hat. Fickt die Gewalt, die er hervorbringt. Fickt die Ungleichheit, die er als Tugend preist. Fickt die Verwüstungen, die er unserer Umwelt zufügt. Fickt den endlosen Kreislauf der Akkumulation und auf den Wachstumskult. Fickt die Mont Pelerin Society und alle Think Tanks, die sie fortwährend unterstützen und bewerben. Fickt Friedrich Hayek und Milton Friedman, die uns ihre Ideen aufgedrückt haben. Fickt die Thatchers, Reagans und all die feigen, eigennützigen Politiker, die sich einzig der Habgier unterwerfen. Fickt eine durch Panikmache erzeugte Ausgrenzung, die „andere" zwar als würdig befindet, unsere Klos zu putzen und unsere Böden zu wischen, aber nicht als Mitglieder unserer Gesellschaft akzeptiert. Fickt den immer stärker werdenden Hang zum Messen und Quantifizieren—als könnte alles, was zählt, auch gezählt werden. Fickt die Tatsache, dass die Gier nach Profit über den Bedürfnissen der Gemeinschaft steht. Fickt einfach absolut alles, wofür der Neoliberalismus steht, und fickt das trojanische Pferd, auf dem er hereingeritten ist.

Viel zu lange wurde uns seine Alternativlosigkeit gepredigt: dass „die steigende Flut alle Boote hebt"; dass wir in einer darwinistischen Alptraumwelt leben würden, jeder gegen jeden, in der nur das Gesetz vom „Survival oft the Fittest" gilt. Wir haben das Konzept der „Tragik der Allmende" völlig verinnerlicht. Dabei ist sie tatsächlich nur ein Täuschungsmanöver, das die „Tragik des Kapitalismus" und seine endlosen Plündereien widerspiegelt[14]. Der Schwachpunkt in Garrett Hardins Überlegungen[15] war, nicht zu berücksichtigen, dass die beschriebenen Rinderherden zuvor in Privatbesitz waren. Wie würde es dagegen aussehen, wenn wir eine tatsächliche Allmende wieder als Allmende ins Leben riefen—ohne die Vorbedingung einer privaten Eigentümerschaft[16]? Wäre es nicht großartig, wenn wir uns mehr auf die Präfiguration schon stattfindender Alternativen konzentrieren und diesen bei der Wahl unserer Organisationsformen den Vorzug geben würden[17]? Statt die bittere Pille von Wettberwerb und Leistung zu schlucken und auf die Eigenbehandlung mit neoliberalen Rezepten zu setzen, könnten wir unsere Energien auf die tiefere Heilung konzentrieren, die aus Kooperation und gegenseitiger Hilfe erwächst[18].

Jamie Peck[19] hat den Neoliberalismus einmal als „radikalen politischen Slogan" bezeichnet. Ein solches Verweilen in der Sphäre der Kritik reicht aber nicht mehr aus.

Seit wir unseren Gegner ausgemacht und benannt haben, sind schon viele Jahre ins Land gegangen. Durch unsere Schriften und Proteste haben wir ihn inzwischen noch besser kennengelernt. Und jedesmal, wenn wir ihn endlich besiegt glaubten—wie nach der Finanzkrise 2008 und der daraus entstandenen Occupy-Bewegung—, hat der Zombie sich in einer neuen, noch widerlicheren Form wieder aus dem Staub erhoben[20]. Japhy Wilson[21] bezeichnet diese fortbestehende Macht als „neoliberale Gotik". Zur Überwindung dieses Gruselkabinetts müssen wir meiner Ansicht nach unsere Strategien in die Sphäre des Enaktivismus verlagern[22]. Könnte „Fick den Neoliberalismus" nicht ein Mantra für eine neue Art der Politik werden? Ein bestärkender, ermächtigender Slogan, der nicht nur zur politischen Aktion aufruft, sondern auch zur Reklamation unseres eigenen Lebens dann und dort, wo es tatsächlich stattfindet? Jedesmal, wenn wir diesen Satz benutzen, können wir anerkennen, dass damit ein Aufruf zum enaktiven Handeln gemeint ist, die über bloße Worte hinausgeht und Theorie und Praxis zur wunderschönen Tätigkeit der Präfiguration verbindet. In unserer Ablehnung des Neoliberalismus ist ein mehrgleisiger Ansatz notwendig. Wir können den Neoliberalismus zwar nicht komplett ignorieren oder vergessen. Aber wir können aktiv gegen ihn vorgehen: durch ein Handeln, das über eine reine Performanz der Rhetorik und die Rhetorik der Performanz hinausgeht. Lasst uns einen neuen, radikalen politischen Slogan in Umlauf bringen. Mit dem Hashtag #fuckneoliberalism können wir dafür sorgen, dass sich unsere Verachtung wie ein Lauffeuer verbreitet. Bei diesem Ausdruck unserer Empörung darf es aber nicht bleiben. Wir müssen unseren Entschluss auch in die Tat umsetzen und unsere Hoffnung als etwas verwirklichen, das unserer körperlichen Erfahrung im Hier und Jetzt innewohnt[23]. Wir müssen die Welt eigenhändig erneuern, und zwar sofort.

Durch unseren ständigen Appell an das bestehende politische Repräsentationssystem haben wir uns bewusst selbst getäuscht und entmächtigt. Immer noch warten wir blind vertrauend auf einen Erlöser, der vom Himmel fällt. Dabei hat sich das System doch als durch und durch korrupt erwiesen. Immer wieder entpuppt sich der nächste großartige Kandidat nur als die nächste Niete. In der jetzigen Phase des Neoliberalismus geht es aber nicht mehr nur darum, welche fragwürdigen Individuen an der Macht sind. Unser Glaube an das System ist der eigentliche Kern des Problems. Die institutionellen Bedingungen, in denen der „Luzifer-Effekt" sich entfalten kann[24], werden durch uns erst produziert und ermöglicht. „Die Banalität des Bösen" besteht ganz einfach darin, dass die Politiker in einem System arbeiten, wo die Perversion der Macht belohnt wird, indem alles darauf ausgerichtet ist, den Gesetzen des Kapitalismus zu gehorchen[25]. Aber wir müssen nicht gehorchen—wir sind diesen Gesetzen nicht verpflichtet. Durch Direkte Aktion und die Organisation von Alternativen können wir das gesamte System anklagen und den Teufelskreis des Missbrauchs durchbrechen. Ein politisches System, das durch den Kapitalismus definiert, für ihn geschaffen, in ihn verstrickt und von ihm abgeleitet ist, kann niemals repräsentativ dafür sein, wie wir diese Welt erkennen und in ihr leben. Also müssen wir dieses neue Leben selbst in die Hand nehmen und unsere kollektive Praxis zurückfordern. Wir müssen mit einer enaktiven Politik beginnen und eine relationalere Solidarität befürworten, die anerkennt, dass die Unterdrückung und das Leid eines Einzelnen tatsächlich ein Anzeichen für die Unterdrückung aller ist[26]. Durch die hingebungsvolle Praxis von gegenseitiger Hilfe, von Gemeinschaft, Gegenseitigkeit und nichthierarchischen Organisationsformen—Formen von Demokratie im ursprünglichen Sinn des Wortes, als Macht für die Menschen—können wir ein Leben beginnen, das in andere mögliche Welten hineinführt. Letztendlich ist der Neoliberalismus doch nur eine besonders obszöne und widerliche Idee, die mit einer ganzen Fülle ekelhafter Folgen und haarsträubender Annahmen einhergeht. Dafür verdient er, dass ihm mit genauso vulgärer Sprache und Aktionen begegnet wird. Unsere Gemeinschaft, unsere Kooperation und unsere Sorge füreinander sind dem Neoliberalismus zuwider. Was wir lieben und feiern, ist ihm verhasst. Wenn wir also sagen: „Fick den Neoliberalismus!", so soll damit mehr ausgedrückt werden als Worte: Lasst uns damit unserem Eintreten füreinander Ausdruck verleihen. Sagt es also laut und mit mir zusammen, und sagt es jedem, der euch zuhört— aber vor allem: Lasst es einen Aufruf zur Aktion und zur Verkörperung unserer präfigurativen Kraft werden, diese verdammte Welt zu ändern. Fick den Neoliberalismus!

εΛληνικά – Greek

Γάμα το Νεοφιλελευθερισμό

Translated by Χαράλαμπος Τσαβδάρογλου –
Charalampos Tsavdaroglou

Translator's Commentary

The article "Fuck Neoliberalism" is an excellent and accurate expression of the political duty of today's radical scholars. Giorgio Agamben felicitously said that "the profanation of the unprofanable is the political task of the coming generation."* Neoliberalism ought to be profaned, and what better than "fuck it, fuck it to hell."†

The Greek translation of Springer's article took place at a time when the tide of social movements against neoliberal austerity policies gave way to the mediation and representation policies of a so-called "left" government. However, the limits of social struggles have been confronted for almost a decade in the context of the deepest political and social crisis. To overcome this crisis, neoliberalism has implemented a series of violent social, economic, sexist, racist, and xenophobic policies. In recent years, processes of neoliberalization in Greece took place amid the implementation of three memorandums (austerity agreements) between the Greek government and the Troika (IMF, European Central Bank, European Commission), an activation of the all-time classic,

---

* Giorgio Agamben, *Profanations*, (New York: Zone Books, 2007), 92.
† Simon Springer, "Fuck Neoliberalism," *Acme: A Journal of Critical Geographies* 15, no. 2 (2016): 285.

Friedman's "shock doctrine," and a state of emergency as a permanent exception. The neoliberal policies brought new restrictions to labor rights, a dramatic increase in unemployment from 8 percent to 27 percent, drastic reductions of up to 50 percent in salaries and pensions, privatization and commercialization of state property and public services (airports, ports, trains, and highways). On a spatial level in particular, new enclosures have been imposed through land grabbing, fast-track spatial and urban planning policies, evictions of political squats, and the auctioning off of family homes when people were unable to make mortgage payments. Moreover, we witnessed the emergence of the neo-Nazi-fascist Golden Dawn, the criminalization of HIV-positive sex workers, extreme police brutality, and media negativity toward anti-austerity mobilizations.

At the same time, neoliberalism exploits the very destruction it produces with its urban gentrification, creative city, and city branding policies. The Airbnbfication, as a form of tourist neoliberalization, conquers the city center and neighborhoods in cities. The mayor of Athens was elected under the radical Lefebvrian slogan "right to the city," which corresponds to the tourists' and investors' right to the city, accompanied by criminalization and exclusion of undesirable groups, such as squatters, sex workers, migrants, and the homeless; the very avant-garde exhibition "Documenta 14," with a neo-orientalist view, discovers in Athens the "new Berlin," while famous international agencies organize tourist trips to the Greek neighborhoods in crisis. Last but foremost, in this neo-liberal dystopia, newly arrived refugees from the war zones of the Middle East are forced to live in state-run camps at the outskirts of cities and at abandoned industrial sites, in unsafe and precarious conditions, and are thereby excluded from the right to the city. Consequently, as Springer has argued, "there is nothing about neoliber-alism that is deserving of our respect."[*]

In these turbulent times, social relations, modes of communication, and communities are constantly strug-gling against neoliberalization processes. In Greece, the previous decade was marked by an extraordinary outbreak of creative struggles that overwhelmingly shouted, "fuck neoliberalism." The resistance to gold mining, the strug-gles for land and freedom, the hundreds of labor strikes, the resistance to patriarchy, transphobia, and sexism, the struggles against evictions, and the struggles of immi-grants to abolish the borders and gain the right to the city indicate that, across the world, neoliberalism is being challenged.

In the above context Simon Springer's article is an important contribution, as it invites us to a reflective process "toward production, invention, and creation as the satisfaction of the desire of community."[†] It is an excel-lent call to (re)open our politico-intellectual imaginations in ways that could (re)imagine "an enactive agency that went beyond mere words, combining theory and practice into the beautiful praxis of prefiguration."[‡]

Γάμα το Νεοφιλελευθερισμό

Γάμα τον Νεοφιλελευθερισμό. Αυτό είναι το οξύ μήνυμά μου. Θα μπορούσα ίσως να κλείσω την συζήτησή μου σε αυτό το σημείο και πραγματικά δεν θα πείραζε. Η θέση μου είναι σαφής και ήδη γνωρίζετε την ουσία αυτού που θέλω να πω. Δεν έχω τίποτα θετικό να προσθέσω στην συζήτηση περί νεοφιλελευθερισμού, και για να είμαι ειλικρινής, με αρρωσταίνει να σκέφτομαι για αυτό. Έχω απλά βαρεθεί.

---

[*]   Simon Springer, "Fuck Neoliberalism," 288.
[†]   Simon Springer, "Fuck Neoliberalism," 287.
[‡]   Simon Springer, "Fuck Neoliberalism," 289.

Για μια στιγμή είχα σκεφτεί να βάλω ως τίτλο για το άρθρο το «Ξέχνα τον Νεοφιλελευθερισμό», καθώς κατά κάποιον τρόπο αυτό είναι ακριβώς που θέλω να πω. Έχω γράψει για πολλά χρόνια πάνω στο θέμα[1] και πλέον έχω φτάσει σε ένα σημείο που απλά δεν θέλω να ξοδέψω περισσότερη ενέργεια σε αυτή την προσπάθεια, για το φόβο ότι η συνέχιση της ενασχόλησης γύρω από αυτή την ιδέα έχει λειτουργήσει στο να διαιωνίσει τον έλεγχό της. Για περαιτέρω προβληματισμό επίσης αναγνωρίζω ότι ως πολιτικός ελιγμός είναι δυνητικά πολύ επικίνδυνο να εγκλωβιστεί το κεφάλι μας στην άμμο και συλλογικά να αγνοήσουμε ένα φαινόμενο το οποίο έχει τέτοιες καταστροφικές και εξουθενωτικές συνέπειες στον κοινό μας κόσμο. Υπάρχει μια διαρκής δύναμη στο νεοφιλελευθερισμό την οποία δύσκολα μπορούμε να αρνηθούμε και δεν είμαι πεπεισμένος ότι η στρατηγική της άγνοιας είναι πραγματικά η σωστή προσέγγιση[2]. Έτσι οι πραγματικές σκέψεις μου ήταν «λοιπόν γάμα τον», και ενώ ένα λιγότερο θορυβώδες και πιο ευγενικό όνομα για αυτό το άρθρο θα μπορούσε να μετριάσει το πιθανό αδίκημα που προκαλείται από τον τίτλο που επέλεξα, στη συνέχεια το ξανασκέφτηκα. Γιατί θα πρέπει να ανησυχούμε για την χρήση της βωμολοχίας από ότι για την πραγματική χυδαία συζήτηση του ίδιου του νεοφιλελευθερισμού; Αποφάσισα ότι ήθελα να παραβιάσω, να ανατρέψω και να προσβάλλω, ακριβώς διότι ο νεοφιλελευθερισμός οφείλει να μας προσβάλει, είναι ανατρεπτικός και για αυτό ακριβώς πρέπει να τον παραβιάσουμε. Εάν μαλάκωνα τον τίτλο δεν θα ήταν άλλη μια παραχώρηση στην εξουσία του νεοφιλελευθερισμού; Αρχικά ανησύχησα για το τι θα μπορούσε να σημαίνει ένας τέτοιος τίτλος όσον αφορά τη φήμη μου. Θα υπονόμευε τη μελλοντική μου προβολή ή τις προσφορές εργασίας και την κινητικότητά μου ως ακαδημαϊκού είτε σε κάποια ανώτερη θέση είτε σε κάποια άλλη τοποθεσία; Αυτό το ένιωσα σαν να αποδέχομαι μια προσωπική ήττα απέναντι στη νεοφιλελεύθερη πειθαρχία. Γάμα τα.

Επίσης ένιωσα σαν να έκανα μια παραδοχή ότι δεν υπάρχει μια καθομιλουμένη απάντηση που θα μπορούσε κατάλληλα να προσφερθεί για την αντιμετώπιση του νεοφιλελευθερισμού. Όπως και το γεγονός ότι μπορούμε να ανταποκριθούμε μόνο σε ένα ακαδημαϊκό πλαίσιο χρησιμοποιώντας πολύπλοκες γεωγραφικές θεωρίες περί πολυχρωμίας, υβριδισμού και μετάλλαξης για να αποδυναμώσουμε το οικοδόμημα του νεοφιλελευθερισμού. Αυτό φαίνεται ως αποδυνάμωση, και παρόλο που και εγώ έχω συνεισφέρει στην συνάρθρωση μερικών από αυτών των θεωριών[3], συχνά νιώθω ότι αυτού του τύπου τα πλαίσια είναι ενάντια στο είδος του επιχειρήματος που στην πραγματικότητα θέλω να πραγματοποιήσω. Είναι ακριβώς στην καθημερινή, απλή, μη μεγαλόστομη και κοσμική διάσταση που νομίζω ότι η πολιτική της άρνησης πρέπει να τοποθετείται. Για αυτό επιμένω στο «Γάμα τον Νεοφιλελευθερισμό», διότι πιστεύω ότι αποδίδει καλύτερα αυτό που πραγματικά θέλω να πω. Το επιχείρημά μου είναι λίγο πιο διαφοροποιημένο εννοιολογικά και με οδήγησε να σκεφτώ περισσότερο από κάθε άλλη φορά στη ζωή μου σχετικά με τον όρο «γάμα». Πόσο φανταστικά πολύχρωμη λέξη! Το «γάμα» [fuck] λειτουργεί τόσο ως ρήμα όσο και ως ουσιαστικό, και ως επίθετο είναι ίσως η πλέον χρησιμοποιούμενη λέξη που εκφράζει θαυμασμό στην αγγλική γλώσσα. Μπορεί να χρησιμοποιηθεί για να εκφράσει οργή, περιφρόνηση, ενόχληση, αδιαφορία, έκπληξη, ανυπομονησία, ή ακόμα και ανούσια έμφασή επειδή απλά λέγεται πολύ εύκολα. Μπορείς να «γαμήσεις (καταστρέψεις) κάτι» [fuck something up], να «γαμήσεις (αδικήσεις) κάποιον» [fuck someone over], να «γαμήσεις (σπαταλήσεις) το χρόνο σου» [fuck around], να «μη δώσεις δεκάρα» [not give a fuck], και υπάρχει αναμφίβολα γεωγραφικό σημείο αναφοράς στη λέξη στο βαθμό που θα μπορούσαν να σε διατάξουν «να πα να γαμηθείς». Σε αυτό το σημείο ενδεχομένως να σκεφτείτε «εντάξει, αλλά ποιος δίνει δεκάρα [who gives a fuck?]; Λοιπόν, εγώ δίνω, και εάν σας ενδιαφέρει το σταμάτημα του νεοφιλελευθερισμού, το ίδιο θα πρέπει να κάνετε και εσείς. Οι ισχυρές ικανότητες που συνοδεύουν τη λέξη προσφέρουν μια πιθανή πρόκληση για τον νεοφιλελευθερισμό. Για να έρθουν στην επιφάνεια και να αποκαλυφθούν αυτές οι ικανότητες χρειάζεται να εκτιμήσουμε τις αποχρώσεις του τι θα μπορούσε να σημαίνει η φράση «γάμα τον νεοφιλελευθερισμό». Την ίδια στιγμή, γάμα τις αποχρώσεις. Όπως ο Kieran Healy πρόσφατα έχει ισχυριστεί οι αποχρώσεις «συνήθως εμποδίζουν να αναπτυχθεί η θεωρεία που είναι πνευματικά ενδιαφέρουσα, εμπειρικά παραγωγική ή πρακτικά πετυχημένη».[4] Έτσι λοιπόν χωρίς να φετιχοποιούμε τις αποχρώσεις ας εργαστούμε γρήγορα μέσω αυτού που πιστεύω ότι πρέπει να είναι η προτεραιότητα μας στο να γαμήσουμε τον νεοφιλελευθερισμό.

Η πρώτη αίσθηση είναι πιθανώς η πιο προφανής. Λέγοντας «γάμα τον νεοφιλελευθερισμό» μπορούμε να εκφράσουμε την οργή μας απέναντι στη νεοφιλελεύθερη μηχανή. Αποτελεί μια ένδειξη της οργής μας, της επιθυμίας μας να διατρανώσουμε τη δυσαρέσκειά μας, να διασπείρουμε δηλητήριο στο πρόσωπο του επιβλαβούς δόλου που έχει γίνει φανερός σε όλους μας. Μπορεί να έρθει με τη μορφή της κινητοποίησης περισσότερων διαμαρτυριών ενάντια στο νεοφιλελευθερισμό ή γράφοντας περισσότερα άρθρα και βιβλία κριτικάροντας τις επιδράσεις του. Το τελευταίο αφορά τη μετατροπή και το αρχικό την ελπίδα ότι όσοι έχουν διαστρεβλωθεί από το νεοφιλελευθερισμό είναι πρόθυμοι να αλλάξουν τους τρόπους τους. Δεν προεξοφλώ ότι αυτές οι μέθοδοι δεν είναι σημαντικές τακτικές στην αντίστασή μας, αλλά είμαι σχεδόν σίγουρος ότι δεν θα είναι ποτέ αρκετές για να μετατραπούν σε ένα κύμα υπέρ μας και ενάντια στο νεοφιλελευθερισμό. Πραγματοποιώντας μεγάλες δημόσιες χειρονομίες αμφισβήτησης επιδιώκουμε πολλές φορές να προκαλέσουμε τους φορείς εξουσίας σε μια συνομιλία, και λανθασμένα πιστεύουμε ότι αυτοί

ενδέχεται να μας ακούσουν και να δεχθούν τη λαϊκή φωνή
της άρνησης⁵. Αντ' αυτού δεν θα πρέπει λοιπόν εμείς να
μιλάμε; Εδώ βρίσκεται η δεύτερη έννοια του «γάμα τον
νεοφιλελευθερισμό», η οποία βρίσκεται στην έννοια της
απόρριψης. Αυτή θα μπορούσε να υποστήριξη το τέλος
του νεοφιλελευθερισμού (όπως τον ξέρουμε) με τον τρόπο
που έχουν προβάλει οι J.K. Gibson-Graham⁶, σύμφωνα με
τις οποίες μπορούμε απλά να σταματήσουμε να μιλάμε για
αυτόν. Ειδικότερα, οι μελετητές θα μπορούσαν να αποσυν-
δέσουν τον νεοφιλελευθερισμό από το επίκεντρο της προ-
τεραιότητας τους στις μελέτες τους. Ίσως να μην τον ξεχά-
σουν ή να τον αγνοήσουν εντελώς, γεγονός το οποίο έχω
ήδη αναγνωρίσει ως προβληματικό, αλλά αντ' αυτού να
εστιάσουν τα γραπτά τους σε άλλα πράγματα. Για άλλη μια
φορά αυτό είναι εξαιρετικά σημαντικό σημείο επαφής για
εμάς καθώς η εργασία μας είναι πέρα από τη νεοφιλελεύθερη κοσμοθεωρία, αλλά και εδώ επίσης δεν είμαι απόλυτα
πεπεισμένος ότι αυτό είναι αρκετό. Όπως ισχυρίζεται ο
Mark Purcell⁷, «είναι αναγκαίο να στραφούμε πέρα από
το νεοφιλελευθερισμό και να κοιτάξουμε τον εαυτό μας,
για να ξεκινήσουμε τη δύσκολη—αλλά επίσης και ευχάρι-
στη—δουλειά της διαχείρισης των δικών μας υποθέσεων
για εμάς τους ίδιους». Ενώ η άρνηση, η διαμαρτυρία και
η κριτική είναι αναγκαίες, εμείς επίσης χρειάζεται να σκε-
φτούμε ενεργά την έννοια γάμα τον νεοφιλελευθερισμό,
κάνοντας πράγματα έξω από την εμβέλειά του.

Η άμεση δράση πέρα από το νεοφιλελευθερισμό ανα-
φέρεται στις προεικονιστικές πολιτικές⁸, οι οποίες αποτελούν την τρίτη και πιο σημαντική αίσθηση σε αυτό που
νομίζω ότι θα πρέπει να εστιάσουμε όταν επικαλούμαστε
την ιδέα του «γάμα τον νεοφιλελευθερισμό». Η προεικόνιση αφορά την απόρριψη της κεντρικότητας, της ιεραρ-
χίας και της εξουσίας, οι οποίες συνοδεύουν τις πολιτικές
της αντιπροσώπευσης, τονίζοντας αντ' αυτού τις ενσω-
ματωμένες πρακτικές θέσπισης οριζόντιων σχέσεων και

μορφών οργάνωσης που επιδιώκουν να αντικατοπτρίσουν την προς αναζήτηση μελλοντική κοινωνία[9]. Πέρα από το να «πράττουμε μιλώντας», η προεικόνιση και η άμεση δράση υποστηρίζουν ότι ποτέ δεν υπάρχει μια συζήτηση εκ των ουκ άνευ, αναγνωρίζοντας πως οτιδήποτε θέλουμε να κάνουμε, μπορούμε να το πράξουμε από μόνοι μας. Παρ' όλα αυτά, έχει δοθεί ιδιαίτερη προσοχή στους τρόπους με τους οποίους ο νεοφιλελευθερισμός έχει την ικανότητα να συλλαμβάνει και να σφετερίζεται όλα τα είδη πολιτικού λόγου και πολιτικών επιταγών[10]. Για τις κριτικές του τύπου David Harvey[11] μόνο άλλη μια δόση κράτους μπορεί να επιλύσει το ζήτημα του νεοφιλελευθερισμού, και συγκεκριμένα ο Harvey με ευκολία απορρίπτει τη μη-ιεραρχική οργάνωση και τις οριζόντιες πολιτικές ως γρασάρισμα στις ράγες για ένα βέβαιο νεοφιλελεύθερο μέλλον. Ωστόσο στην απαισιόδοξη οπτική του, παρανοεί εντελώς τις προεικονιστικές πολιτικές, οι οποίες αποτελούν ένα μέσο και όχι ένα τελικό σκοπό[12]. Με άλλα λόγια, υπάρχει μια σταθερή και διαρκής επαγρύπνηση που ήδη οικοδομείται σε προεικονιστικές πολιτικές, ώστε η πραγματική πρακτική της προεικόνισης δεν μπορεί να συναγωνιστεί. Είναι αναστοχαστική και προσεκτική αλλά πάντα έχει ως προοπτική την παραγωγή, την εφεύρεση και τη δημιουργία για την ικανοποίηση των επιθυμιών της κοινότητας. Με αυτόν τον τρόπο οι προεικονιστικές πολιτικές είναι σαφώς αντί-νεοφιλελεύθερες. Συνιστούν την κατάληψη των μέσων, ως δικών μας μέσων, μέσων χωρίς απώτερο τέλος. Το να προεικονίζεις είναι να αγκαλιάζεις την ευθυμία και την χαρά που συνοδεύει το να βρισκόμαστε μαζί ως ριζοσπαστικά ίσοι, όχι ως πρωτοπορία ή ως προλεταριάτο που αποβλέπει στην υπερβατική κενού περιεχομένου υπόσχεση της ουτοπίας ως «μη-τόπος», αλλά ως η γειωμένη εμμένεια του εδώ και τώρα που πραγματώνει τη δημιουργία ενός νέου κόσμου «στο κέλυφος του παλιού» και την αέναη σκληρή δουλειά και επαναβεβαίωση που αυτό απαιτεί[13].

Δεν υπάρχει τίποτα στο νεοφιλελευθερισμό που να αξίζει το σεβασμό μας, και σε συμφωνία με τις προεικονιστικές πολιτικές της δημιουργίας, το μήνυμα είναι πολύ απλό «γάμα τον». Γάμα την αναμονή που επιφέρει στο πολιτικό φαντασιακό μας. Γάμα τη βια που αυτός γεννά. Γάμα την ανισότητα που αυτός εκθειάζει ως αρετή. Γάμα τον τρόπο που έχει ρημάξει το περιβάλλον. Γάμα τον ατελείωτο κύκλο της συσσώρευσης και τη λατρεία της ανάπτυξης. Γάμα την Mont Pelerin society και όλα τα think tanks που συνεχίζουν να τον στηρίζουν και να τον προωθούν. Γάμα τον Friedrich Hayek και τον Milton Friedman που μας επιβαρύνουν με τις ιδέες τους. Γάμα τους Θατσερικούς, τους Ριγκανικούς και όλους τους δειλούς και ιδιοτελείς φιλάργυρους πολιτικούς. Γάμα τον φόβο που διασπείρει τον αποκλεισμό, που βλέπει τους «άλλους» ως άξιους μόνο για να καθαρίζουν τις τουαλέτες μας και να σφουγγαρίζουν τα πατώματά μας, αλλά όχι ως μέλη των κοινοτήτων μας. Γάμα την εντεινόμενη κίνηση προς υπολογισμούς και την αποτυχία να εκτιμηθεί ότι δεν υπόκεινται όλα σε υπολογισμούς. Γάμα την επιθυμία για κέρδος πάνω από τις ανάγκες της κοινότητας. Γάμα οτιδήποτε σημαίνει ο νεοφιλελευθερισμός και γάμα τον δούρειο ίππο πάνω στον οποίο κινείται! Για πολύ καιρό μας λένε ότι «δεν υπάρχει εναλλακτική», ότι «η αυξανόμενη παλίρροια σηκώνει όλες τις βάρκες», ότι ζούμε σε ένα κόσμο δαρβινικού εφιάλτη όλων ενάντιων όλων στον οποίο «επιβιώνει ο ισχυρότερος». Έχουμε καταπιεί την ιδέα της «τραγωδίας των κοινών» όταν στην πραγματικότητα αυτή αποτελεί το τέχνασμα που αντανακλά την «τραγωδία του καπιταλισμού» και τους ατελείωτους πολέμους λεηλασίας[14]. Η αχίλλειος πτέρνα του Garrett Hardin[15] ήταν ότι ποτέ δε σταμάτησε να σκέφτεται πως η βόσκηση βοοειδών ήταν ήδη ιδιωτική ιδιοκτησία. Τι θα μπορούσε να συμβεί όταν εκ νέου συλλάβουμε τα πραγματικά κοινά ως κοινά χωρίς τις προϋποθέσεις της ιδιωτικής ιδιοκτησίας[16]; Τι θα μπορούσε να συμβεί όταν αρχίσουμε να δίνουμε περισσότερη προσοχή στην προεικόνιση εναλλακτικών που ήδη συμβαίνουν και ευνοώντας αυτές τις εμπειρίες ως τις πιο σημαντικές μορφές οργάνωσης[17]; Τι θα μπορούσε να συμβεί όταν αντί να καταπίνουμε τα πικρά χάπια του ανταγωνισμού και της αξίας εστιάζουμε τις ενέργειές μας όχι στο να θεραπεύουμε τον εαυτό μας με νεοφιλελεύθερες συνταγές, αλλά με την βαθύτερη θεραπεία που προκύπτει από τη συνεργασία και την αλληλοβοήθεια[18].

Ο Jamie Peck[19] κάποτε αποκάλεσε το νεοφιλελευθερισμό ως ένα «ριζοσπαστικό πολιτικό σύνθημα», αλλά αυτό δεν είναι πλέον αρκετό για να βρίσκεται στη σφαίρα της κριτικής. Έχουν περάσει πολλά χρόνια από τότε που εντοπίσαμε για πρώτη φορά τον εχθρό και από τότε τον γνωρίζουμε καλά μέσα από τα γραπτά και τις διαμαρτυρίες μας. Αλλά ακόμα και εάν είμαστε σίγουροι για την ήττα του, όπως στον απόηχο της χρηματοπιστωτικής κρίσης του 2008 και το επακόλουθο κίνημα Occupy, αυτός συνεχίζει να ασθμαίνετε για αέρα και να ξαναζωντανεύει στη μορφή του ζόμπι[20]. Ο Japhy Wilson[21] αποκαλεί αυτή την συνεχιζόμενη δύναμη ως «νεοφιλελεύθερο γκόθικ» και είμαι πεπεισμένος ότι για να ξεπεραστεί αυτή η φρικτή παράσταση πρέπει να προχωρήσουμε τις πολιτικές μας στη σφαίρα της αυτοθέσμισης[22]. Τι θα συμβεί εάν το «γάμα το νεοφιλελευθερισμό» γίνει το μάντρα για ένα νέο είδος πολιτικής; Μια δυνατή φράση που μιλάει όχι μόνο για δράση, αλλά για την ανάκτηση των ζωών μας στους χώρους και τις στιγμές στις οποίες ενεργά ζούμε; Τι θα συμβεί εάν κάθε φορά που χρησιμοποιούμε αυτή τη φράση αναγνωρίζουμε ότι αυτή σημαίνει ένα κάλεσμα για αυτοθεσμισμένη δράση που προχωράει πέρα από απλές λέξεις, συνδυάζοντας θεωρία και πρακτική σε μια όμορφη πράξη προεικόνισης; Πρέπει να λάβουμε μια πολύπλευρη προσέγγιση στην απόρριψη του νεοφιλελευθερισμού. Ενώ δεν μπορούμε να τον αγνοήσουμε ή να τον ξεχάσουμε εντελώς, μπορούμε ενεργά να εργαστούμε εναντίον του με τρόπους που εκτείνονται πέρα από την επιτέλεση της ρητορικής και τη ρητορική της επιτέλεσης. Με όλα τα μέσα, ας προωθήσουμε ένα νέο ριζοσπαστικό πολιτικό σύνθημα. Χρησιμοποιήστε το hashtag (#fuckneoliberalism) και κάντε την περιφρόνηση μας να γίνει viral! Αλλά πρέπει να κάνουμε πολύ περισσότερα από το να εκφράζουμε απλώς την αγανάκτησή μας. Πρέπει να θεσπίσουμε την αποφασιστικότητά μας και να συνειδητοποιήσουμε την ελπίδα μας ως ενυπάρχουσα στις ενσώματες εμπειρίες στο εδώ και το τώρα[23]. Χρειάζεται να ξαναφτιάξουμε το κόσμο από μόνοι μας, μια διαδικασία που δεν πρέπει να αναβληθεί.

Έχουμε εσκεμμένα εξαπατηθεί και αποδυναμωθεί από τη συνεχιζόμενη προσφυγή στις υφιστάμενες πολιτικές διευθετήσεις της αντιπροσώπευσης. Η τυφλή μας πίστη μας έχει κάνει να περιμένουμε ατέρμονα να πέσει ο σωτήρας από τον ουρανό. Το σύστημα έχει αποδείξει ότι είναι τελείως διεφθαρμένο, όταν ξανά και ξανά κάθε επόμενος σπουδαίος πολιτικός υποψήφιος αποδεικνύεται ότι είναι μια αποτυχία. Σε αυτή τη νεοφιλελεύθερη στιγμή δεν αποτελεί περίπτωση ότι απλώς κάποια προβληματικά άτομα βρίσκονται στην εξουσία. Αντιθέτως, είναι η μεγάλη μας πίστη στο ίδιο το σύστημα που αποτελεί την επιτομή του προβλήματος. Εμείς παράγουμε και ενεργοποιούμε τις θεσμικές συνθήκες για να παίζει μαζί μας το «φαινόμενο Λούσιφερ»[24]. «Η μπαναλιτέ του κακού» είναι τέτοια ώστε αυτοί οι πολιτικοί κάνουν απλά τη δουλειά τους σε ένα σύστημα που ανταμείβει τις διαστροφές της εξουσίας διότι είναι όλα σχεδιασμένα να υπηρετούν τους νόμους του καπιταλισμού[25]. Αλλά δεν πρέπει να υπακούσουμε. Δεν είμαστε υποχρεωμένοι ακολουθήσουμε αυτή τη τάξη. Μέσω της άμεσης δράσης μας και της οργάνωσης εναλλακτικών μπορούμε να καταδικάσουμε ολόκληρη της δομή και να σπάσουμε τον φαύλο κύκλο της κακοποίησης. Όταν το πολιτικο σύστημα ορίζεται, ρυθμίζεται, μπερδεύεται και προέρχεται από τον καπιταλισμό, ποτέ δεν μπορεί να εκπροσωπήσει τους τρόπους μας να γνωρίζουμε και βρισκόμαστε στον κόσμο και ως εκ τούτου πρέπει να αναλάβουμε την ευθύνη αυτών των τρόπων ζωής και να επαναδιεκδικήσουμε τη συλλογική μας δράση. Πρέπει να αρχίσουμε να γινόμαστε ενεργοί στις δικές μας πολιτικές και να ξεκινήσουμε να αγκαλιάζουμε έναν πιο σχεσιακό τρόπο αλληλεγγύης που αναγνωρίζει ότι η υποταγή και η δυστυχία του ενός είναι ενδεικτική της καταπίεσης όλων μας[26]. Μπορούμε να ξεκινήσουμε να ζούμε σε άλλους πιθανούς κόσμους μέσω από μια ανανεωμένη δέσμευση στις πρακτικές της αλληλοβοήθειας, της συντροφικότητας, της αμοιβαιότητας και των μη-ιεραρχικών μορφών οργάνωσης που συλλαμβάνουν εκ νέου τη δημοκρατία στην ετυμολογική της βάση της λαϊκής εξουσίας. Τελικά ο νεοφιλελευθερισμός είναι μια ιδιαίτερα αποκρουστική ιδέα που συνοδεύεται από μια ολόκληρη σειρά από χυδαία αποτελέσματα και γελοίες υποθέσεις. Ως απάντηση, του αξίζει να βρεθεί αντιμέτωπος μια εξίσου προσβλητική γλώσσα και δράση. Η κοινότητά μας, η συνεργασία μας και η αμοιβαία φροντίδα μας είναι όλα απεχθή στο νεοφιλελευθερισμό. Μισεί αυτό που εμείς πανηγυρίζουμε. Έτσι όταν εμείς λέμε «γάμα τον νεοφιλελευθερισμό» αυτό δεν είναι μια απλή φράση, σημαίνει πολλά περισσότερα, συνιστά την αμοιβαία μας δέσμευση. Πείτε το δυνατά, ας το πούμε όλοι μαζί, και ας το πούμε σε κάθε έναν που θέλει να ακούσει, αλλά πάνω από όλα αποτελεί ένα εγερτήριο σάλπισμα για δράση, είναι η ενσάρκωση της προεικονιστικής μας δύναμης να αλλάξουμε αυτόν τον γαμημένο κόσμο. Γάμα τον Νεοφιλελευθερισμό!

नवउदारवाद भाड़ में जाए!

Translated by जय कौशल – Jai Kaushal

Translator's Commentary

Being a linguist and translator, it is always fascinating for me to work on something with mind-storming content. I find Simon's work to be a profound piece of intelligence loaded with basic realities about neoliberalism. It is sometimes slightly difficult to reproduce the same intensity of content in the same ways as in original work, but, in this instance, the intensity and clarity on neoliberalism helped me to translate it into the same register. Interestingly, the central expression revolves around the word "fuck," and sometimes this word makes academics nervous and uncomfortable, so as a translator it was quite a challenge for me to find the correct word in Hindi.

नवउदारवाद भाड़ में जाए!

ये नवउदारवाद भाड़ में जाए! जी हाँ, मैं यही कहना चाहता हूँ। अगर मैं अपनी बात यहीं खत्म कर दूँ तो भी कोई फ़र्क नहीं पड़ेगा। मेरी स्थिति बिल्कुल स्पष्ट है और आप भी समझ ही गए होंगे कि मैं वास्तव में क्या कहना चाहता हूँ। नवउदारवाद के बारे में चर्चा करने के लिए मेरे पास कुछ भी सकारात्मक कुछ भी नहीं है, सच कहूँ तो मुझे इस बारे में सोचकर ही बुखार आने लगता है. बस, बहुत हो चुका. मैं वास्तव में जो कहना चाहता था, उसके लिए एक समय मुझे इस पत्र का शीर्षक 'नवउदारवाद को भूल जाओ' देना ज्यादा उचित जान पड़ रहा था. मैं कई वर्षों से इस विषय पर लिख रहा हूँ[1] और अब मैं इस बिंदु पर आ खड़ा हुआ हूँ, जहाँ से इस विचार पर और

अधिक ऊर्जा नहीं खपाई जा सकती, क्योंकि मुझे डर है कि इससे आगे काम करने का मतलब है इस मुद्दे को बेवजह स्थायीत्व प्रदान करना। बल्कि मुझे लगता है कि एक राजनीतिक पैंतरेबाजकी तरह अगर हम सब शुतुरमुर्ग की तरह रेत में अपने सिर घुसाकर अपनी साझी दुनिया में नवउदारवाद के विनाशकारी और गंभीर परिणामों को नजरअंदाज करने लगेंतो स्थिति और बुरी हो जाएगी। असल में, नवउदारवाद की लगातार बढ़ती शक्ति को नकारना मुश्किल है और मुझे यकीन है कि इसे नकारना रणनीतिक ढंग से भी सही तरीका नहीं होगा². सो, इस बारे में मेरे सटीक विचार यही हैं कि 'यह, भाड़ में जाए'. मेरे द्वारा इस पेपर के लिए अगर थोड़ा शालीन शीर्षक चुन लिया जाता तो शायद यह इसके अपराध को कमतर ही व्यंजित करता। इसे बाद में देखा जाएगा। कोई गालियाँ दे रहा हो तो हम समाज को लेकर बहुत चिंतित क्यों हो उठते हैं जबकि हमारे सामने चिंतन करने के लिए नवउदारवाद जैसी उससे भी घृणित चीज मौजूद है! मैंने सोच लिया कि अब मुझे नियमोल्लंघन करने हैं, मैं परेशान हो गया था, मुझे नवउदारवाद द्वारा किया जा रहा अपमान और शोषण साफ़-साफ़ दिखाई पड़ रहा था। यह अच्छी बात नहीं है, बस इसीलिए हम सबको इसका उल्लंघन और विरोध करना चाहिए. अगर मैं अपने पेपर का शीर्षक चुनने में थोड़ी नरमी बरतता तो क्या यह इसकी शक्ति को देखते हुए भी इसके प्रति उदारता नहीं मानी जाती! हालांकि मैं भी शुरुआत में जरा-सा चिंतित हुआ था कि कहीं ऐसा शीर्षक मेरी साख तो नहीं गिरा देगा? कहीं इससे मेरी अगली पदोन्नति, नई नौकरी के ऑफ़र, मेरी शैक्षिक गतिविधियाँ अथवा कहीं अन्यत्र जाने या उन्नति करने के अवसर तो बाधित नहीं हो जाएंगे! एकबारगी यह मुझे नवउदारवाद के सामने अपनी निजी हार लगी, बखैर, अब यह भाड़ में जाए! ऐसा महसूस हुआ, इसलिए मैं मानता हूँ कि नवउदारवाद के विमर्श का प्रतिवाद करने के लिए वास्तव में कोई मजबूत वैचारिक उत्तर मौजूद नहीं है. तो क्यों नहीं इसे लोग सीधे-सीधे क्यों नहीं नकार देते! बस, हम लोग अकादमिक जगत में रंग-बिरंगी दिखने वाली, दोगली और अपनी सामाजिक नींव को खुद कमजोर करने वाली उत्परिवर्तन की भौगोलिक सैद्धांतिकियों का उपयोग कर इस पर बात करके शांत हो जाते हैं, जिससे बहुत फर्क नहीं पड़ता. अपने लेखन में मेरा योगदान भी ऐसे ही कुछ सिद्धांतों का उपयोग है³. पर मैं वास्तव में उक्त विचार के विरोध में ऐसा कुछ करना चाहता था. क्योंकि अपने दैनिक सोच-विचार में, अपने क्रिया-कलापों में मैंने

इस पर एक अरुचिकर तरीके से नकार की राजनीति महसूस की। ब इसीलिए मैंने इसका शीर्षक 'फक नियोलिबरेलिज्म' रखा क्योंकि यही वह सही पद है, जो मेरे कहे को पूरी तरह व्यंजित कर सकता है. असल में, मैं एक बारीक बिंदु की ओर इशारा कर रहा हूँ और इसके लिए मैंने 'फक' शब्द पर इतना अधिक सोचा है कि जीवन में किसी और शब्द पर कभी ऐसे नहीं सोचा. गज़ब का शब्द है ये! विस्मय व्यक्त करने के लिए अंग्रेजी में सबसे ज्यादा काम में लिए जाने वाले इस शब्द को हम कभी संज्ञा, क्रिया अथवा विशेषण के रूप में प्रयोग करते हैं. इसेक्रोध, अवमानना, झुंझलाहट, उदासीनताओं- रआश्चर्य व्यक्त करने के साथ-साथ अक्सर बिना किसी मतलब के भी बोल दिया जाता है, जैसे 'फ़क समथिंग अप', 'फ़क समवन ओवर', 'फ़क अराउंड', 'नॉट गिव अ फ़क' आदि, यहाँ तक कि कभी-कभी सीधे-सीधे किसी को इंगित करते हुए कह दिया जाता है, 'गो फ़क योअरसेल्फ़' . इस पॉइंट पर आकर आप सोचने लगते हो कि, अच्छा!, किसके साथ फ़क? खैर, अगर आप वास्तव में नवउदारवाद का अंत करने के इच्छुक हैं तो आपको कुछ करना पड़ेगा. इस शब्द में जो ताकतवर शक्तियाँ ध्वनित होती है, वही उसकी चुनौती भी हैं. 'फ़क नियोलिबरेलिज्म' पद की सही व्यंजना और बारीकी तक पँहुचकर ही हम इसको ठीक से समझ सकते हैं और खत्म करने के औजार पा सकते हैं. जी हाँ, तब तक 'फ़क नियोलि- बरेलिज्म' और 'फ़क नूआन्स' दोनों झेलें.हाल ही में कीरन हीली[4] ने तर्क दिया है कि, विकास की यह तथाकथित बाधापूर्ण थ्योरी न केवल बौद्धिक रूप से रोचक और आनुभाविक दृष्टि से उपजाऊ है, वरन् सफल भी'. तो इस बारीकी से सम्मोहित हुए बिना आइए, तुरंत यह जानें और काम में लग जाएँ जैसा कि मैं इस बेहूदा नवउदारवाद पर सोच रहा हूँ. इसका पहला अर्थ तो बिल्कुल स्पष्ट है.'फ़क नियोलिबरेलिज्म' कहकर हम इस नव उदारवादी व्यवस्था के प्रति अपना रोष प्रकट कर रहे हैं. जो हमारे गुस्से, आक्रोश और हम सबके सामने आ खड़ी हुई इस घटिया, दुर्भावनापूर्ण स्थिति के मुँह पर थूकने का संकेत है. नवउदारवाद और इसके दुष्प्रभावों के खिलाफ़ प्रतिरोध दर्ज करवाकर, जुलूस निकालकर और अधिक संख्या में आलेख एवं किताबें लिखकर भी इसे व्यक्त किया जा सकता है. इससे न केवल उपदेश का रूप बदल जाएगा वरन् पहले से ही विकृत चुकी आकाँक्षाएँ अपने तेवर बदलने को मजबूर हो जाएँगी.मैं यह नहीं कह रहा कि उक्त पद्धतियाँ हमारे प्रतिरोध करने के सटीक

तरीके सिद्ध होने वाले हैं बल्कि मुझे यकीन है कि ये सभी उपाय न
तो नवउदारवाद को पूरी तरह बाँधने में समर्थ हैं और न ही हमारे पक्ष
में हैं. इस मुद्दे पर जनता का विशाल रक्षात्मक प्रतिरोध दर्ज
कराने के लिए शक्तिशाली कारकों को आपसी संवाद का हिस्सा
बनाना होगा. हमारा यह सोचना गलत होगा कि वे प्रतिरोध की
आवाज को सुनने और शामिल करने की पहल करेंगे[5]. क्या हमें बात
नहीं करनी चाहिए? अब हम 'फ़क नियोलिबरेलिज़्म' के दूसरे पॉइंट
पर आते हैं. इसे नवउदारवाद के अस्वीकार पर आधारित है (जैसा कि
हमें लगता है) जे.के गिब्सन-ग्राहम[6] द्वारा विकसित किया गया यह
तरीका नवउदारवाद के खात्मे के लिए काफ़ी उपयोगी जान पड़ता है.
इसके अंतर्गत हमें सीधे-सीधे नवउदारवाद पर बात करना बंद कर
देना होगा. विद्वानों एवं शोधार्थियों को इसे ध्यान में रखते हुए
नवउदारवाद पर अपने शोध और अध्ययन को प्राथमिकता देना बंद
करना पड़ेगा.हो सकता है हम इसे पूरी तरह न भूल पाएँ अथवा
उपेक्षित न कर पाएँ, मैंने स्वयं भी इसे एक समस्या ही माना है,
लेकिन हम इसे अन्य बातों की तुलना में कम महत्व तो दे ही सकते
हैं, या इस पर लिखना नगण्य कर सकते हैं. एक बार फ़रि यह हमारे
लिए संपर्क का एक महत्वपूर्ण बिंदु बन गया है कि हम नवउदारवाद
की दुनिया से ऊपर हैं. हालांकि मुझे अच्छी तरह पता है कि इतना भर
पर्याप्त नहीं है. जैसा मार्क परसेल[7] का तर्क है, "हमें न केवल
नवउदारवाद की दिशा उलटने की जरूरत है, वरन् अपनी भी. ताकि हम
अपने मुश्किल मुद्दों को खुद के लिए हल करने की आनंददायक
शुरुआत कर सकें." 'निषेध, विरोध और आलोचना जरूरी हैं, पर हमें
सचेत होकर यह भी सोचना चाहिए कि कैसे इस कम्बख्त नवउदारवाद
की पहुँच से चीजों को दूर रखा जाए. अब तीसरा और सबसे
महत्वपूर्ण पॉइंट, जिस पर मुझे लगता है कि हमें 'फ़क नियोलिबरे-
लिज़्म' पर विचार करते समय बखूबी फोकस करना चाहिए, और वह
है- पूर्व-निर्धारित राजनीति के तहत नवउदारवाद के परे जाकर इस
पर सीधी कार्यवाही करना[8].इसके लिए केंद्रिकता, पदानुक्रम और
आधिकारिकता का नकार जरूरी है, इस आधिकारिकता में प्रतिनिधि
राजनीति प्रमुख होती है और इसके लिए समानांतर संबंधों तथा
संगठन के ऐसे रूपों पर फ़ोकस करना पड़ता है जिनका प्रतिबिंबन
इच्छित भावी समाज में दिखाई दे[9]. इस तरह बिना 'संवाद-स्थापन',
पूर्वनिर्धारण और सीधी कार्यवाही के कुछ भी नहीं हो सकेगा.
ध्यान रहे, हमें जो भी करना है, खुद से ही करना होगा.फिर भी, उन

सभी प्रमुख तरीकों पर ध्यान जरूर दिया गया है, जिसमें नवउदारवाद कब्जा करने में सक्षम रहा और सभी तरह की राजनीतिक बहसों और आदेशों में सही ठहराया जाता रहा[10]. डेविड हार्वे[11] जैसे आलोचकों की मानें तो नवउदारवाद के प्रश्न को राज्य स्वयं प्रमुखता देकर हल कर सकता है. खासकर, उसे गैरश्रेणीबद्ध संगठन और क्षैतिजि राजनीति को सबसे पहले खारिज करना चाहिए, जो रेलगाड़ी में ग्रीस की तरह नवउदारवादी भविष्य की जरूरत बन रहे हैं. वस्तुत: अभी अपनी हताशा में वह पूरी तरह पूर्व-निर्धारित राजनीति को गलत-समझ बैठा है, जबकि यह रास्ता है, भविष्य के लिए एक जरूरी रास्ता, मंजिल नहीं[12] दूसरे शब्दों में, वहाँ पहले से ही पूर्वनिर्धारित राजनीति को लेकर लगातार ऐसी सतर्कता बनाए रखी गई है, ताकि वास्तविक प्री-फ़िगरेशन की वास्तविक प्रेकटिस शामिल ही न हो पाए. यह एक प्रभावी और चौकस स्थिति तो है ही, साथ ही इसे उत्पादन, आविष्कार और समुदाय की इच्छा की संतुष्टि के रूप में निर्माण की दिशा में एक अच्छा कदम भी माना जाएगा. इस नजरिए से पूर्वनिर्धारित राजनीति स्पष्ट रूप से नवउदारवाद विरोधी है. वे साधनों, रास्तों को हमारा समझकर उनपर कब्जा कर रहे हैं, पर हमारे रास्ते अंतहीन हैं. इसे प्रकल्पित करने के लिए एकता और सबके साथ बराबरी से चलने की जरूरत है, और इससे जो प्रफ़ुल्लता एवं आनंद है, वह न तो अगुआ बनकर मिलेगा और न कट्टर सर्वहारा वर्ग साथ झूठे आदर्श-राज्य बल्कि कहना चाहिए 'शून्य-राज्य' के भावभीने वादे करने में है. हाँ, यह यथार्थ की कठोर और पुरानी जमीन पर नई और वास्तविक दुनिया के निर्माण में है, जिसके लिए कड़ी मेहनत और एक बार फ़िर पक्के इरादों की आवश्यकता है[13]. नवउदारवाद में ऐसा कुछ नहीं है कि हम इसे महत्व दें, इसीलिए निर्माण की पूर्वनिर्धारित राजनीति के संदर्भ में मेरा सीधे तौर पर यही कहना है- नवउदारवाद हो बरबाद! हमारे राजानीतिक कल्पनालोक में भी इस बदतमीज की घुसपैठ हो गई है. इसकी वजह से हिंसा बढ़ी है. असमानता अब एक सद्गुण बन गया है. इसने पर्यावरण को तबाह कर डाला है. इसने संचय की अंतहीन प्रवृत्ति और विकास के छद्म को बेतरह बढ़ावा दिया है. भाड़ में जाएँ मोंट पेलेरिनि सोसाइटी और उसके थिंकटैंक, जो लगातार इसे न केवल सहारा दिए हुए हैं, वरन् बढ़ावा भी दे रहे हैं. फ़्रेडरिक हाएक और मिल्टन फ़्रायडमेन को लानत है, जो वे नव उदारवाद पर टिके हुए अपने विचार हम पर थोप रहे हैं. लानत है उन थैचरों, रीगनों और लोभ

में अंधे हो चुके ऐसे सभी कायर, आत्मकेंद्रित राजनीतिज्ञों को! भाड़ में जाएँ वे लोग, जो जानबूझकर जनता को इसका डर दिखाकर अपने व्यापार में लगे हैं, जिनकी नजर में दूसरों की औकात सिर्फ़ उनका संडास साफ़ करने और फर्श पर पोंछा लगाने वाले से ज्यादा नहीं है. ऐसे लोग किसी को भी अपने समाज का सम्माननीय नागरिक नहीं गिनते. मेट्रिक्स की ओर तेजी से मुड़ते और इस बात से बेपरवाह कि वे जिसे बेमायने समझ रहे हैं, उसके भी मायने हो सकते हैं. लानत है, लाभ कमाने की उस इच्छा को जो समाज के हितों की उपेक्षा करती है. सीधे तौर पर कहें तो, हर उस चीज को लानत है, जिसकी बात नवउदारवाद करता है. उस ट्रोजन हॉर्स को भी, जिस पर यह सवार है! बहुत समय से हमको यही समझाया जा रहा है कि 'इस व्यवस्था का कोई विकल्प नहीं है'। यह उसी प्रकार की स्थिति है, जैसे 'समुद्र में उठता ज्वार सारी नावों को अपनी चपेट में ले लेता है, और हम एक डरावने डार्विनियन संसार में रहते हैं, जहाँ सब एक-दूसरे के विरोधी हैं. सब के सब 'योग्यतम की उत्तरजीविता' के सिद्धांत के ही खिलाफ हो गए हैं. यहाँ संघर्ष का सिद्धांत काम करता है. हम पूरी तरह 'कॉमन्स की त्रासदी' के विचार में डूब गए, जबकि असलियत में यह चाल है, जो 'पूंजीवाद की त्रासदी' और उसके द्वारा युद्धस्तर पर की गई अंतहीन लूट के रूप में सामने आती है.[14]. गैरेट हार्डिन[15] की दुखती रग यही थी. वह कभी यह सोचना बंद नहीं कर सका कि खुले में चरते दिखाई देते आम पशु किसी की निजी मिल्कियत कैसे बन गए थे. कैसा रहे, अगर हम असली कॉमन्स से उसके बारे में निजी मिल्कियत की इस पूर्वधारणा के बिना मिलें[16]? कैसा रहे, अगर हम विकल्पों के पूर्व-प्रारूपों पर गौर करना शुरू कर दें जो कि पहले से संगठन के सबसे महत्वपूर्ण प्रकार सिद्ध हो चुके हैं[17]? कैसा रहे, अगर हम प्रतियोगिता और मेरिट की कड़वी गोलियाँ खाने के बजाय अपनी ऊर्जा नवउदारवादी नुस्खों द्वारा इलाज में खर्च न करें, बल्कि सहयोग और आपसी सहायता की गहरी हीलिंग का उपयोग करें[18]? एक बार जेमी पेक[19] ने नवउदारवाद को 'एक कट्टरपंथी राजनीतिक नारा' घोषित किया था, पर अब यह आलोचना के क्षेत्र से ही बाहर हो गया है. हमने सालों पहले अपने दुश्मन को पहचान लिया था पर तब हम इसे अपने लेखन और प्रतिरोध के बल पर ही जान सके थे. अब हम इसके खात्मे को लेकर निश्चिंत हो चुके हैं, 2008 के वित्तीय संकट और कब्जा आंदोलन के परिणाम आने के बाद यह लगातार हाँफ रहा है और अपनी खराब

हालत को किसी तरह शक्तिशाली ढंग से उबारने के लिए संघर्ष कर रहा है[20]. जेफ़ी वलिसन[21] ने इसकी बढ़ती शक्ति को 'नवउदारवादी असभ्य' कहा है और मैं यकीनी तौर पर कह सकता हूँ कि इस हॉरर शो पर काबू पाने के लिए हमें अपनी राजनीति को कानूनी दायरे में लाना होगा[22]. अगर यह 'फ़क नवउदारवाद' हमारी राजनीति में घुसकर उसे बदलने का एक नया मंत्र बन गया तो क्या होगा? एक ऐसे मुहावरे को जीवंत किया जाना चाहिये जो न सिर्फ हमको सक्रियता प्रदान करे वरन् उस स्थान और उन लम्हों को भी सुधारे जिसमें हम अपना जीवन जीते हैं? क्या हर बार जब हम इस मुहावरे का प्रयोग करते हैं तो हमको ऐसी निष्क्रिय संस्था याद नहीं आती जो महज शब्दजाल में उलझती और सिद्धांतों के संकलन तथा व्यवस्था के पुरातन स्वरूप को संरक्षित करने के दिलचस्प अभ्यास में लिप्त रहती है? हमको नवउदारवाद को अस्वीकार के लिए बहुविधि का प्रयोग करने चाहिये। जबकि हम नव उदारवाद न पूरी तरह से नकार सकते है और न ही भूल सकते हैं अतः हमको इसका इस तरह विरोध करना होगा जिससे बात इसके प्रदर्शन के शाब्दिक प्रतिवाद से आगे बढ़े। किसी भी सूरत में हमको नए और उग्र राजनीतिक नारे को प्रबल करना होगा। (#fuckneoliberalism) इस हैशटैग का प्रयोग करके हम अपनी नाराजगी को वायरल कर सकते है। परन्तु हमको अपने रोष को प्रकट करने से भी अधिक बहुत कुछ करना होगा। हमको अपने-अपने हल और अपनी अभिलाषाओं को अभी और इसी वक़्त मजबूती से कहना होगा। हमको दुनिया को यह अहसास कराना होगा कि यह विरोध का दौर रुकने वाला नहीं है। हम स्वेच्छा से इस व्यवस्था पर मोहित हुए और बार-बार वर्तमान राजनीतिक संरचना से प्रतिनिधित्व की मांग करके स्वयं को कमजोर किया। हमने लम्बे समय तक आकाश से एक बूँद पाने की निरर्थक प्रतीक्षा की। इस व्यवस्था ने स्वयं साबित किया है कि यह पूरी तरह से भ्रष्ट है। इस व्यस्वथा के कारण आने वाले समय में हमारे महान उम्मीदवार भी असफल साबित होंगे। इस नवउदारवादी संरचना में परेशानी का कारण यह नहीं है कि समस्याग्रस्त व्यक्ति सत्ता में था वरन् हमारा इस व्यवस्था के प्रति अंधविश्वास मूल समस्या है। हमने एक ऐसी संस्थागत समस्याओं को जन्म दिया और बढ़ाया है जिसने "ल्युसिफ़िर इफ़ेक्ट" को खुलकर अपना प्रभाव दिखाने का अवसर दिया।[24]. इस समस्या की कुरूपता यह है कि इसमें काम करने वाले ये राजनीतज्ञि अपनी नौकरी सिर्फ इसलिए कर रहे हैं क्योंकि

व्यवस्था इनको सत्ता के उलटफेर का अवसर देती है क्योंकि ये सब इस तरह से तैयार किये गए हैं ताकि पूंजीवाद का समर्थन कर सकें।[25]. परन्तु हम उनकी आज्ञा का पालन नहीं करते हैं। हम इस व्यवस्था के प्रति आभारी नहीं है।अपनी सीधी कार्यवाही और संगठनात्मक बदलाव के द्वारा हम व्यवस्था के सभी दोषों और शोषण के बृहद् चक्र को तोड़ सकते हैं। जब राजनीतिक व्यवस्था अंदरुनी तौर उलझी हुई तथा उदारवाद के अनुरूप परिभाषित और नियमित हो तो ये कभी भी हमारी समझ को और उसके उसके अनुरूप बनने वाली दुनिया का प्रतिनिधित्व नहीं कर सकती है। अत: अब हमको अपने तय किए गये जीवनपथ की जिम्मेदारी उठानी होगी और एक समग्र संस्था के निर्माण की प्रबल मांग करनी होगी। हमको अपनी राजनीति में सक्रिय होना आरम्भ करना होगा और सम्बन्धों की इस समझ के प्रति अपना समर्थन दर्शाना होगा जो कि यह रेखांकित करती है कि एक की पीड़ा और अपमान वास्तव में सभी का शोषण है।[26]. हम सम्भावनाओं से भरी ऐसी दुनिया में इस आपसी प्रतिबद्धता के साथ रहना आरम्भ कर सकते हैं कि उसमें आपसी सहयोग, फेलोशिप, पारस्परिक आदान-प्रदान तथा अश्रेणीबद्ध संगठन हो। ऐसी व्यवस्था जो कि लोकतंत्र की मूलभावना के अनुरूप लोगों की शक्ति पर आधारित होगी। मूलत: नवउदारवाद एक बेहद बकवास विचार है जोकि अपने साथ बेहूदा परिणाम और मूर्खतापूर्ण मान्यताओं को लेकर आता है। बदले में यह उतनी ही प्रतिरोधात्मक भाषा और आंदोलन का सामना करने योग्य है. हमारा समुदाय, हमारा संगठन और हमारा एक-दूसरे की चिंता करना इसको नागवार गुजरता है. हम जिसका जश्न मनाते हैं ये उससे नफरत करता है. अत: हम कह सकते हैं 'फ़क नियोलिबरेलिज्म'. आइए, इसे जोर से कहें, मेरे साथ कहें, जहाँ तक आवाज पहुँचे, सबसे कहें! लेकिन इन सबका एक ही मतलब है कि यह शक्ति के पुरातन स्वरूप में बदलाव का एक पुरजोर आह्वान है ताकि इस विभेदकारी दुनिया को बदला जा सके। ये नवउदारवाद भाड़ में जाए!

CHAPTER 10

Bahasa Indonesia – Indonesian

Neoliberalisme Sialan

Translated by Okty Budiati

Translator's Commentary

When I read an essay from Simon Springer, entitled "Fuck Neoliberalism," I knew the article would be the key to undetstanding the tangled conditions in my country, Indonesia. Why are there still so many texts that are used as guidelines to see its social politics? This old social psychology is obsolete, made of old texts and writings that are no longer relevant to the contemporary situation in Indonesia. I see Simon's article more as a penetrating voice, as an arrow in reading world political history that reminds us that it is important to pay attention to the details. This essay will have a positive impact on ways of thinking and on the individual minds.

Some things were quite difficult, like determining the meaning of the word *fuck* in Bahasa Indonesia, so that in the delivery its meaning could be understood by the readers. However, "neoliberalism" has come to dominate all social in Indonesia, and this may be difficult for those who cannot think freely to grasp. I believe any action comes with a risk, and, therefore, I dare to translate this essay without using a pseudonym.

In my translation, I followed the author's intent in every detail without altering the force and meaning. The essay must be read in its entirety, each word conveying meaning. I compiled it into sentences that flow easily for comprehension and read flexibly. It was quite difficult, especially in the Indonesian language, where each word has various meanings. But, the language of literacy remains pluralistic and communicative in free speech. I hope this translation will encourage people in Indoneisa to connect with the global movement against neoliberalism and will encourage those who can to speak out against injustice in all situations. This is as an invitation to dare to speak out.

Neoliberalisme Sialan

Neoliberalisme Sialan (*Fuck Neoliberalism*). Itulah pesan tumpulku. Aku mungkin dapat mengakhiri diskusi ini sekarang, dan itu tidak masalah. Posisiku tetap jelas, dan Anda menangkap inti dari apa yang ingin kukatakan. Aku tidak memiliki sesuatu yang positif untuk ditambahkan dalam diskusi tentang neoliberalisme ini, dan jujur saja, aku sudah terlalu muak untuk memikirkannya. Aku sudah mempertimbangkan, dan menyebut makalahku ini menjadi 'Neoliberalisme Sialan' sebagai gantinya, seperti dalam beberapa hal, tepatnya apa yang ingin kulakukan, aku telah menulis tentang masalah ini selama bertahun-tahun,[1] hingga aku tiba pada satu titik, di mana tidak lagi mau menguras banyak energi hanya untuk mengabadikan ketakutan sebagai pegangan penciptaan ide. Refleksiku menyadari bahwa sebagai manuver politik, hal itu sangat berbahaya, seperti hanya menempelkan kepala kita di dalam pasir, dan secara kolektif mengabaikan fenomena yang berdampak pada penghancuran, hingga melemahkan dunia kita bersama. Seperti ada kekuatan berkelanjutan dari sebuah neoliberalisme yang sulit ditolak, dan aku tidak yakin, bahwa pendekatan yang tepat tidak lain strategi yang membodohkan[2]. Jadi, apa yang aku pikirkan akan seperti; *'baiklah mengalaminya semua itu'*, dan sementara menulisnya dengan ketenangan yang lembut dapat mengurangi potensi pelanggaran atas pilihan judul tulisanku sebagai pertimbangannya. Mengapa kita harus menjadi khawatir menggunakan kata-kata kotor tentang wacana keji neoliberalisme itu sendiri? Aku memutuskan untuk melakukan pelanggaran dengan kesal, dengan menyinggung perasaan, karena kita memang harus tersinggung kepada neoliberalisme yang sangat membingungkan, dan karena itu, kita harus melanggarnya. Tidakkah akan melunakkan gelar dengan konsesi lain dalam kekuatan neoliberalisme? Awalnya aku pun khawatir dengan reputasiku atas pilihan judulku ini. Apakah akan menghambat promosi, dan penawaran pekerjaanku di masa depan, seandainya aku ingin mempertahankannya di akademisi, baik ke wilayah atas atau ke wilayah yang baru? Ini terasa seperti rentetan kekalahan bagi disiplin neoliberal. Persetan dengan itu.

Hal itu sama saja membuatku mengakui bahwa tidak akan ada tanggapan yang tepat untuk melawan wacana neoliberalisme. Seakan kita hanya dapat menanggapi format akademis hanya melalui teori geografis yang kompleks tentang variegasi, hibriditas, dan mutasi untuk melemahkan bangunannya. Ini tampak tidak berdaya, dan walaupun aku telah berkontribusi dalam artikulasi untuk beberapa teori ini[3], dan aku sering merasa bahwa jenis pembingkaiannya sesuai dengan jenis argumen yang ingin kubuat. Sedangkan di keseharian, biasa, tidak biasa, bahkan duniawi, menurutku harus ada penolakan politik. Maka aku memilih 'Fuck Neoliberalism', karena inilah yang ingin kusampaikan. Aku menginginkan argumenku memiliki nuansa itu dengan lebih banyak menggunakan istilah 'fuck' yang mungkin akan kulakukan di lain waktu dalam hidupku. Betapa kata yang sangat bagus! Ia bekerja sebagai kata benda atau kata kerja, dan sebagai kata sifat itu mungkin merupakan tanda seru yang paling sering digunakan dalam bahasa Inggris. Istilah ini memang biasa digunakan dalam mengekspresikan kemarahan, penghinaan, gangguan, ketidakpedulian, kejutan, ketidaksabaran, atau bahkan dapat menjadi penekanan yang tidak berarti karena hanya bantalan lidah. Anda bisa 'mengacaukan sesuatu', 'bercinta dengan seseorang', 'bercinta di sekitar', 'tidak bercanda', dan ada titik geografis yang jelas untuk merujuk pada kata sejauh yang Anda mampu perintahkan untuk 'pergi bercinta sendiri'. Pada titik ini Anda mungkin bahkan berpikir 'ok, tapi siapa yang memberikan "*fuck*"?' Baiklah, aku tahu, jika Anda tertarik untuk mengakhiri neoliberalisme, seharusnya Anda melakukannya. Kemampuan yang kuat dengan menyertakan kata akan mampu menantang potensi neoliberalisme. Untuk menggali dan membongkar kemampuan ini, kita perlu menghargai nuansa apa yang bisa diartikan dengan ungkapan '*fuck neoliberalism*'. Namun pada saat yang sama, bercinta dengan nuansa itu. Seperti yang dikemukakan Kieran Healy[4], ini "*biasanya menghalangi perkembangan teori yang secara intelektual menarik, secara empiris generatif, atau hampir berhasil*". Jadi tanpa bernafaskan nuansa ini, mari kita percepat kinerja ini bersamaku, dan kita harus berani mengacaukan neoliberalisme.

Dalam hal pertama, dan yang paling jelas. Dengan mengatakan '*fuck neoliberalism*' maka akan mengekspresikan kemarahan kita terhadap mesin neoliberal. Ini adalah indikasi kemarahan, keinginan, kebencian, dan memuntahkannya kembali racunnya tepat di wajah kejahatan yang paling jahat, dan yang telah ditunjukkannya kepada kita semua. Hal ini akan mampu hadir hanya dalam bentuk memobilisasi lebih banyak demonstrasi melawan neoliberalisme atau dalam menulis lebih banyak makalah, dan buku yang mengkritisi pengaruhnya. Hingga untuk yang terakhir, berkhotbah kepada pertobatan, dan yang pertama berharap, bahwa orang yang sesat akan bersedia untuk mengubah cara-cara mereka. Bukan saya berbagi metode, namun hal ini mampu menjadi taktik penting dalam perlawanan kita, dan saya meyakini bahwa mereka sama sekali tidak cukup kuat untuk mengubah arus dalam melawan neoliberalisme yang menguntungkan kita. Dalam membuat gerakan massa yang agung, maka kita harus berusaha menarik aktor yang berpengaruh ke dalam percakapan yang serius, bahwa mereka mungkin mendengarkan serta mulai mengakomodasi suara penolakan terpopuler[5]. Bukankah sebaiknya kita berbicara? Inilah pemikiran yang kedua tentang makna dari '*fuck neoliberalism*', yang tidak lain merupakan gagasan penolakan. Ini akan menjadi advokasi untuk mengakhiri neoliberalisme (seperti yang kita ketahui) dengan cara yang lebih maju oleh JK. Gibson-Graham[6] namun kita berhenti membicarakannya. Para ilmuwan, pada khususnya, lebih memprioritaskan fokusnya hanya kepada studi mereka. Mungkin tidak sepenuhnya melupakan atau mengabaikan neoliberalisme, yang selama ini saya anggap bermasalah, tapi berlanjut dengan tulisan tentang hal-hal lain. Sekali lagi ini adalah titik kontak yang sangat penting bagi kita saat kita bekerja melampaui pandangan dunia neoliberal, tapi di sini juga saya tidak sepenuhnya yakin bahwa ini sudah cukup. Seperti yang dikatakan Mark Purcell[7], "Kita perlu berpaling dari neoliberalisme, dan menuju diri kita sendiri, untuk memulai usaha yang sulit—tapi juga menyenangkan—untuk mengelola urusan kita, untuk diri kita sendiri". Sementara ini sebuah penyangkalan, protes, dan kritik sanagatlah diperlukan, dan kita juga perlu memikirkan secara aktif bagaimana mengacaukan neoliberalisme, yaitu, dengan melakukan hal-hal di luar jangkauannya.

Tindakan langsung di luar wilayah neoliberalisme adalah berbicara ke dalam politik prefiguratif[8], yang merupakan pengertian ketiga, dan paling penting dari apa yang kupikir, bahwa kita harus fokus pada saat membuat gagasan *'fuck neoliberalism'*. Prefigure sendiri berarti adalah menolak sentinis, hierarki, dan otoritas yang datang melalui politik representatif dengan menekankan praktik dalam hubungan horizontal, dan tentunya membangun organisasi yang mencerminkan apa yang dicari oleh masyarakat di masa depan[9]. Setelah memasuki tahap prefigurasi, lalu memasuki tindakan langsung yang berpendapat bahwa tidak pernah ada percakapan yang harus dilakukan, dan menyadari bahwa apa pun yang ingin kita lakukan, kita dapat melakukannya sendiri. Walau demikian, hal yang perlu diperhatikan secara signifikan terhadap cara-cara di mana neoliberalisme dapat menangkap, menyesuaikan semua jenis wacana, dan imperatif politik[10]. Bagi para kritikus seperti David Harvey[11], dan hanya badan negara yang mampu menyelesaikan pertanyaan neoliberal dengan cepat, menolak organisasi non-hirarkis, melakukan politik horizontal, dan mengecohkan masa depan neoliberal yang terjamin. Namun pesimisnya, sepenuhnya salah dalam memahami makna dari politik prefiguratif yang akan menjadi sarana tanpa akhir, selain membuat sarana masa depan[12]. Dengan kata lain, perlunya kewaspadaan secara terus-menerus, dan terus-menerus, hingga terbangun politik prefiguratif hingga praktiknya tidak terkooptasi. Ini bersifat refleksif sekaligus pandangan menuju produksi, penemuan, dan penciptaan sebagai kepuasan atas keinginan masyarakat. Dengan cara ini, politik prefiguratif secara eksplisit adalah gerakan anti-neoliberal. Mereka memanfaatkan sarana sebagai sarana kita, sarana tanpa akhir. Untuk prefigure yang merangkul keramahan, dan kegembiraan yang datang bersamaan dengan persamaan radikal, bukan sebagai pelopor, dan proletar di jalan menuju janji utopia kosong yang transendental atau 'tempat yang kosong', namun sebagai bukti iman yang kokoh di sini, sekarang saatnya membuat sebuah dunia baru 'di dalam cangkang yang lama' dengan kerja keras, dan penegasan kembali yang terus-menerus[13].

Tidak ada apa-apa tentang neoliberalisme yang pantas untuk kita hormati, dan karena itu dalam konser politik prefiguratif penciptaan, pesan saya cukup sederhana '*fuck it*'. Persetan dengan politik imajinasi kita. Persetan dengan kekerasan yang ditimbulkannya. Persetan dengan ketidak-setaraan yang dianggapnya sebagai kebajikan. Persetan karena semua itu telah merusak lingkungan. Persetan siklus akumulasi, dan kultivasi pertumbuhan tanpa henti. Persetanlah masyarakat Mont Pelerin, dan semua '*think tank*' yang terus menerus menopang, dan promosikan-nya. Fuck Friedrich Hayek, dan Milton Friedman, karena telah membebani kita dengan gagasan mereka. Persetan para Thatcher, Reagans, dan semua politisi pengecut yang mementingkan diri sendiri dengan berusaha mengga-ruk bagian belakang ketamakan. Persetan pengecualian rasa takut yang melihat 'orang lain' layak membersih-kan toilet kita, dan mengepel lantai kita, tapi bukan sebagai anggota komunitas kita. Persetanlah langkah intens menuju metrik, dan kegagalan untuk menghar-gai, bahwa tidak semua hal yang diperhitungkan dapat dihitung. Persetan keinginan untuk keuntungan atas kebutuhan masyarakat. Fuck seluruh neoliberalisme, fuck yang menaiki kuda Troya! Telah lama kita diberi-tahu 'tidak ada alternatif', bahwa 'pasang naik meng-angkat semua kapal', bahwa kita hidup di dunia mimpi buruk Darwin, dari semua melawan semua, 'survival of the fittest'. Kami telah menelan gagasan tentang 'tragedi the commons' hook, line and sinker; padahal kenyataan-nya semua ini adalah tipu muslihat yang benar-benar mencerminkan 'tragedi kapitalisme' dengan perang pen-jarahannya yang tiada akhir[14]. Garrett Hardin[15] dalam Achilles' heels adalah; bahwa dia tidak pernah berhenti untuk memikirkan bagaimana ternak penggembalaan telah dimiliki secara pribadi. Apa yang mungkin terjadi ketika kita menemukan kembali hakekat yang sebenar-nya sebagai milik bersama tanpa prasangka kepemilikan pribadi[16]? Apa yang mungkin terjadi ketika kita mulai memperhatikan lebih dekat pada pilihan alternatif yang telah terjadi dengan mengistimewakan pengalaman ini sebagai bentuk organisasi yang paling penting[17]? Apa yang mungkin terjadi ketika alih-alih menelan pil pahit persaingan dan pernikahan, sebaliknya kita malah mem-fokuskan energi untuk tidak mengobati neoliberal kita, namun pada penyembuhan yang lebih dalam yang diser-tai kerjasama dan bantuan timbal balik[18]?

Jamie Peck[19] pernah menyebut neoliberalisme sebagai 'slogan politik radikal', namun tidak lagi cukup berta-han lama dalam wilayah kritik. Sudah bertahun-tahun berlalu, sejak kami pertama kali mengidentifikasi musuh, dan sejak saat itu kami telah mengetahuinya dengan baik melalui tulisan dan protes kami. Tetapi bahkan ketika kami pun meyakini kekalahannya, karena setelah krisis keuangan 2008 dalam Gerakan Pendudukan berikutnya, ia akan terus mengudara, berhijrah dengan bentuk zom-bikasi yang lebih kuat[20]. Japhy Wilson[21] menyebutnya kekuatan sebagai 'gothic neoliberal', dan aku meyakini bahwa untuk mengatasi kejadian horor ini, kita harus pindahkan politik ke dalam dunia yang tidak aktif[22]. Bagaimana jika *'fuck neoliberalism'* kita jadikan sebagai mantra untuk jenis politik baru? Frasa yang memungkin-kan untuk berbicara, tidak hanya untuk tindakan, tapi juga untuk reklamasi kehidupan kita di ruang, dan waktu, di mana kita aktif menjalaninya? Bagaimana jika setiap kali kita menggunakan ungkapan ini, kita menyadari bahwa itu berarti panggilan untuk agen yang tidak aktif, yang melampaui kata-kata belaka, menggabungkan teori dan praktik ke dalam praksis prefigurasi yang indah? Kita harus mengambil pendekatan multi penolakan terhadap

neoliberalisme. Meskipun kita tidak dapat mengabaikan-
nya sepenuhnya atau melupakannya, kita dapat secara
aktif berupaya melawannya dengan cara yang melampaui kinerja retorika, sekaligus retorika kinerja. Dengan
segala cara; mari maju sebuah slogan politik radikal baru.
Gunakan hashtag (#fuckneoliberalism), jadikanlah penghinaan ini sebagai virus! Tapi kita harus melakukan lebih
dari sekadar mengungkapkan kemarahan kita. Kita harus
memiliki tekad dengan mewujudkan harapan sebagai
iman dari pengalaman kita yang terkandung di sini, dan
sekarang[23] Kita perlu membuat ulang dunia kita sendiri,
sebuah proses yang tidak dapat ditunda.

Dengan sengaja kami menipu, dan melemahkan diri
dengan terus mengajukan banding atas pengaturan repre-
sentasi politik yang ada. Iman kita yang buta membuat
kita menunggu tanpa henti agar seorang penyelamat
turun dari langit. Sistem ini telah terbukti benar-benar
rusak parah, di mana berkali-kali kandidat politik besar
berikutnya terbukti gagal. Saat ini neoliberal bukanlah
masalah individu yang berkuasa. Sebaliknya, kepercayaan
terhadap sistem itu sendiri yang menjadi inti dari masalah.
Kami memproduksi dan mengaktifkan kondisi kelem-
bagaan demi 'Lucifer Effect' untuk dimainkan sendiri[24].
'Kejahatan yang binal' sedemikian rupa sehingga para
politisi ini hanya melakukan pekerjaan mereka dalam
sistem yang hanya memberi imbalan penyimpangan
kekuasaan, karena semuanya dirancang untuk melayani
hukum kapitalisme[25]. Tapi kita tidak harus taat. Kita tidak
terikat dalam pesanan ini. Melalui tindakan langsung,
dan pengorganisasian alternatif, kita dapat mendakwa
seluruh struktur dalam memutus jaring lingkaran pele-
cehan ini. Ketika sistem politik didefinisikan, dikondi-
sikan, terjerat, dan berasal dari kapitalisme, maka tidak
akan pernah dapat mewakili cara kita untuk mengetahui
keberadaan di dunia ini, jadi kita perlu mengendalikan

jalan hidup ini, dan merebut kembali kolektif kita. Kita harus mulai menjadi tidak aktif dalam politik kita, dan mulai merangkul rasa solidaritas yang lebih relasional, sebuah solidaritas yang mengakui bahwa penaklukan, dan penderitaan seseorang sebenarnya menunjukkan penindasan semua[26]. Kita bisa memulai hidup di dunia lain yang mungkin melalui komitmen baru terhadap praktiknya untuk saling membantu, membuat persekutuan, melakukan timbal balik, membentuk organisasi non-hirarkis demi sebuah demokrasi untuk rakyat. Pada akhirnya, neoliberalisme adalah gagasan yang sangat kotor, yang datang dengan serangkaian konsekuensi vulgar, dan asumsi kasar. Sebagai tanggapan, pantas untuk dipenuhi dengan bahasa, dan tindakan yang sama menyinggungnya. Komunitas kita, kerja sama kita, dan kepedulian kita terhadap satu sama lain sangat menjijikkan bagi neoliberalisme. Mereka membenci apa yang kita rayakan. Jadi ketika kita mengatakan '*fuck neoliberalism*' berarti hanya kata-kata saja, biarlah itu menjadi komitmen kita satu sama lain. Ucapkan dengan suara keras, ucapkan bersamaku, dan katakan pada siapa saja yang mau mendengarkannya, tapi yang paling penting, seruan untuk bertindak sebagai wujud nyata dari kekuatan prefiguratif dalam mengubah dunia yang sialan ini. Neoliberalisme Sialan!

Fotti-'Fanculo il neoliberismo

Translated by Fabrizio Eva

Translator's Commentary

I agreed to translate Simon's article, because I appreciate the author, and the topic (and the title) was inviting. In Italian we call neoliberalism "neoliberismo," with a different meaning from "neoliberalismo" (considered more of a sociopolitical approach). The issue is well understood and neoliberalism is treated as "the enemy" within radical left political movements and organizations. The difficulties of translating were related to the fact that I'm not a professional translator. But I know the topic, so I translated some phrases contextually rather than literally. The main problem was translating the title: curse words are the hardest to translate. I found the closest words for "fuck"and decided to combine two Italian words, *fotti/fanculo*, which, in my opinion, together capture the sense, based on what I saw watching movies and reading fiction in English. I didn't try to predict how the audience would interpret the translation.

There is, in fact, no political risk in Italy in dealing with or addressing the topic neoliberalism/neoliberismo. Perhaps a slight "academic" risk, but I'm already known as a libertarian leftist and have already paid the academic cost for it. In Italy, with the exception of very few geographers, the discipline of geography doesn't pay attention to "political" topics like "neoliberism": in the past with a

Marxist approach, now with a post-modern and post-colonial approach. There is always the risk that a translator will "produce" a hybrid text, but this is less likely when the translator knows the topic than it is with a professional translator who might misunderstand the meaning of some phrases. Translations are relevant to counter the hegemony of English within academia and beyond.

Fotti/'Fanculo il neoliberismo

Fotti/'Fanculo il neoliberismo. Questo è il mio messaggio senza peli sulla lingua. Potrei probabilmente terminare la mia discussione a questo punto e non farebbe nessuna differenza. La mia posizione è chiara e probabilmente avete già capito qual è l'essenza di quello che voglio dire. Non ho niente di positivo da aggiungere al dibattito sul neoliberismo e per essere del tutto onesto sono piuttosto stufo di doverci pensare. Ne ho semplicemente abbastanza. Ad un certo punto avevo pensato di chiamare questo articolo "Dimenticare il neoliberismo" perché in qualche modo è esattamente quello che vorrei fare. Ho scritto sul tema per molti anni[1] e sono giunto al punto che non voglio più impegnare energie in questo sforzo per paura che continuare a lavorare su questa idea sia funzionale a perpetuarla. Come ulteriore riflessione io però riconosco che come azione politica è potenzialmente piuttosto pericoloso semplicemente ficcare la testa nella sabbia e ignorare collettivamente un fenomeno che ha avuto così devastanti e debilitanti effetti sul nostro mondo condiviso. E' difficile negare che il neoliberismo sia forte e continuamente sostenuto e non sono convinto che la strategia dell'ignoranza sia effettivamente l'approccio giusto[2]. Così il mio preciso pensiero è stato "e allora fottilo/'fanculo", e mentre un più calmo e gentile nome per questo articolo avrebbe potuto smussare la potenziale offesa del titolo che ho scelto, alla fine ci ho ripensato. Perché dovremmo essere più preoccupati sull'uso della volgarità piuttosto che della concreta ignobile "incensazione" del neoliberismo stesso? Ho deciso che volevo trasgredire, disturbare e offendere esattamente perché noi *dovremmo* essere offesi dal neoliberismo; esso è totalmente traumatizzante e per questo *dovremmo* alla fine cercare di distruggerlo. Ammorbidire il titolo non sarebbe una ulteriore concessione al potere del neoliberismo? Inizialmente mi sono preoccupato di quanto un tale titolo potesse significare per la mia reputazione. Avrebbe potuto incidere su future promozioni o offerte di lavoro e avrei potuto mantenere le mie possibilità di "mobilità" accademica sia come carriera che come trasferimenti? Questo sembra ammettere una sconfitta personale nei confronti del potere "disciplinare" del neoliberismo. Si fotta.

Mi è anche sembrato che potesse essere una ammissione che non sia possibile una risposta informale, nel linguaggio ordinario, che possa essere delineata in modo appropriato per contrastare gli argomenti del neoliberismo. E' come se potessimo rispondere solo in modo accademico e usando complesse teorie geografiche per indebolire il suo edificio concettuale. Questo sembra essere impotenti, e sebbene io stesso abbia contribuito nell'articolazione di queste teorie[3], spesso sento che questo è una sorta di ingabbiamento che lavora contro il tipo di argomenti che concretamente vorrei usare. E' precisamente nel quotidiano, nell'ordinario, nel non significativo e nell'abituale che io penso che la politica del rifiuto deve essere collocata. Così ho deciso per Fotti/'Fanculo il neoliberismo perché penso che illustri la maggior parte di quello che effettivamente voglio dire. Gli argomenti che voglio sostenere sono molto più morbidi di così, cosa che mi ha fatto molto riflettere sull'uso del temine fotti/'fanculo, più di quanto non mi capiterà nel corso della mia vita. Che fantastica e colorata parola ("fuck", *N.d.T.*)! Funziona come sostantivo e come verbo, e come aggettivo è forse il più usato modo di esclamazione della lingua inglese. Può essere usato per esprimere rabbia, disprezzo, fastidio, indifferenza, sorpresa, impazienza o anche un'enfasi generica solo perché scivola facilmente fuori dalla bocca.

A questo punto potreste pensare, okay, ma chi è che fotte? Beh, io lo faccio e se siete interessati a metter fine al neoliberismo dovreste farlo anche voi. Le potenti possibilità che derivano dal termine offrono potenziali sfide al neoliberismo. Per liberare queste abilità abbiamo bisogno di apprezzare le sfumature di quello che potrebbe significare la frase "Fotti/'Fanculo il neoliberismo". Nello stesso modo 'fanculo le sfumature. Come ha sostenuto recentemente Kieran Healy[4] "impediscono solitamente lo sviluppo di teorie intellettualmente interessanti, empiricamente produttive o di successo sul piano pratico". Così, senza fare delle sfumature un feticcio, analizziamo velocemente quello a cui dovremmo dare la priorità nel fottere il neoliberismo.

Il primo significato è forse il più ovvio. Dicendo Fotti/'Fanculo il neoliberismo possiamo esprimere la nostra rabbia contro la macchina neoliberista. E' una indicazione di rabbia, del nostro desiderio di gridare il nostro risentimento, di rimandare al mittente il veleno della nociva malvagità che ci è stata propinata. Questo può prendere la forma dell'organizzare ancor più proteste contro il neoliberismo o nello scrivere ancor più articoli e libri criticando la sua influenza. Nel secondo caso si predica ai convertiti, nel primo si spera che i già contaminati vogliano cambiare il proprio atteggiamento. Non ignoro che questi metodi siano importanti tattiche nella nostra resistenza, ma sono anche piuttosto sicuro che mai possano essere concretamente abbastanza per deviare la marea contro il neoliberismo e a nostro favore. Facendo grandi gesti pubblici di sfida cerchiamo di attirare potenti attori in un confronto, credendo erroneamente che possano ascoltare e comincino a soddisfare la voce popolare del rifiuto[5]. Non dovremmo smettere di discutere? Questo è il secondo significato di "Fotti/'Fanculo il neoliberismo", che è basato sulla nozione di rifiuto. Ciò significa auspicare la fine del neoliberismo (così come lo conosciamo) nel modo suggerito da J.K. Gibson-Graham[6] per cui semplicemente smettiamo di discuterne. Gli studiosi in particolare dovrebbero smettere di dargli la priorità nei loro studi. Forse non completamente, cosa che ho già detto essere problematica, ma piuttosto orientare i nostri scritti verso altri temi. Una volta di più questo è un punto cruciale di contatto per noi che operiamo oltre la visione neoliberista, ma ancora una volta non sono totalmente convinto che sia abbastanza. Come ha sostenuto Marc Purcell[7]: "dobbiamo reindirizzarci dal neoliberismo verso noi stessi per iniziare il difficile, ma anche gioioso, lavoro di gestire le nostre cose per noi stessi". Mentre se negazione, protesta e critica sono necessarie abbiamo anche bisogno di pensare su come fottere attivamente il neoliberismo facendo cose al di fuori della sua portata.

L'azione diretta oltre il neoliberismo mette in evidenza la *politica prefigurativa*[8] che è il terzo e più importante significato di quello che io penso sia ciò cui prestare attenzione quando evochiamo l'idea del "Fotti/'Fanculo il neoliberismo". Prefigurare significa rigettare il centralismo, la gerarchia e l'autorità che deriva dalla politica rappresentativa, enfatizzando la pratiche connesse di attivazione di relazioni orizzontali e forme di organizzazione che cercano di riflettere la società futura che si desidera[9]. Più ancora del "continuare a discutere", la prefigurazione e l'azione diretta sostengono che non c'è mai stato un confronto da fare e riconoscono che, qualunque cosa sia quello che vogliamo fare, possiamo farlo da noi stessi. Ciò nonostante è stata prestata molta attenzione ai modi in cui il neoliberismo è abile nel catturare e appropriarsi di tutti i modi del discorso politico e dei suoi obblighi[10]. Per critici come David Harvey[11] solo una ulteriore dose di stato può risolvere la questione neoliberista e in particolare è molto sbrigativo nel respingere le politiche non gerarchiche e orizzontali definendole come fattori utili ad assicurare un futuro neoliberista. Certo nel suo pessimismo fraintende completamente la politica prefigurativa, che consiste in mezzi non rivolti ad un fine certo, ma rivolti a mezzi futuri[12]. In altre parole c'è una costante e continua autoriflessione insita nella politica prefigurativa così che le pratiche concrete della prefigurazione non possano essere cooptate. E' riflessiva e attenta, ma sempre con lo sguardo teso alla produzione, invenzione e creazione come modi di soddisfare i desideri della comunità. In questo modo la politica prefigurativa è esplicitamente anti neoliberista. E' una politica che fa suoi i mezzi, come "nostri" mezzi; mezzi senza una conclusione predefinita. Prefigurare significa aderire alla convivialità e alla gioia che deriva dall'essere uniti in quanto uguali radicali, non avanguardia e proletariato sulla via verso una trascendentale vuota promessa di utopia o di un "non luogo", ma come la concreta immanenza del *qui e ora* in cui si fa un nuovo mondo "nel quadro del vecchio" e il perpetuo duro lavoro di riconferma che la cosa richiede[13].

Non c'è niente del neoliberismo che merita il nostro rispetto e così, in linea con la politica prefigurativa della creatività, il mio messaggio è piuttosto semplice. "si fotta/'fanculo". Fanculo il potere che ha sulla nostra immaginazione politica. Fanculo la sua violenza intrinseca. Fanculo la disuguaglianza che esalta come virtù. Fanculo al modo i cui devasta l'ambiente. Fanculo il ciclo infinito dell'accumulazione e il culto della crescita. Fanculo alla Mont Pelerin Society [gruppo ristretto di "potenti" come la Trilaterale, Bilderberg, ecc., *N.d.T.*] e a tutti i Think-tank che continuano a sostenere e proporre le sue idee. Fanculo Freidrich Hayek e Milton Friedman che ci intristiscono con le loro idee. Fanculo alle Tatcher, ai Reagan, a tutti i codardi, opportunisti politici che cercano solo di soddisfare i loro interessi e la loro avidità. Fanculo all'esclusivismo dei mercanti di paura che vedono gli "altri" solo come buoni a pulire i nostri gabinetti e a lavare i nostri pavimenti, ma non come membri della nostra comunità. Fanculo la sempre più intensa "misurazione" di tutto e il corrispondete calo di considerazione che non tutto ciò che conta può essere "contato". Fanculo il desiderio del profitto che sovrasta i bisogni della comunità. Fanculo totale a tutto ciò che il neoliberismo rappresenta e fanculo al cavallo di Troia che usa! Per troppo tempo ci è stato raccontato che "non c'è alternativa", che "la marea che sale alza tutte le barche", che viviamo in un incubo darwiniano di tutti contro tutti in cui "sopravvivono i più forti". Ci siamo bevuti completamente la "tragedia delle cose in comune" [del comunismo in senso lato, *N.d.T.*], quando in realtà è un trucco concettuale che riflette la "tragedia del capitalismo" e le sue guerre di saccheggio senza fine[14]. Nell'articolo "The Tragedy of Commons" di Garrett Hardin[15] il tallone d'Achille era che non aveva considerato nel suo esempio a come le mandrie al pascolo comune fossero in effetti già possedute da privati. Cosa potrebbe succedere, invece, se noi convertissimo una cosa comune nella pratica in un reale "comune" senza il presupposto della proprietà privata[16]? Cosa potrebbe succedere se cominciassimo a prestare maggiore attenzione alla prefigurazione di alternative che già stanno avvenendo e privilegiassimo quelle esperienze come le principali forme di organizzazione[17]? Cosa potrebbe succedere se invece di ingoiare la pillola amara della competizione/competitività e del merito noi invece focalizzassimo le nostre energie non a medicare le nostre ferite con prescrizioni neoliberiste, ma a curarci più nel profondo con la cooperazione e il mutuo aiuto[18]?

Jamie Peck[19] ha definito il neoliberismo come uno "slogan politicamente radicale", ma non è più tempo di indugiare nel campo della critica. Sono passati molti anni da quando abbiamo identificato il nemico e da allora lo abbiamo ben analizzato tramite scritti e proteste. Ma anche se siamo certi della sua sconfitta, come dopo la crisi finanziaria del 2008 e il susseguente Movimento di Occupy, il neoliberismo continua a succhiare l'aria e si rianima in una forma ancora più potente di morto vivente[20]. Japhy Wilson[21] chiama questo continuo potere il "gotico neoliberista" e sono convinto che per poter battere questo spettacolo dell'orrore dobbiamo spostare la nostra politica nel campo dell'azione[22]. E se "fotti/fanculo il neoliberismo" diventasse il mantra per un nuovo tipo di politica? Una frase capace di parlare non solo all'azione, ma anche alla rivendicazione delle nostre vite negli spazi e nei momenti/tempi nei quali attivamente li viviamo? E se ogni volta che usiamo questa frase noi riconoscessimo che è un richiamo ad un'azione efficace che vada oltre le parole, combinando teoria e pratica lungo la bella strada della "prefigurazione"? Dobbiamo avere un approccio molto ramificato nel nostro rifiuto del neoliberismo. Mentre non possiamo ignorarlo completamente o dimenticarlo noi possiamo lavorargli contro in modi che vanno oltre l'esibizione della retorica e della retorica dell'esibizione. Portiamo avanti un nuovo, radicale slogan politico. Usiamo l'hashtag #fuckneoliberalism [#fanculo-neoliberismo] e rendiamo virale il nostro disprezzo! Ma dobbiamo fare di più che esprimere la nostra indignazione. Dobbiamo trasformare in pratica la nostra determinazione e realizzare le nostre speranze nel *qui e ora* delle nostre esperienze di vita[23]. Dobbiamo rifare il mondo da noi stessi, un processo che non può essere rimandato.

Ci siamo volontariamente disillusi e indeboliti continuando a riferirci al'esistente sistema di rappresentatività. La nostra cieca fiducia ci ha fatto attendere continuamente che apparisse un "vecchio saggio". Il sistema ha dimostrato di essere intrinsecamente corrotto; in cui di volta in volta il nostro nuovo, grande candidato politico mostra di essere un fallimento. In questo contesto neoliberista non è una semplice questione di individui problematici che sono al potere. Al contrario è la nostra cieca fiducia nel sistema stesso che incarna il cuore del problema. Noi produciamo e rendiamo effettive le condizioni istituzionali perché l' "effetto Lucifero" si manifesti[24]. "La banalità del male" è che i politici stanno solo facendo il loro mestiere in un sistema che ripaga la perversione del potere in quanto tutto è configurato per servire le leggi del capitalismo[25]. Ma non dobbiamo obbedire. Non dobbiamo fare il suo gioco. Tramite l'azione diretta e l'organizzazione di alternative possiamo mettere sotto accusa l'intera struttura e rompere il circolo vizioso dell'abuso. Quando il sistema politico è definito da, condizionato per, invischiato con, e derivato dal capitalismo, non può mai rappresentare in nostro modo di conoscere e essere nel mondo e così dobbiamo farci carico di questi modi di vita e rivendicare la nostra azione collettiva. Dobbiamo cominciare a diventare più concreti nella nostra politica e cominciare ad praticare un maggior senso relazionale di solidarietà che riconosca che sottomissione e sofferenza di uno è segno dell'oppressione dei molti[26]. Possiamo cominciare a vivere in un altro possibile mondo grazie ad un rinnovato impegno nelle pratiche di mutuo aiuto, amicizia, reciprocità e forme di organizzazione non gerarchica che riconducano la demo-crazia al suo senso etimologico di *potere* del *popolo*. In definitiva il neoliberismo è una particolare ributtante idea che si accompagna ad una massa di volgari risultati e di rozzi assunti. Come risposta merita di essere trattato simmetricamente con linguaggio e azione offensivi. La nostra comunità, la nostra cooperazione e il nostro curarsi l'un l'altro sono tutti odiosi per il neoliberismo. Odia quello che festeggiamo. Così quando diciamo "fotti/fanculo il neoliberismo" vogliamo significare più che una semplice frase, è una messa in pratica del nostro impegno verso gli altri. Ditelo forte, ditelo con me e ditelo a chiunque voglia ascoltare, ma soprattutto mostratelo come un richiamo all'azione e al compimento del nostro potere prefigurativo di cambiare il fottuto mondo. *Fotti/Fanculo il Neoliberismo!*

CHAPTER 12

日本人 – **Japanese**

くたばれ、ネオリベラリズム

Translated by 渡邊小百合 – Sayuri Watanabe

Translator's Commentary

When I first received a request to translate an academic paper from English to Japanese, I was slightly hesitant. But after reading it I realized its importance, and that it ought to be read more widely, and so my reluctance vanished. I accepted the request more willingly and more enthusiastically than a usual translation job, because I adamantly support the message communicated in this paper: put an end to neoliberalism. I viewed my translation of this paper as a great opportunity to spread Simon Springer's words among the Japanese-speaking community, thereby making a modest contribution to humanity's endeavor to achieve a better world.

I spent quite a bit of time familiarizing myself with some of the technical words and ideas in the paper, however, the word I had the most difficulty putting into Japanese was the key word—*fuck*. Although I was quite surprised when I first read the title, I very much admire the decision to both use the word and the justification for doing so. So then I asked myself; "What would it be in Japanese?" As far as I know, there is no Japanese counterpart with the same degree of vulgar gusto, multifaceted use, and emotional versatility as the word *fuck*. It is a colorful word, indeed! I had to think carefully about how to put it in Japanese so that the author's intent in using this word would be conveyed in the translation. When I saw the cover art for the book, which seems to represent the author's sentiment toward neoliberalism, I was convinced that my choice of Japanese word was accurate.

There are so many things I would love to see changed in this world. I consider myself to be reserved, and I'm quite careful about what I say and how I act, but I don't hesitate in joining Simon Springer and other like-minded people in saying, loudly: fuck neoliberalism!

くたばれ、ネオリベラリズム

くたばれ、ネオリベラリズム(Fuck Neoliberalism)。これが、本稿が伝える飾りのない率直な主旨である。この主旨をもって、本議論を終了することもできるだろうし、そうしたとしてもたいした変わりはない。私の所論は明確であり、私がここで何を述べようとしているのか、その要旨はすでに伝わっているであろう。ネオリベラリズムに関し、その議論で私が付け加えるべきプラスの局面は何一つないし、それを論議せざるを得ないこと自体に全くもってうんざりしているというのが私の本音だ。もうたくさんだ、その一言につきる。ネオリベラリズムを本当に忘れてしまいたいという思いもあり、本稿題名を「Forget Neoliberalism(忘れてしまおう、ネオリベラリズム)」にすることも一時は考えた。長年にわたり、私はネオリベラリズムをテーマとした論文を執筆してきた[1] が、ネオリベラリズムをテーマとした執筆活動を続けることは、結局のところその存続性を強めてしまっているのではないかという不安から、これを主題とした論議にこれ以上の労力を注ぎたくないとさえ思うようになった。しかし同時に、すでに私たちが共有する世界にこれ程の破壊的、弱体化効果をもたらしてきた現象の存在から目をそむけ、集合的に無視するという政治的戦略には大きな危険が潜んでいることもまた私は認識している。ネオリベラリズムには絶え間ない力が注がれていて、それを否定することは困難であるし、またその存在を無視するといった戦略が取るべき適切なアプローチだという確信は全く持てない[2]。そこで私の脳裏に浮かんできた言葉が、「それなら、そんなもの

くたばってしまえ(well fuck it then)」そのものであり、本稿の題名としてより落ち着いた、穏やかなものを採用すれば、私が選択したこの題名で人々を不愉快な気持ちにさせてしまうことは避けられるだろうとも思ったが、結局その後考えを変えた。そもそも私達がより心配すべきは不敬な言葉を使うことではなくネオリベラリズムの下劣な言説(ディスコース)そのものではないだろうか。私達を狼狽させるネオリベラリズムに私達は怒ってしかるべきであり、最終的にその境界線を越えることを目指さなければならない。だから私は、境界線を越え、狼狽させ、そして怒りを買うことこそが私が本当にしたいことなのだという結論に至った。題名の響きを柔らかくすること自体、ネオリベラリズムの力にさらに譲歩したことになるのではなかろうか。私は当初、この題名によって私自身の名声に何らかの影響が出るのではないかと心配した。研究者として引き続きさらなる上を目指すなり、新天地への移動を考えたりした時、将来の昇進や採用の邪魔にならないだろうか。この時私は、ネオリベラリズムが支配する世界に対して敗北を認めたように感じた。冗談じゃない('Fuck that')。

　また私は、ネオリベラリズムの言説に対抗するに十分な口語的応答手段がないことを認めてしまっているようにも感じた。まるでその体系の弱体化を図るには、その雑色や雑種性、突然変異における複雑な地理的理論を用いた学術形式をもって応答するしかないかのようだ。それでは人々は理解できず彼らの無力化を招くように思え、私自身がこうした理論のいくつかを明確化することに寄与してきたわけだが[3]、このような理論的枠組みは私が本当に論じたい事柄とは相反する働きをしていると感じることが多々ある。毎日の、通常の、目立たない、平凡な生活においてこそ政治的手段としての拒絶の行使が活かされるのだと私は思う。こうして私は、「Fuck Neoliberalism(くたばれ、ネオリベラリズム)」に落ち着いたわけであるが、それはなぜなら、私が本当に言いたい事のほとんどをその題名は伝えているからである。もちろん私の論点は題名より多少多くの意味合いを含んではいるが、この題名を考える上で、私はおそらく今までの人生の中で一番「fuck」

という単語についてより深く考えることとなった。なんとすばらしく多彩な単語なのだろう！名詞だけでなく動詞としても使われ、おそらく形容詞として英語で最も使われる感嘆を表す言葉だろう。怒りや軽蔑、苛立ち、無関心、驚き、焦りを表現するのに使われ、また口をついて出てくる意味のない強調語句としても使われる。例えば次のように様々な意味で使われる。「fuck something up（何かをダメにする）」、「fuck someone over（誰かをだます）」、「fuck around（ふざける、どうでもいいことをして時間を無駄にするなど）」、「not give a fuck（関係ない、どうでもいい）」。「go fuck yourself（ふざけるな、勝手にしろ）」のように相手に対して行け（"go"）と指示できるという点で、この単語がここでは明らかに地理的基準点の意味合いを持っていることが分かる。

　　この時点で、「そんなこと、どうだっていいだろう（'who gives a fuck?'）。」という読者もいるかもしれない。少なくとも、私にとってはどうでもよいことではない。もしあなたがネオリベラリズムの終焉に興味があるのなら、是非考えてほしい。この単語が持つ大きな力は、ネオリベラリズムへの対抗手段にもなり得るのだ。この力の可能性を掘り下げて解き放つためには、私達はやはり「fuck neoliberalism（くたばれ、ネオリベラリズム）」の言葉に隠されたニュアンス（意味合い）を理解する必要があるだろう。しかしそうは言いつつも、やはりニュアンスなんてものもクソくらえだ（"fuck nuance"）。Kieran Healy[4] が最近論じたように、ニュアンスというのは「大概、知的観点からは興味深く、経験的に生成する、または実用に優れた理論の発展を妨害する。」ものである。そこで、ニュアンスへの執着をやめ、ネオリベラリズムをぶっ潰す（"fucking up neoliberalism"）ために私達が優先すべき事をさっそく考えてみよう。

　　第一の意味合いは最も明らかであろう。「くたばれ、ネオリベラリズム(fuck neoliberalism)」と叫ぶことで、私達はネオリベラリズムという機械に対する憤怒を表すことができる。それは、私達の怒り、そして憤慨の感情を叫びたい、私達に向かってネオリベラリズムが見せつけてきた有害な悪意に向

かって今度は逆に毒を吐き飛ばしてやりたいと切望する私達の思いの現れである。この思いを伝えるためには、さらに多くのネオリベラリズムに対する抗議集会を発動するか、またはその影響についてもっと論文や書籍を書いて批判するという方法がある。2番目の方法は、ネオリベラリズム反対の立場にすでに転換している人々に向けた説論であり、最初の方法では、邪道に陥った人々が自ら選んで方向転換することに望みをかけて実行される。これらが抵抗運動において大切な方法であることを否定するわけではないが、ネオリベラリズム優勢の現状をひっくり返し、私達に有利な状況を作り出すためにはそれら方法は十分ではないと実際のところ言わざるを得ない。反対姿勢を大々的に公に示そうとして、私達は有力者と話し合いの場を持つことを試みるが、その際、彼らが大多数の人民による反対意見に耳を傾け、便宜をはかってくれるのだという誤った思い込みをしてしまうのである[5]。それより、話し合いをすること自体、もうやめるべきではないだろうか。これこそが「くたばれ、ネオリベラリズム(fuck neoliberalism)」に込められている第二の意味合いであり、これは拒絶の概念として見られるものである。これは、その一切の言及をやめるという、J.K.Gibson-Graham[6]が唱導した方法により、私達が知るところの)ネオリベラリズムの終焉を唱えることである。特に学者の場合で言うと、研究テーマとしてネオリベラリズムを重点的に論じることに終止符を打つことである。それは、ネオリベラリズムを完全に消し去ったり無視したりという、すでに私自身がそうすることの問題性を認識しているやり方ではなく、別のテーマに焦点をあてた執筆に取りかかることであろう。これもまた、ネオリベラリズムの世界観を超えて活動しようとする時、私達にとって非常に重要な接点である。しかし、私はこれで十分だとこの時点においても心から確信を持つことができない。Mark Purcell[7]が述べているように、「私達は、ネオリベラリズムから離れ、私達自身に目を向けて、困難ではあるが喜ばしくもある、自分たちの事は自分たちで管理するための取組みを始める必要がある。」否定や抗議、批判は必要であるものの、ネオリベラリズムを積極的にぶち壊そうとする時、

その影響力が及ばない所で活動することでその目的を達成
することも考える必要がある。

　　ネオリベラリズムの領域を超えた直接行動は、予示的
政治[8]とは何かを物語っており、「くたばれ、ネオリベラリズム
(fuck neoliberalism)」に込められた思いをかきたてようとす
る時、私達がまず着目すべき第三の意味合いであり、また最
も重要な意味合いである。予示することは、目指す将来の社
会像を反映しようとする水平関係構造や組織形態を具現化
することを強調し、それにより代表政治に見られる中央集権
的傾向、階層制度および権力を拒絶することである[9]。「話し
合いはもうしない」の領域を超え、予示的行動、直接行動は、
私達が何を欲しようと、その全ては私達自身で実現可能で
あることを認識しつつ、始めから話し合うことなど何もなかっ
たことを主張するのである。それにも関わらず、あらゆる政治
的言説や要請を掌握、専有するネオリベラリズムのやり方に
あまりにも大きな関心が向けられてきた[10]。David Harvey[11]
のような批評家によると、あとほんの少しの国家権力(影響)
があればネオリベラリズムが抱える問題は解決し得るのであ
り、その考えから、Harveyは非階層的組織や水平政治は、す
でに約束されているネオリベラリズム未来を助ける潤滑油に
過ぎないとしてそれらを即、否定する。しかしそうした悲観的
見方の中で、彼は予示的政治というものが目的を達成するた
めの手段ではなく、未来の手段であるという点を完全に誤解
してしまっている[12]。つまり、予示的政治には、常時的、継続的
な監視態勢が組み込まれているため、予示的行動の実践を
権力の中に組み込むことはできないのである。それが反射的
であれ慎重であれ、常にその視点は、コミュニティーの意思を
実現するものとしての生産、発明そして創造に向けられている。
このように、予示的政治は明らかに反ネオリベラリズムの立
場を取る。それは私達の手段、それ自体が目的である手段と
して、手段全てを結束させる。予示的行動の実施は、人々が、
実現し得ない空約束であるユートピア(ラテン語で「存在し
ない場所」'no place')への到達を目指す政治運動の先駆者
や無産階級としてではなく、「古い殻の中で ('in the shell of

the old")」新しい世界を今、ここで創り出し、永続的勤労と新世界が何を必要としているかの再確認を行うことをその内在性として基盤に置き、急進的平等関係にある者として、共存することで生まれる悦楽と歓喜の情を抱くことである[13]。

　ネオリベラリズムには、私達が尊敬するに価する側面は何一つないのであり、予示的政治の創造的観点に同調する私のメッセージは、端的に、「(ネオリベラリズムよ、)くたばれ('fuck it')。」なのである。私達の政治的想像を阻むその束縛なんか、くたばれ。それによって生み出だされる暴力も、くたばれ。まるで美徳であるかのごとくそれが称揚する不平等もくたばってしまえ。自然に対して猛威をふるってきたその破壊行為よ、くたばれ。終わりなき利殖サイクルと成長信奉よ、くたばれ。それを支持、推進し続けるモンペルラン・ソサイエティーも全てのシンクタンク(頭脳集団)も、くたばれ。自分たちの考えを私達に押し付けたフリードリヒ・ハイエクもミルトン・フリードマンも、くたばれ。サッチャー主義者、レーガン主義者そして欲に目がくらんでいる卑怯で自己愛の強い政治家も、くたばれ。私達のトイレ清掃か床拭きをする者としての価値はあるが、私達のコミュニティーの一員としての価値はないと「他者」を見る、恐怖を利用した排斥もくたばってしまえ。勢いを増すばかりの数値指標への傾倒、そして大切な物全てが計量できるわけではないことの見過ごしも、くたばれ。コミュニティーの要求を犠牲にした利益の追求も、くたばれ。ネオリベラリズムに象徴される全てのもの、そして自ら忍び乗り込んだトロイの木馬もくたばってしまえ！私達は、ずいぶんと長い間、「代替案などない」、「上げ潮は船をみな持ち上げる」のだと、そしてみなが権勢し合う「適者生存('survival of the fittest')」というダーウィン説の悪夢のような社会に生きているのだと言い聞かされてきた。私達は「コモンズの悲劇」論をすっかり鵜呑みにしてしまったのであるが、実はこれは、「資本主義の悲劇」とその終わりなき略奪戦争を反映する策略だったのである[14]。Garrett Hardin[15]の唯一の弱点は、彼が、放牧されている牛がどのようにしてすでに所有物であったかを全く考えなかったことである。　私的所有という前提条件がない共有

地(コモンズ)としての事実上のコモンズを私達が呼び戻したらどうなるだろうか[16]。私達が、すでに始まっている代替案の予示的行動をより注意深く見守り、こうした経験を最も重要な組織の形態であるとして優先したとしたら、どうなるだろうか[17]。競争と手柄という苦渋をなめるのではなく、ネオリベラリズムが出す処方箋を己に投与するかわりに、協力と相互扶助からくるより深く作用する療養にエネルギーを注いだら、どうなるだろうか[18]。

　　Jamie Peck[19]はかつて、ネオリベラリズムを「急進的政治的スローガン('radical political slogan')」と呼んだが、批評という枠組みの中に留まっているだけではもはや不十分なのだ。敵を特定してからすでに何年も過ぎ去ったが、それ以来、私達はネオリベラリズムについて執筆や抗議集会を通してそれについてよく知ることとなった。しかし、2008年の金融危機の爪痕や直後のウォール街占拠運動(Occupy Movement)に示されるように、私達はその敗北を確信しながらも、ネオリベラリズムはわずかな酸素を求め喘ぎ、より強力になったゾンビのように自らを蘇生し続けているのである[20]。Japhy Wilson[21]はこのネオリベラリズムの前進力を、「ネオリベラル・ゴシック('neoliberal gothic')」と呼ぶが、このホラーショーに打ち勝つためには、私達の政治を自律の枠組みに移行させる必要があると私は考える[22]。「くたばれ、ネオリベラル(fuck neoliberalism)」が新しい形の政治を求めるマントラになったらどうだろうか。この句が言及しているのは、行動することのみならず、私達が積極的に己の生を全うすることができる空間(spaces)と瞬間(moments)に生きることへの主張であり、この句はその肯定を叫ぶのである。この句を使う度に、それが単なる言葉としての領域を超えて、理論と実践を合わせて予示的行動を美しく体現化させる自律型活動体の要求であると認識したらどうだろうか。ネオリベラリズムを拒絶しようとする時、私達は多面的アプローチを取らなければならない。ネオリベラリズムを完全に無視、忘れることはできない一方で、私達は、修辞に求める成果や、成果を約束する修辞を超越した方法で反対活動を行うことができる。いずれにしても、こ

こで新しい急進的政治スローガンを掲げよう。ハッシュタグ(#fuckneoliberalism)を使って私達のネオリベラリズム蔑視の気持ちをネットで広めよう！だが、私達の憤りを表すためにはもっと何かしなくてはならない。私達の決意を行動に移し、私達の願望を今('now')、ここ('here')で内在的に具現化し、それを体験することによって実現しなければならない[23]。私達は、自らこの世界を創造し直す必要があるのであり、その過程は将来に先延ばしすることはできないのである。

　　私達は、既存の代表政治体制に訴え続けることで自らを故意に欺き、弱体化させてきた。そこに盲目的に信頼を置いてきた私達は、空から救済の手が下りてくるのを永遠に待つこととなったのである。その制度は隅から隅まで退廃しきっていることを自ら露呈し、事ある度に、私達が選んだ偉大なる次期候補者も結局は無能であったという結果に終わる。このネオリベラリズム時代、問題ある個人が権力の座についているだけなどという程度の話では終わらない。本当に問題なのは、私達がその体制そのものを信じているという点である。それにより、私達自身が「ルシファー効果('the Lucifer Effect')」を顕在化させる組織的条件を生み出してしまうのだ[24]。「悪の陳腐さ ('The banality of evil')」には、ルールを無視した力の逸脱を称賛する体制下で政治家はただその職務を遂行しているに過ぎないが、それはなぜならそうした体制はそもそも資本主義の法則に則るよう作られているという事実がある[25]。しかし私達がそれに追従する必要はない。この法則から私達が受ける恩義もない。私達の直接行動と代替案の結集によって、私達はその全構造を告発し、その乱用の悪循環を打ち破ることができる。政治体制が資本主義により定義され、その目的のために条件付けられ、その中に編み込まれ、そしてそこから派生する時、その体制は、世界における私達の知識獲得と生の手段を反映する存在とは決してなり得ないのであり、そうであるなら、私達はこうした生き方の行方を自らの手中に収め、私達の集団的活動体を取り戻す必要がある。政治において私達は自律しなければならないし、一個人の征服、苦しみは全民に対する抑圧であると認識する、より相関的な団

結感を受け入れなければならない[26]。私達は、相互扶助、仲間意識、相互依存や、民衆 に力を('power to the people')が本来意味するところの民主主義を再編成する非階層的な組織形態に新たに身を投じ、別様の実現可能な世界に生きることが可能となる。結局のところ、ネオリベラリズムは、特に腐敗した理論であり、多くの俗悪な結果や野暮な仮定を生み出す。それに応えて、ネオリベラリズムは、同じくらい侮辱的な言葉と行動をもって扱われるに値する。私達の共同体、協力、そして互いへの思いやりの気持ちは全てネオリベラリズムが厭うものである。私達が歓喜に沸くことを嫌うのである。私達が「くたばれ、ネオリベラリズム('fuck neoliberalism')」と言うとき、それがただの言葉に終わらないことを、そしてそれが私達互いへの約束の成立であることを示そう。大きな声でそう叫ぼう、私と共に叫ぼう。そして耳を傾ける人全てに向かって叫ぼう。そして何より、この言葉を叫ぶとき、それは行動しようとの明快な呼びかけであり、このふざけた世界を変えるための私達の予示的行動力の体現であることを示そうではないか。くたばれ、ネオリベラリズム！

CHAPTER 13

ភាសាខ្មែរ – **Khmer**

សរសើរនិយមមធ្យមវិចេងុរវៃយៈ

Translated by កញ្ញាញ៉ា សុខ – Kanha Sok

Translator's Commentary

I worked with Simon as his Khmer translator for his research project on homelessness in Cambodia back in 2015. What caught my attention to and interest in this essay were its abstract and key words, they were so simple and straight to the core. Having read the article, I felt his intense feelings about neoliberalism, his disgust, and his fearlessness in expressing it to the world, regardless of the consequences.

Frankly speaking, neoliberalism is a foreign word in my country. I have seen the word in English articles online, but it is not commonly talked about or discussed in the Cambodian context. During the translation process, I had moments of doubt as to whether Cambodian people would understand this article in Khmer, as the concept was new: *neoliberalism* is not in the Khmer dictionary. Another thing is the vocabulary. Simon's article is unlike many academic essays, which carefully select the language to express the author's viewpoint on the subject without being directly offensive. Yet with this article, although the viewpoint is clear and straightforward, it is tricky to translate these words into Khmer, as Khmer and English have little in common. I needed to be very careful in balancing the choices of Khmer words to retain the meaning required by the original context. For instance, one of my solutions when I couldn't figure out a better way to translate a phrase and to prevent the idea from being misunderstood was to add the the original phrase in parentheses after the translation, so that the readers could refer to it.

Lastly, I enjoyed translating this article, because I really appreciated the guts the author showed. Though he knew that this article might jeopardize his career path, he still spoke up.

សរសើនិទិយមថ្មមីចងុរវៃយ៎

សរសើនិទិយមថ្មមីចងុរវៃយ៎ ។ នរៈគឺជា
សារវរបសខញញុំ។ ខញញុំអាចនឹងបញចបបស
ការពិភាកុសារបសខញញុំកុរវមនរៈ វាកក
មវិនមៃនជបញញុហាអុរវៃដនៃ។ ជបរវបសខញញុំ
ចបបសលាសនិឯខញញុំកដជេ្ដ្ដជាកចថាអុនក
នឹឯលព៌អុរវៃដនៃលខញញុំចង៎និយាយនៃ។

ខញញុំគុមាានអុរវៃដនៃលរិជដមានចង៎បនុថថនៃ
លសៃសរសើនិទិយមថ្មមីកុនុឯការពិភាកុសានរៈ
ទរៈ និយាយដោយសុមោៈចចៈ ខញញុំខពតើម
សុមុបើតនៃគិតពវិ។ វាពិតជាលើសហាឱើយ។

ខញញុំធ្ុលាបកគិតចង៎ដជាកចចំណងនៃឯចុយ
អកុថទនរៈថាជ "បំកុលរចសរសើនិទិយមថមី"
ប៎ុនុតនៃខញញុំនៃរ៎តនៃគិតថា "សរសើនិទិយមថមី
ចងុរវៃយ៎" គុរុវ៎នឹឯអុរវៃដនៃលខញញុំចង៎និយាយ
ជាឯ។ ខញញុំបានសសរអកុថទដនៃលសុគពវ
បុរធលាបទទនរៈជាចុរវើនន្ុនទាំមកហាឱើយ[1] ខញញុំ
បានសសរដលចចំណាចមួយដនៃលបុរសុវិនបរើ
ខញញុំថនៃរ៎តនៃបនុតបញញូចនពញកមុលវាឯញតើស
ឈាមទនៃលើរាតទនៃទៀត ខញញុំខុលាច
ខញញុំបនុតតមុលៃរបសវាជាឯមុន ។ ខញញុំកក
គិតយើពញបនុតនៃមទនៀតថាសរសើនិទិយមថមីគឺជា

គមនូរោាងនយោលោាយមុយដវែលអាចបងុកទុយមខាន
បញនុហាោបូរសុវិនបលើយេលើងមិនបខានពិចារណាោ
បខានគុវើមគុរូវ ធ្វើរោេសបុរេំសនូរុវទទុុទិពល
ដវែលរោាពោាំនោាំដលលសំសងុកមរុុមរសេពុកយលើង។

អំំណាោចនិងតទុុទិពលរបសេសរោេនិនុិយមចំមីើ
កខានេតវែខុុលោាំងឡ្យលើងវែលខុំញេនំយលេចារោា
មនិមខែនផោាយុទទុុផសវាសុរុុគតុុវើមគុរូវកៃុុនុុងកោ
រសវិរវីរវរលេនេនុងគមុុរោាងនយោលោាយមុុយនោេ
ទៃ[2] ខុំញុុំកេបខានពិចារណាោឡ្យលើងវិញ្អំពីកោរ
ជាកេចំណាោងដលើងអេគុុបបទទុុយយសុុរសំើរដ្ាងនោេ
ដែរ បៃុុនុុតៃ "ចងុុរឱ"។ ហាេគុុអុុវើបខានជាពុុក
យលើងបោារមុុកជាខុុលោាំងអំំពីកោរបុុរោើពោាកុុយ
បុុមេមោាចជាជាងមតៃិអរវិជុុជមខានដវែលសរោេនិនំិយម
ចំមីើនោេពោាំនោាំដលលសំសងំគមនោេ? ហាេគុុ
ដំូចនោេហាលើយយបខានជាខុំញុុំចងេបំពខាន ចងេថាោ
សុុគីើ ចងេសុុគៃិបនុុទោាសចំខដោាយសោារពុុក
យលើងគបុុបើខេិងសមុុបោារជាមុុយនៃិងសរោេនិនិយម
ចំមីើនោេមខែន។ រោា(សរោេនិនិយមចំមីើ)ពិគជាោ
មនិលុុអ ដំូចនោេពុុកយលើងគបុុបើបំពខានរោា។

គលើចំណាោងដលើងដវែលសមសុុនជាងនោេអាោចនិង
កវែបុុរំើកោរយលេយលើញ្រសេមនុុសុុសចំពោេ
សរោេនិនិយមចំមីើ ទៃ? ដំបុុង ខុំញុុំធុុលោាបេ
បោារមុុកថាោកេនុុគៃិៃិឈុុមេលោេរបសេខុំញុុំអាោច
និៃិគុុរូវបខានបេពោាលេដោាយសោារចំំណាោងដលើង
មុុយនោេទៃ។ គលើរោាបងុុអាោកេកោរឡ្យលើងគំណំវែង
ឬ៉ឆិកោាសកោារងោារខុំញុុំកៃុុនុុងសុុចោាបេនេិង
កុុរោៅសុុចោាបំនវែលុុ្ទៃ? អារុុមុុមណៃិទោាំងនោេ
ហាោកេបៃើៃុុរូវិចុុយខុំញុុំចៃោាញ្នេិងសរោេនិនិយម
ចំមីើទៃោៅហាលើយ។ ចងេឱ។ ទៃុុទៃិមគុុនខានោេ
ដែរ

ខុំញុុុំមខានអារុុមុុមណៃិចាោខុំញុុុំកំពុុង

បង្កើតការស្រកាសមួយដែលពិបាកសម្រាប់ការពិភាក្សាបន្ទាប់ក្នុងសេរីនិយមថ្មី។ មានអត្ថបទសិក្សាជាច្រើនប្រើប្រាស់ទ្រឹស្តីភូមិវិទ្យាដ៏ស្មុគស្មាញដូចជា Variegation, hybridity, and mutation ក្រោមគោលបំណងធ្វើឲ្យឥទ្ធិពលសេរីនិយមថ្មីកាន់តែចុះខ្សោយ។ យ៉ាងណាមិញ វាមិនមានប្រសិទ្ធិភាពដូចតែការគិតនោះទេ។

ការខិតខំប្រឹងប្រែងរបស់ខ្ញុំកន្លងមកទៅលើអត្ថបទសិក្សាដែលផ្អែកលើទ្រឹស្តីទាំងនេះ[3] មិនបានបញ្ជាក់យ៉ាងក្បោះក្បាយលើអ្វីដែលខ្ញុំចង់និយាយនោះទេ។ ខ្ញុំប្រែជាយល់ឃើញថាអ្វីដែលកើតឡើងជារៀងរាល់ថ្ងៃ ជាធម្មតា សមញ្ញ និងដដែលៗគឺអ្វីដែលយើងគប្បីលើកឡើងមកពិភាក្សា។ ហេតុនេះហើយបានជាខ្ញុំសសេរ "សេរីនិយមថ្មីចង្រៃយ៊"នេះឡើងដោយសារវាបង្ហាញពីអត្ថន័យដែលខ្ញុំពិតជាចង់និយាយ។ ការពិភាក្សាដែលខ្ញុំចង់បង្ហាញមានភាពខុសប្លែកគ្នាជាងនេះបន្តិច ដែលធ្វើឲ្យខ្ញុំគិតពីពាក្យ "ចង្រៃយ៊" (fuck) ជាច្រើនលើកច្រើនសារជាងពេលណាៗទាំងអស់ក្នុងជីវិតខ្ញុំ។ ពាក្យនេះពិតជាមានអត្ថន័យសន្ធឹកសន្ធាប់ និងសម្បូរបែបមួយ! វាអាចប្រើជានាមឬជាកិរិយាសព្ទ វាក៏អាចប្រើជាគុណនាមដែលត្រូវបានគេប្រើប្រាស់ជាច្រើនបំផុតក្នុងអក្សរសាស្ត្រអង់គ្លេស។ វាត្រូវបានប្រើប្រាស់នៅពេលដែលមនុស្សបង្ហាញភាពខឹងក្រោធ មិនពេញចិត្ត ភាពអាក់អន់ស្រពន់ចិត្ត រំភើប ភាពធុញទ្រាន់ ភាពអន្ទះ:

សារ ឬគ្រាន់តែនិយាយចោលក៏បាន។ អ្នកអាច “ធ្វើអ្វីមួយខុស” (fuck something up) “ប្រព្រឹត្តអំពើអយុត្តិធម៌ទៅលើនណាម្នាក់” (fuck someone over) “ភាពខ្ជិលច្រអូស” (fuck around) “មិនខ្វាយខ្វល់ពីអ្វីទាំងអស់” (not give a fuck) ពាក្យនេះក៏ត្រូវបានប្រើប្រាស់ខុសគ្នាទៅតាមតំបន់ផងដែរដូចជា “ទៅចុះនរកទៅ” (go fuck yourself)។ នៅពេលនេះអ្នកប្រហែលជាគិតថា “បាន ប៉ុន្តែតើមានអ្នកណាខ្វល់ពីរឿងនេះ? (who gives a fuck)”។ ខ្ញុំខ្វល់ប្រសិនបើអ្នកទាំងអស់គ្នាចាប់អារម្មណ៍ក្នុងការបំបាត់សេរីនិយមថ្មីដែរនោះអ្នកទាំងអស់គ្នាគប្បីធ្វើដូចនេះ។ ឥទ្ធិពលដែលពាក្យនេះមានអាចជាអ្វីដែលប្រឆាំងនឹងសេរីនិយមថ្មី។ ដើម្បីយល់ឲ្យកាន់តែច្បាស់ពីសមត្ថភាពទាំងនេះ ពួកយើងត្រូវតែឲ្យតម្លៃទៅលើភាពខុសប្លែកគ្នាដែលឃ្លា “សេរីនិយមថ្មីចង្រៃយ៍” (fuck neoliberalism) ពាំនាំ។ ទន្ទឹមគ្នានេះដែរ ភាពខុសប្លែកចង្រៃយ៍។ ដូចដែល Kieran Healy[4] បានលើកឡើងក្នុងពេលថ្មីៗនេះ វា “រមែងរារាំងដល់ការអភិវឌ្ឍនៃទ្រឹស្តីដែលទាក់ទាញ មានភស្តុតាងសិក្សាត្រឹមត្រូវ និងរមែងទទួលបានជោគជ័យ”។ ហេតុនេះដោយយល់ពី”ភាពខុសប្លែកគ្នា” (nuance)នេះឲ្យកាន់តែច្បាស់ទើបពួកយើងអាចចាប់ផ្តើមធ្វើអ្វីដែលខ្ញុំយល់ថាសំខាន់ក្នុងការបំបាត់ (fucking up) សេរីនិយមថ្មីនេះ។

ជាដំបូងនិងជាក់ស្តែងបំផុតនោះ ដោយនិយាយថា “សេរីនិយមថ្មីចង្រៃយ៍” (fuck neoliberalism) ពួកយើងអាចបញ្ចេញអារម្មណ៍

ខឹងគូររវាធចំពោះយនានៗគបុុរលើបុុររាស់់រសស់
សេរើនិយមចមួយ១ ។ នេះគឺជាការរៀបបងុុហាញពី
ភាពខឹងសមួបការ ចំណាងំកុុនុុងកការបញ្ចុចុញ
ភាពមិនពេញចិត្តុុ ខុុជាកំ់ពិសទទៅលើមុុខ
សតុុរចងុុរំ់ដំ់អាកុុរកំ់ដែលបបានបងុុហាញ
ចំ់ពោះមុុខពួកយលើង១។ ការបងុុហាញទៅំងនេះ
មានរនៅកុុនុុងទទមុុងំ់ដុុផជា កការបងុុកលើតចលនា
បុុអធទៅំងនិងសេរើនិយមចមួយលើ្យុកការសសេរ
អគុុចបទសិកុុសាវិងសៀវរៅ ់ដែលវិះគនំ់អំពី
ទទុុផធវិពលរបសំ់រ៉ា១។ ការសសេរអគុុចបទទៅំងនេះ
គឺសងុុយ័ឺមទុុយមានកការក ៃបុុរ ់ ចំ់ន ៃកងកា
រធុុរលើចលនាមមានបំណងកុុនុុងកការ ៃកទសុុសសនៈ
ទ ងុុរលើរបសំ់ពួកគ ៉ា១។ ខុុ ញុុ ់ំ មិនម ៃននវិយាយថា
រ៉ាធិឺសាសុុរុុតសំ់ខ ៉ាន ់់ ទ ៉ាំងនេះមិនចុុ លរួម
ចំ់ន ៃកបនុុតិចសរ ៉ោះនរ ៉ោះ ទ ៉ា ។ គ ៃខុុញុុ ់ំ បុុ ររ ៉ាក ជ
ចារ ៉ាមមិនទ ៉ាន់ គុុ រប ំ់ គុុ ររ ៉ាន់ ទ ៉ាលំ់ គ ៃ សរ ៉ោះ១។
ពួកយលើងយលំ់ច ៉ាបុុ រសវិនបលើទ ៉ាញជនសវ ៉ាធការណៈ
ទ ៉ៅកុុនុុងកការសនុុ ទទ ៉ាមមុុ យនេះ នេ ៉ោះយលើង
និឹងមមានសកមុុមជនដ ៃលមម ៉ានតទុុផធវិពលចុុ រលើន១។
ពួកយលើងយលំ់ច ៉ាពួកគ ៉ាបុុ រហ ៃលជ ៉ាវុុ តច ៉ាបំ់
និ ងចវ ៉ាបំ់ផ ៃុ តលើមទទុុ លយកសម ៉ាុ ល ៉ោឹ ៃនកការ
បងវិ សរ ៉ាធ១[5] គ ៃពួកយលើងគបុុ រ ើណយប ់ នវិ យ ៉ាយ
ព ើរ ៉ា? ការបងវិ សរ ៉ាធគឺជ ៉ាហ ៉ោត ៉ាផលទ ើព ើរដ ៃល
ធុុ រលើ ើ ចុុ យខុុ ញុុ ំ់ យ ំំ យលំ់ច ៉ា"សេរើនិ ៉ យមចមួ យមើព ិត
ជ ៉ាចងុុ រំ ើយ ្"១ យ ៉ោ ៉ំ ងទ ៉ៅ ៉ត ៉ាម J.K Gibson-Graham[6]
ដលើ មុុ បុុ បបើ ញុុ ចបំ់ រសេរើនិ វិ យមចមួ លើ(គ ៉ាមដ ៃលពួ ក
យលើ ងធុុ ល ៉ាបំ់ ដ ើ ង) នេ ៉ោះពួ កយលើ ងយលំ់ នវិ យ ៉ាយ
ព ើរ ៉ា១។ អុុ នកបុុ ររ ៉ាជធុុ ញ ជ ៉ាព ើសវសស បញុុ ណយបំ់
កការសវិកុុ សារបសំ់ ខុុ លុុ នដ ៃលផុុ តលៅ ៉ាកទ ៉ៅលើ
បុុ រធ ៉ាន ៉ តទ១នេ ៉ោះ១។ បុុ ររ ៉ា ៃលជ ៉ាពួកគ ៉ៅ ៉ មិនប ៉ាន
បំ់ ភុុ លួ ៉ោ ចទ ៉ាំ ងសុុ រុុ ងទ ៉ោ គ ៃពួ កគ ៉ៅ ៉ ៃន ើ ៃរ ជ ៉ាសសេរ

ព័ត៌អ្នករវើផ្សេងទេ។ វៀងវិញ ដវែលខ្ទុញ្ញ្ចុំយលៈថ្ងាន រៈ
គឺជាបញ្ញាហា។ មនុតងទៀត ខ្ពុញ្ញុំគិតតថ្ងាារ៉ាព័តិកជា
សច់ខ្ទាន់ណាស់ដវែលព័ត្តិកយណើងបន្ទុតសច៊ិកខ្ពុស្សា
កខ្ទរវៅព័ឆ្វឆ្ងប់រង៉ិរណ៌ណសវេ៊វិនិ៊យ័មធ្ញុ៉ម៊ិនៈ ប៉ុន្ទុក៊តវៃ
ខ្ពុញ្ញុំគិតតធ្ងារ៉ាវានវៅ៊តវៃម៊ិនគ្ម្រ្លប់គ្ញរ៉ាន់។ ដ្ឋុច
Mark Purcell[7] និ៊យ័ាយ័ផ្ងាន៉ "ព័តិ៊យ័ណើ៊គប្ម្រុប៊ណើ៊ង៉ាក
ចណ្ញ្ញ្ញ៌ព័រ៉ិវ៊វិនិ៊យ័ម៌ធ្ញ្ម៉ិក៊វៃប៉ៃរ៉េម៊ី៊កម៌ណើ៊លខ្ញុល្ញ្ល៌ន
យ៊ណើងវិញ ច៉ាប៊ផ្ញុក៌វើម៌អ្ញរ៉ើ៊ដវែលលៈបា៉កត៌វៃ៊ផ្ញុ៊កល៌
ភា៊ព័សប៊ញ៌ប៉ាយ័ ធ្ញុ៊រ៊ីវ៊ទ៊ញ្លើ៊ងដ៊ណ៉ាយ័ច៊ា៊ប់ផ្ញុ៊ក៌ម៊ើ៉ន៊ធ្ង
ទ៌វៅកធ្ង៌ខ្ញុ៊ល្ញ្ឍ៌នឌ៉ងផ្ញ្ុ៉ទ៉ាល៊។" សារ៌ៈសុំ៌ខ៌ធ្ងន៌
នវៃ៊ការ៌បដ៊ិសរ៊ណ៌ធ ការ៌បញ្ញ្ផ៌វ៉ាងន៊ិ៊ងការ៊វិៈ៊គន៌
គប្ម្រុប៊ិគ្ញ៉រ៊ិក៌វៃបន្ញ្ុ៌ត គ្វៃ៊ព័រ៊ិយ័ណើ៊ងគ្ញ្រ៌ញរ៊ិគ្វៃ៊គ៊ិគត៌ច៊ញុយ័
ច៊ញុ៊វ៉ីន៊ធ្ងាក៊ម៌ើ៊គ្ញ្ុ៊ធ្ញ្ុ៊រ៊ីវ៉ែប៉ៃ៊ណ៉ា៊ធ្ងម៌ើ៊ប៉ៃ៉ធ្ញ្ុ៊ម៌ើ៊ច៊ញ្ុ៊យ័
សរ៉ើ៊វ៊វិនិ៊យ័ម៊ធ្ញ្ម៉ិ៊ច៊ង្ញ្ុ៊រ៊ី៊ណ៉ាយ័៌ន៉៉រ៊៉ល៊វ៉ាយ័ដ៊៉ណ៉ាយ៌រ៉ិ៊ធ៊ី
ផ្ញ្ុ៊ស៊រ៊ង្វ៉ខ៉ទ៉ៀ៊ត៉។

    សកម៊ញ្ុ៌មភា៊ព័ច៊ញ្ុ៊ប៉ា៊ស់៌ខ៉ដវៃលធ្ញ្ុ៊រ៊ិ៊ណើ៊ល៊ណើ៊ស
ព័រ៊ិសរ៉ើ៊វ៊វិនិ៊យ័ម៊ធ្ញ្ម៊ើ៊គ៌ណ៉៉៉ហា៊៉៉ៅ៌ថ្ងាន៊៉យ័ណ៉ាប៉៉ាយ័
ន៉ំ៌យ័ាធ្ញ៌ៀ៉ប (Prefigurative politics)[8] ដវែលជា៌ច៉ំ៌ណ្ញ្ុ៊ច
ទ៉ីព័ានវិ៊ជា៌ច៌ំ៌ណ្ញ្ុ៊ច៊ស់៌ំ៌ខ៌ធ្ង៌ន់៌ម៊ញ្ុ៊យ័ដ៊ៃលខ្ញ្ុ៊ញ្ញ៌ំ
គិតតធ្ងា៌ព័ត៌៊យ័ណើ៊ងគ្ញ្ុ៊ត៊វៃ៊ផ្ញ្ុ៊ត៊វៅ៌តល៊ណើ៊ជា៌ព័ត៌៊ិ៊សរ៉េ៊ស
ព័ណ៉ល៊យ័ណើ៊ងព័ត៌៊ភា៊ក៊ញ្ុ៊ស្សា៊ក៌ព័ត៌៊គ៌ប់៌ន៊ិ៌ត "សរ៉ើ៊វ៊វិនិ៊យ័ម
ធ្ញ្ុ៊ម៉ើ៊ច៊ង្ញ្ុ៊រ៊ី៊ណ៉ាយ័៌"ន៉៉ៈ។   ការ៊បញ្ញ្ុ៊រ៊ៀ៊បធ្ញ្ៀ៉ប៊ក៊ញ្ុ៊ន៊ូ៊ង
នំ៌យ័ន៌វៅ៌ទ៌ៅ៊ន៉៉ៈគ៊ើ៊ជ៉ាក៌ការ៊បដ៊ិ៊សរ៊ណ៌ធ៉យ័៉ណ៉ាប៉៉ាយ័
គ៌ណ្ញ្ុ៊ត៌ាលន៊ិ៊យ័ម៊ បា៌ន៉៉ៈន៊ុ៊ក៊ញ្ុ៊ម៌ន៌ន៊ិ៊ងអ៊ញ្ុ៊ញ៉៉ាធ៌រ៊ដ៊ៃ៊ល
ស៊ញ្ុ៊ច៌ិ៊ត៌ក៊ញ្ុ៊ន៊ូ៊ងន៉យ័៉ណ៉ាប៉៉ាយ័គ៌ ៌ំ៌ណ៉៉ាង។ ន៌យ័៉ណ៉ាប៉៉ាយ័
នំ៌យ័ធ្ញ្ៀ៉ប៌មា៌ន៌ទ៌ៅ៊ង់៌ន៊ិ៊ងការ៊គ៊ញ្ុ៊រ៌ប់៌គ៊ញ្ុ៊ងដ៊ណ៉៉ាយ័៌មា៌ន
ទ៌ំ៌ន៉ាក់៌ទ៌ំ៊ន៌ន៌រ៊ា៉ង៌រ៊ ៉ៀ៉បស៊ញ្ុ៊ម៌ណើ៊ព័ណ៉ាល៌គ៊ើ៊គ៊ម៌ាន
ឌ៌ការ៊ន៊ិ៊ងប៊ា៌ន៉៉ៈ ន៊ុ៊ក៊ញ្ុ៊ម៊ទ្ទ៌ណើ៊យ័។ ន៉៉ៈគ៊ើ៊ជ៉ាបញ៌ភ៊ា៉៉ៅ៌ទ
ន៉យ័៉ណ៉ាប៉៉ាយ័ម៊ុ៌យ័ដ៊ៃ៊ល៊ធ្ញ្ុ៊ល៉៉ៈបញ្ញ្ុ៊ច៉៉ា៌ ៉ងព័ើ៊អ៊ន៉៉ាក៌
គ៌ដ៊ៃលសង្ញ្ុ៊ក៌ម៊ស៊ញ្ុ៊ រ៌វៃ៉ង៌រ៊ ៉ក៉៉ៈ។ ជ៌៉ាជ៌៉ា៉ង"ការ៊ដ៊ជ៌ល៌វៃ៊ក"គ៌វ៉ៃ
ម៉៉៉ញ្ុ៊យ័៌៉ង ការ៊ធ្ញ្ៀ៉ប សកម៌ញ្ុ៊មភា៊ព័ច៊ញ្ុ៊ប៉៉ា៉ស់៌ខ៉៉ន៊ិ៊ងច៌ ៉ំ៊ខ

ពួកុ៍គុ៖រុ៖រកការកការនវិទ្យាយរវៃកញ្ញៃកចុ៖រៅននៅៈ
ទៅ អុ៖រៅដៃលតុ៖រុ៖រកការនៅៈគុ៍កុំណត់គៅលដៅ
ឱ្យយចុ៖បាសៗ៍លនុ៖អុ៖រៅដៃលយៅៀងៗងុ៍បានហៅយ
យៅៀងុធុ៖រៅរៀៗៅទៅៗៗ៕ មវិនតៃបៗ៍ុំណ្ឌុណៅៈ មៗៃន
ចៃណ្ឌុៗចមុ៖ុយចៃនុៗនុៗនុៗដៃលសៗៃរៅនវិទ្យយមថុមៅៀទទុៗល
បានចៃណ្ឌៗៅបៗ៍អៗៃរុៗមណ្ឌៅ៍កុៗនុៗងៗៅការសៗនុៗៗៃនៗៃ
នុៗយៅៀៗៅៗៅ៕[10]   សមុៗៗៅៗៅៗ៍អុៗៗៃនៗៃកៗៃវិភៗៃៗៅៗៅៗៃ
David Harvey[11] លៗៅៗៅៗយៗៅៗ៍ៗៅៗៃៗៃៗៃៗៃសៗៗៗៅៗ៍ៗៃៗៃ
មុៗៗៅៗៗៅៗៃៗៗៗៅៀៗៃៗៃៗៃៗៃៗៃៗៗៗៃៗៅៗៃៗ៍ៗៃ
រៗៃៗ៍ៗៗៃៗៅៗៃៗៃៗៃៗៃៗៗៗៃៗៃ ៗៃៗៃៗៅៗៃៗៅៗៅៗៃៗៃៗៃៗៃ
ៗៗៗៗៃៗៃៗៃៗៃៗៃៗៗ៍ៗៃៗៃៗៃៗៃៗៅៗៃ៍ៗៃៗៅៗ៍ៗៃៗៗៃៗៃ
ៗៗៗៃៗៗៃៗៗៃៗៃៗៃៗៃៗៗៗៃៗៗៃៗៃៗៃៗៃៗៃៗៃៗៅៗៃ
ៗៅៀៗ៍ៗៃៗៗៃៗៗៃៗៃៗៗៃៗៃៗៃៗៃៗៗៃៗៃ
ៗៃៗៃៗៗៃៗៃៗៃៗៃៗៃៗៃៗៃៗៃៗៗៃៗៃៗៃៗៃៗៗៃៗៃ
ភៗៃៗៗៗៅៗ៍ៗៃៗៅៗ៍ៗៅៗៗៗៃៗៃៗៃៗៗៗៃៗៃៗៃៗៃៗ៍ៗៅៗៃៗៃ
ៗៗៗៗៃៗៃៗៃៗៗៗ៍ៗៅៗៅៗ៍ៗៃៗៃៗៃៗៗៃៗៅៗៃ
ៗៅៀៗៗៗៅៀៗៃៗៅៗៅៀៗៃៗៅៗៃៗៅៗៗៗៃ៕ ៗៃៗៅៗៅៗៃៗៃៗៅៗៅៗៃ
ៗៗៗៗៗៅៗៃៗៅៗៗៗៅៗៃៗៅៗៃៗៃៗៗៗ៍ៗៃៗៗៗៃៗៅៗៃ
ៗៗៗៗៅៗៃៗៅៗៃៗៃៗៗៃៗៃៗៗៗៃៗៗៃៗៃៗៃៗៗៃៗៃ[12]
ៗៗៃៗៗៗៗៅៗៃ ៗៃៗៅៗៗៗៗៅៗៅៗៗៗៗៅៗៃៗៗៃៗៃៗៗៅៀៗៃៗ
ៗៗៃៗៗៗៅៗៃៗៃៗៅៗៃៗៗៗៃៗៗៃៗៅៗៃៗៃៗៗៅៀៗៗៃ
ៗៗៃៗៃៗៗៃៗៅៀៗ៕ ៗៃៗៗៃៗៃៗៃៗៃៗៅៗៗៗៗៗៃៗៃៗៅៗៗៃៃៃ
ៗៗៗៗៃៗៗៗៗៃៗៗៗៃៗៃៗៗៗៃៗៃៗៗៗៃៗៗៃៗៅៀៗៃ៍ៗៃ ៗៃៗៃ
ៗៗៗៗៃៗៗៗៗៅៗៃៗៃៗៗៅៀៗៗៗៃៗៅៗៃៗៗៅៗៃៗៗៃៗៅៀៗៃ៕ ៗៃៗៃ
ៗៗៗៗៗៗៗៗៃៗៗៗៗៅៀៗៃៗៅៗៃៗៗៗៗៗៗៃៗៗៃៗៗៃ៍ៗៃ
ៗៅៀៗៅៀៗៅៗៃៗៗៃៗៃៗៃៗៗៗៗៗៗៃៗៃៗៗៃៗៃៗៗៃៗៗៃៗៅៗៃ
ៗៗៗៗៃៗៃៗៃៗៃៗៗៗៃៗៃៗៗៅៗៗៗៃៗៅៗៃៗៅៗៃៗៃ
ៗៗៗៗៃៗៗៃៗៃៗៅៀៗៃៗៗៃៗៗៗៗៅៀៗៃៗៃៗៅៗៗៗៃៗៗៃៗៗ៍
ៗៅៗៃៗៗៃៗៗៅៗៗៗៅៗ៍ៗៃៗៗៗៗៃៗ៍ៗៃៗ៕ ៗៗៗៗៃៗៗៃៗៗៃៗៃៗៗ៍ៗៃ
ៗៗៗៗៃៗៅៀៗៗៃៗៃៗៅៀៗៃៗ៍ៗៗៗៗ៍ៗៃៗៗៃៗៅៗៃៗៅៗៃ
ៗៗៗៃៗៃៗៗៗៗៃៗៗៗៗ៕ ៗៃៗៅៗៗៗៃៗៅៀៗៃៗៃ
ៗៗៗៗៗៃៗៅៗៗៗៗ៍ៗៃៗៃៗៃៗ៍ៗៗៃៗៗ៍ៗៃ ៗៗៗៗៃៗៅៗៃ

របស់ៗពួកយើង មធ្យោបាយៗបាយដែលគួមៗមានការ
បញ្ចូៗចប់។ ការធ្ងៀបគឺជាកាងឋិបកួរសៗបភាៗ
វ៉ើករ៉ាយ រ០ៗសរ៉ាយរ៉ាក់ៗ។ៗក់ដែលៗ៉ាំៗនៗ៉ាំមក
ជ៉ាមៗយនៗឯភ៉ាៗពសៗមៗើគៗ៉ន៉ា គៗមៗានការសនៗយ៉ា
ខៗយល់ៗនៗខែៗភ៉ាៗពបៗៗៗ៉ាំៗៗៗៗៗៗៗ៉ាៗ៉
ព៉ិតបៗៗ។ៗ៉ៗ៉ៗៗ៉ៗ៉ៗ៉ៗ៉ៗ៉ៗ៉ៗ៉៉
វ៉ាៗ៉ៗ៉ៗ៉ៗ៉ៗ៉ៗ៉ៗ៉ៗ៉ៗ៉ៗ"ៗៗ៉ៗ
សៗ៉ៗៗ៉ៗ៉ៗៗ៉ៗ៉ៗ"៉ៗៗៗៗៗៗៗ៉ៗ៉ៗ៉
ជ៉ាៗៗៗ៉ៗៗ៉ៗៗ៉ៗៗ៉ៗៗ៉ៗ៉ៗ៉។[13]

គៗមៗានអៗៗ៉ៗៗ៉ៗៗ៉ៗៗៗ៉ៗៗៗៗ៉ៗ៉ដែល
៉ៗៗៗ៉ៗៗៗ៉ៗៗ៉ៗៗ៉ៗៗៗ៉ៗ៉ៗ៉ៗ៉ៗ មៗាន
គៗ៉ៗៗៗៗ៉ៗៗៗ៉ៗៗ៉ៗៗៗ៉ៗៗ៉ៗៗ៉ៗៗៗៗ
រៗមៗៗៗៗ៉ៗៗៗ៉ៗៗ៉ៗៗ៉ៗ៉ៗ៉ៗ៉ៗ៉ៗ៉ មៗាន
ស៉ាៗមៗៗៗៗៗៗៗៗ៉ៗ "៉ៗ៉ៗៗ៉ៗៗ៉ៗ"។ ខៗ៉ៗៗ៉ៗៗ៉
ព៉ៗៗៗៗៗៗៗៗៗៗ(ៗៗៗៗៗៗៗៗ៉ៗៗ)ៗ៉ៗៗៗៗៗ
ៗៗៗៗៗៗៗ៉ៗៗ៉ៗៗៗៗ៉ៗៗៗៗ។ ខៗ៉ៗៗ៉ៗៗ៉
ព៉ៗៗៗៗៗៗៗៗៗ៉ៗៗៗៗៗៗៗៗៗៗ៉ៗ។ ខៗ៉ៗៗ៉ៗៗ៉
ព៉ៗៗៗៗៗៗៗ៉ៗៗៗៗៗៗ៉ៗៗៗៗៗៗ៉ៗ។
ខៗ៉ៗៗ៉ៗៗ៉ៗៗៗៗ៉ៗ៉ៗៗៗៗៗៗ៉ៗៗៗៗៗ៉។
ខៗ៉ៗៗ៉ៗៗ៉ៗៗ៉ៗៗៗៗៗៗ៉ៗៗៗៗៗៗៗ៉ៗៗៗ
ៗៗៗៗៗៗៗៗ៉ៗៗៗៗៗៗ៉ៗៗៗៗៗៗៗៗៗ៉ៗៗៗ
ៗៗៗៗៗៗៗៗៗៗ៉ៗៗ (cult of growth)។ ខៗ៉ៗៗ៉ៗៗ៉
ៗៗៗៗៗៗ Mont Pelerin ៗៗៗៗៗៗៗៗៗៗៗៗៗៗៗៗៗ
ៗៗៗៗៗៗៗៗៗៗៗៗៗ។ខៗ៉ៗៗ៉ៗៗ៉ៗៗៗៗៗៗៗ Friedrich
Hayek ៗៗៗ Milton Friedman ៗៗៗៗៗៗៗៗៗៗៗៗៗៗៗ
៉ៗៗៗៗៗៗៗៗៗៗៗៗៗៗ៉ៗៗៗៗៗៗ៉ៗៗ។ ខៗ៉ៗៗ៉
ៗៗៗៗៗ៉ Thatchers The Reagans ៗៗៗៗៗៗៗៗៗៗៗៗៗ
ៗៗៗៗៗៗៗៗៗៗ៉ៗៗៗៗៗៗៗៗៗៗ៉ៗៗៗៗៗ។
ខៗ៉ៗៗ៉ៗៗ៉ៗៗៗៗៗ៉ៗៗៗៗៗៗៗៗ៉ៗៗៗៗៗ៉
"៉ៗៗៗៗៗ៉ៗៗៗៗៗៗៗ៉ៗៗៗៗៗៗ៉ៗៗៗៗៗៗ៉ៗ
៉ៗៗៗៗៗៗៗៗៗ៉ៗៗៗៗៗៗ៉ៗៗៗៗៗៗៗៗ៉ៗៗ៉

ក៏ជាសមាជិកម្នាក់ក្នុងសហគមន៍របស់ពួកយើងទេ។ ខ្ញុំដៀលពីការមិនឲ្យតម្លៃថាមិនមែនអ្វីទាំងអស់សុទ្ធតែសំខាន់នោះទេ។ ខ្ញុំដៀលពីទង្វើដែលឲ្យតម្លៃលើតែផលប្រយោជន៍ជាជាងតម្រូវការរបស់សហគមន៍។ ខ្ញុំដៀលអ្វីដែលសេរីនិយមថ្មីគាំទ្រលើកស្ទួយទាំងអស់មិនតែប៉ុណ្ណោះខ្ញុំថែមទាំងដៀលដល់ល្បិចនៅពីក្រោយសេរីនិយមថ្មីផងដែរ! ជាយូរណាស់មកហើយដែលមានមនុស្សប្រាប់ខ្ញុំថា “គ្មានដំណោះស្រាយផ្សេងនោះទេ”ដែល “រលកធំនឹងបោកទូកទាំងអស់” ដែលពួកយើងកំពុងរស់នៅក្នុងពិភពសុបិនអាក្រក់របស់ដាវីន (Darwinian nightmare) ពោលគឺពិភពដែលអ្នករាល់គ្នារស់ដោយផ្ទុយពី “ឱកាសរស់រាន្តរបស់អ្នកខ្លាំង” (survival of the fittest) ពួកយើងបានទទួលយកគំនិតមួយដែលថា “សោកនាដកម្មរបស់ជនសមញ្ញ”។ ជាការពិតវាគ្រាន់តែជាល្បិចដែលឆ្លុះបញ្ចាំងពី “សោកនាដកម្មនៃមូលធននិយម” និងសង្គ្រាមដណ្តើមដែលគ្មានថ្ងៃបញ្ចប់[14]។ Garrett Hardin[15] ពួកយើងមិនដែលឈប់ហើយគិតថាតើគោដែលស៊ីស្មៅក្លាយជាកម្មសិទ្ធិឯកជនដោយរបៀបណាទេ? តើវានឹងមានអ្វីកើតឡើងនៅពេលដែលយើងផ្គុំភាពសមញ្ញទាំងនេះឲ្យទៅជាបណ្តុំដោយមិនគិតពីកម្មសិទ្ធិឯកជនជាមុន[16]? តើមានអ្វីកើតឡើងនៅពេលដែលយើងចាប់ផ្តើមបង្វែរចំនាប់អារម្មណ៍របស់យើងមកដាក់លើសារៈសំខាន់នៃការសង្កើតដំណោះស្រាយនិងបទពិសោធន៍ដែលមានស្រាប់វិញនោះ?

[17] តើនឹងមិនមានអ្វីកើតឡើងលើបុរសសិនបើពួកយើង
បទោះបង្ហាញចោលការបញ្ឈប់ណាទាំងបុរសដែលឯងដែលយើងលើ
មានសពេវផងដែលនិងឯងាកមកលើការអភិវឌ្ឍ
ផុសរោលផុសរោដៀមប្ញុយភាពសហការកុន្ឋានវិងផំនួយ
ទៅវិញ្ញទៅមកនរោះ?[18]

Jamie Peck[19] ផុលោបប់ហាចៅសរោវិនិយមថុមីថា
ផា "ពាកុយសុូលរៀកនយរៀបាយទុលំទុលាយ"
បំ៉ុនុតកៃ៎កុន្ឋងភូន្ឋកៃ៎ករុូនករវិនៈគន់ វាមចិនទានំ
គុរប់គុរៈានំនៃះទៅ៑ ផាចុូរើនឯនុូនទាំបាន
កនុូលឯផុសតៃៃៅបនុូទៅរាបំពេពពុៈកយៅឯបានកំណត់
សគុរូ្ឋនវិឯគាំឯពើពៃលនោះមក ពុៈកយៅឯ
សុូគាលបំ៑ាកៃ៎ានបំគ៎ៃចុូបាសំគ៎ាមរយៈអគុូចបទ
និឯ៑ការគរៈ៎ៅ៑ យំ៎ាឯណ៎ាមិញ្ញ ទោះបើផា
យៅឯ៑ចុូបាសំ៑ៅ៑ យៅឯយកល្ឋុ៎ៈវ៑ាហ៑ើ៑យ វ៑ា
ប៑ៃ៎ៅ៑កៃ៎ាន៑ត៑ៃ៎ម៑ានៈ៑ទ៑ុ៑ផ៑ិ៑ព៑ល៑ផ៑ាៈ៑ម៑ន៑ទ៑ៅ៑ទ៑ៀ៑ត៑
បនុូទៅបំព៎ើរ៎ើ៑បតុ៎តិ៑សៈដុូបកៈ៑ច៑ុ៑ធ៑ុ៑ន៑ាំ ២០០៨
និ៎បនុូទ៑ាំ៑ប៑ំព៑ើ៑ចលន៑ៅ៑យ៑រោ៑ាយ៑អនុូ៑ក៑រ៑ផ៑ាត៑ិ៑
ផៃ៎ៅ៑ម៑ាន៑ឈ៑ុ៑ម៑រ៑ោ៑ៈ៑ផ៑ាក៑ោ៑ស៑ា៑រ៑ៈ៑ង៑ំ៑គ៑ុ៑ល៑ៅ៑ស Occupy
Movement[20] Japhy Wilson[21] បានហាចៅតុ៑ធ៑ិ៑ព៑ល៑
បនុូតបនុូ៑ទ៑ាំ៑ប៑ំ៑ន៑ៈ៑ៈ៑ថ៑ាផ៑ា "សរោ៑វ៑ិ៑ន៑ិ៑យ៑ម៑ថ៑ុ៑ម៑ី៑
ឯ៎ឯ៎ំ៑ត៑" (Neoliberal gothic) ខ៑ុ៑ញ្ញ៑ុ៑ំ៑ត៑ិ៑ត៑ផ៑ាផ៑ល៑ៃ៑ម៑ុ៑ប៑ើ៑
យកល្ឋុ៎ៈ៑តុ៎ធ៑ិ៑ព៑ល៑ន៑ៈ៑ៈ៑ ពុៈកយៅឯ៑តុ៎រ៑ូ៑ត៑ៃ៎
បឯុ៎វៃ៑ៃ៑នយ៑រោ៑ាយ៑របសំ៑ពុៈកយៅឯ៑ទ៑ៅ៑កុ៎ន៑ុ៑ឯ
ពភ៑ិ៑ផ៑ន៑វ៑ៃ៑ៃ៑ស៑ក៑ម៑ុ៑ភ៑ាព៑ញ្ញ៑ ច៑ល៑ន៑ៅ៑[22] តើនឹងមានអ្វីរ
កើតឡើងបុរសសិនបើ "សរោវិនិយមថុមីឯងរ៎ៃ៑
យំ៎"កុូលោ៎យ៑ផ៑ាម៑ន៑ុ៑ត៑ោ៑ាផ៑ារ៑ប៑ស៑ំ៑ន៑យ៑រ៑ោ៑ាយ៑ថ៑ុ៑ម៑ី៑
ន៑ោះ? តើវ៑ាន៑ិ៑ឯ៑កុ៎ល៑ោ៑យ៑ផ៑ាយ៑ុ៑ល៑ារ៑ម៑ុ៑យ៑កុ៎ន៑ុ៑ឯ
ផ៑ើ៑រ៑វ៑ិ៑ត៑រ៑ប៑ស៑ំ៑យ៑ៅ៑ឯ៑ផ៑ៃ៑ៃ៑ម៑ិ៑ន៑ក៑ុ៑រ៑ឺ៑ម៑ក៑ៃ៑ផ៑ាច៑ល៑ន៑ៅ៑
ត៑ៃ៑ម៑ុ៑យ៑ម៑ុ៑ខ៑ន៑ៅ៑ះ៑ទ៑ៅ៑ តៃ៎ៅ៑ថ៑ៃ៑ម៑ទ៑ៅ៑ាំ៑ឯ៑អ៑ក៑ំ៑យ៑ក
ឱកាសនៃ៑ល៑ំ៑ហ៑រ៑កុ៎ន៑ុ៑ឯ៑ផ៑ើ៑រ៑វ៑ិ៑ត៑ផ៑ៃ៑ៃ៑យ៑ៅ៑ឯ៑រ៑ស៑ំ៑ន៑ៅ៑
យំ៎៎ាឯ៑ស៑ុ៑វ៑ិ៑ត៑ស៑ុ៑វ៑ាញ្ញ៑ទ៑ៀ៑ត៑ផ៑ឯ៑?

បុរសविនិនបเรีเวาលถពេលដแែលយเเលยเเหิង
បុរเเหีบบ្รរាស่ยพูលเเหางยพูលការដแែលយเเหิงចำณาំ
ถ่ารเเวาជ์ាกพ្นុនวាก่ังกារสกម្មម្យูยดแែលលเเหิស
ถ่ีเ Tទ្រ័ీสพ្តីนิงกาัรอនเุรត្តุตนเวาะ? ถำุกยเเหิง
ต្ุរុรต្តเ็เมเเมเวានยพュ Tधซวាស់រុรตជ๊ាต្ចต្รเิเนเกุขุนเ้เง
సσ್ುಲುಭ್ಲ:నเ্าเกเวាลេ์ัีసเรនเุีផซ่เริเเน์ิเយម្ธ่าម្ธ្ีเฯ

บเชีเ Tเวាะบเชีដวาถแกยเเหิงมิនอวាัធ่រុรเ็เืเ็เถูวงเเหัย
ถុ្ถបัาคุพូลเเชเวเรรเ Tเ Tเवาฃ้ัងสพ្រុะุตุเ្เ็วាน ต្เ่ัีเยี่เวาหาเวเวาច
ถำุกยเเหិงอวาัธ่រុรเ้เิเ์ិเเ์ิเกាัร้รพិ่่่อเวา้่ัีเงเวาयี่่ัీเเวาเ้เวามม្เวាੀ្ญ្ีเก
ดุ่่ำเ้เ้เเ्วาสถ្ีเหอ្เเ์ิเ្เ้เ्วादแแ្เเลเเ์ิเหบวាธ្เ្เต្เเិเกตุเ្เेเ्เเ
มก้เฯ ฃพ៊ุ៊ญ្ุ៉ำม៊ี่เวាันเเ้เ្ญ យថวาถำุกยเเหิง ต្ุถรเวาบ้เ์่่าๆ เตตเ้เเ่ี่เืเว៊ีเม
ถวាก្ธ្ยស์พ្លเวาก้เនยเเวาลบเวายថม្ธ្ีเម្ธ្ី្ुยฯ

អ៊ុនកនយលោបាយធ្នុនលើមរបស់ឃយលើង។ នលៅក៊ុនុង
សមាំយសលៅលីនិឃយមថ្ងមុមលីនលេះ បញ្ចុហាមាមិនមលៃន
ស៊ុថ្ងតិកនលៅលលីបុគ្គតលទលកលៃសង្ថ្ងតិកនលៅក៊ុនុង
បច្ចុរពាំន៊ុធ្ធថាំនរៀរបស់ឃលើងដលៃលជលាបលណ្ណុតុល
បញ្ចុហាមាតលៃមុគ្គង។ ពុកឃយលើងបងុ្ងកលើតនិន្ធិញ៉ាវាំង
ទ៊ុឃលក៊ុខណ្ណុខស៊ុថ្ងថាបាំនអាំណពោយផលទ៊ុឃ
មាំន "Lucifer Effect" (នលេះគឺជាសុថ្ងថានភាាព
មុឃយដលៃលមាំនលក៊ុខណ្ណុខឪ៊ុរលើទ៊ុឃយមនុស្ថុស
"ល៊ុអ"បុច្ចុរពុលើតុគតិអាំពលើអាកុ៊ុរកាំទលៅលលីជនដទ៉ុលៃ)[24]
"អាំពលើសាកុ៊ុរកាំដលៃលតុ្មមាំនតមុ៊ុលលៃ" គឺជាអ៊ុរលើ
ដលៃលអ៊ុនកនយលោបាយទវាាំងនលេះធុ៊ុរលើជាបុ៊ុរចាាំ
ក៊ុនុងបុច្ចុរពាំន៊ុធមុ៊ុឃយដលៃលទឃយរងុ្ងវាន់ទលៅលលី
អាំណពោយចខុ៊ុសបុ៊ុរក៊ុតលៃដលៃលទវាាំងអសាំន់លេះ
សុ៊ុទុ៊ុធតលៃតុ៊ុរ៊ុរបាំនភកលៃតាកាំតលៃងឡុ៊ុរលើងលលើមុ៊ុបលើ
បមុ៊ុរលើផលបុ៊ុរឃរលោជនាំមុ៊ុលលធននិឃយម[25] បាំ៉ុន៊ុតលៃ
ពុកឃយលើងមិនចវាាំបវាចាំគុ៊ុរ៊ុរតលៃតលោលរាពតាម
នលោះទលៅ។ ពុកឃយលើងមិនមៃនចវាាមកទ៊ុឃយធុ៊ុរលើតាម
បញ្ចុជាមុ៊ុឃនលេះទលៅ។ តាមររយៈសកមុ៊ុមភាាពជលោយ
ផ៊ុទវាលាំនិនិ៍ដជមុ៊ុរលើសផ៊ុសលោងខដលៃលពុកឃយលើងមាំន
ពុកឃយលើងអាចកលៃបុ៊ុរលៃទម៊ុឃរងាំន៊ុធិបបៃក៍រផុ៊ុតដាំ
កាាចសាវាហាវារនលេះបាំន។ នលៅពលៃលដលៃលបុ៊ុរពាំន៊ុធ
នឃយលោបាយតុ៊ុរ៊ុរបាំនកាំណតាំ រៀបររៀងដលោយ
និនិរ៊ុ៊ុមបញ្ចុចុ៊ុលនិនិបងុ្ងកលើតពមីុ៊ុលធននិឃយម
បុច្ចុរពាំន៊ុធនលោះមិនអាចកាំណវាងការរសាំន់វាន៊ុត
មាំនដជុ៍រិតនិនិការរឃលាំដជលៃនិរបស់ពុកឃយលើងបាំន
ឡុ៊ុលើឃ ហាលតុ៊ុននលេះឃលើងតុ៊ុរ៊ុរតលៃកវាន់ក៊ុតាំបាំ
ន៊ុរដជរិ៍រិតរបស់ឃលើងនិឃយកសិ៊ុទ៊ុធិរិសាំនលៅជា
លក៊ុខណៈបុច្ចុរមុ៊ុលផ៊ុតុំតុ៊ុរ៊ុរឡុ៊ុរប់មករិ៍ញ៉ា។ ពុកឃយលើង
តុ៊ុរ៊ុរតលៃចវាបាំផ៊ុតលើមឃកចិ៍តុ៊ុតទុ៊ុកដជាកាំទលៅលលើ
នឃយលោបាយរបស់ពុកឃយលើងនិឃផុ៊ុតលើមឃបកក៊ុ៊ុរសលោយ
សាវាមតុ៊ុតីភាាពទ៊ុឃយបាំនចុ៊ុរលីនជាាងនលេះ   ពុក

យើងគប្បូបពីទទួលសុគតពាល់ការពាិតមួយដែលថា
ការឈឺចាបរ់បស់បុគ្គលសម្ងួយរូបគឺគំណាងការ
គេប្រៀបសង្ខុគត់ទៅពាលនៅពកយើងងចាំងរស់គុនៗ។
[26] ពួកយើងអាចចាបផុ្គតលើមរស់សារជាថមើ
មុគទៀតក្ងុនងពាិភពពលពកមួយដែលអនុរកុត
ការផុយគុនៗទៅវិញទៅមក មិតុតភពាត ភាព
ដើងទុកុខធុរៈគុន ឥទមុងរៀបចដើយ
គុនបខែងចំកគំណែងបានៈព ពាលគពក ង
ទុលនមកវិញនុរូបុរដាធិបក យុតំណាង
ពើមនុសុសដាតិពិតបុរាកដ។ សារវើនវិមួមើ
គើដាតផនិតអាកុរក់ដលបងុក សលទុធផល
គួរចួយសុអប់ខុតើមដាចុរវើន។ សារវើននិមយ
ថុមើសំកុតសមនឹងទទុលបានសមុតើនឹងទងុរើ
មើលងាយបែបនៈ។ សហាតមនុរបស់ពួកយើង
ភពាសហាការគុនារបស់ពួកយើងឹងការថៃនទ
យកចិតុតទុកដាក់គុនារបស់ពួកយើងគើដា
អុរើដែលសារវើននិមយមថុមើ សុអប់បំផុត។ វា
សុអប់អុរើដែលពួកយើងអអររើករាយដាមួយ។
ហាចគុនៈនទៅព លដែលពួកយើងនិយាយថា
"សារវើនវិមយមថុមើចងុរើ សុមទចុយរាលើសពើ
អកុសរ សុមទចុយពួកយើងបុរកចាន់ខុដាប់នុអុរើ
ដែលពួកយើងនិយាយទ ងអស់គុនៗ។ និយាយ
រាចុយខុលៗងឥលើៗ និយាយរាដាមួយខុញំ
និងនិយាយទៅកាន់អុកដែលបុរាចុនាចង់
សុតាប់បុំនុតសមុនវិយាយកុននឥ យដ់
សុទុធចិតុតធាយើងពិតដាចង់ចាប់ផុតើម
សមានកមុមភពា ទងុរើរដើមបើផុលាស់បុតុរ
ពិភពល កចងុរ មួយនៈ។ សារវើនវិមយមថុមើ
ចងុរ យ!

빌어먹을 신자유주의

Translated by 번역: 이연재 – Jane Yeonjae Lee

Translator's Commentary

I agreed to translate this piece, having previously read and thoroughly enjoyed it. It gave me one of those awakening moments where we reflect on ourselves as academics and how we can push the boundaries and be impactful in the real world. I believe this is an important piece of work not just for advancing resistance to neoliberalism but for reimagining what we mean by a truly critical and responsive scholarship. Although I did not have any previous experience in translation, I had always wanted to try my hand at it at some point, and I thought what better way to start than with this amazing project? South Korea has historically suffered from neoliberalism, and in so many ways the country still is struggling against it. I hope by translating this work, I have played my small part in regenerating interest from Korean scholars, students, and readers who may not have otherwise been exposed to the theory or to this particular article.

In translating this work, I tried my very best to write in an academic voice but stay connected to the playful, angry, and energetic voice of the original writer. I did not translate everything word-for-word but used some of my own understanding of the concepts, reproducing them within the Korean context so that the writing flows and can be easily understood.

빌어먹을 신자유주의

빌어먹을 신자유주의. 본 논문이 이렇게 여기에서 마무리 된다 해도 별 문제 없을 것이다. 신자유주의에 대한 나의 주장은 확고하다. 지금 이 글을 읽기 시작한 독자들은 이미 나의 논점을 이해했을 것이다. 신자유주의의 장점은 더 이상 없다. 좀 더 솔직히 말해서, 나는 신자유주의에 대해 생각하는 것 조차 싫다. 정말 할 만큼 했다. 한때, 본 논문의 제목을 '신자유주의는 잊어라'라고 할까 고민도 해보았다. 지난 몇 년간 신자유주의에 대해 많은 논문들을 쓰다보니,[1] 이 주제에 대해 더 이상 나의 에너지를 쓰고 싶지 않은 시점에 도달하였다. 하지만, 현 연구활동이 일련의 정치적 운동이기 때문에, 사회에 커다란 악영향을 준 신자유주의를 단순히 무시하는 행동은 위험하다는 것을 인식하고 있다. 아직도 신자유주의의 사회적 영향력은 강력하며, 신자유주의의 문제점을 무시한다는 것이 결코 좋은 선택만은 아닌 것 같다[2]. 그래서, 결국 내가 하고자 하는 말은 '빌어먹을'이다. 좀 더 정중하고 부드러운 제목을 선택할 수도 있었지만, 그리하지 않기로 결정했다. 우리가 도대체 왜 신자유주의가 만든 비열한 설교보다, 그것을 비판하고 조롱하는 것을 더 염려해야 하나? 오히려 나는 본 논문을 통해, 신자유주의가 사회를 망친 만큼, 존중과 예의 따위는 버리고 신자유주의를 비판하기로 결심했다. 논문의 제목을 부드럽게 쓴다면 신자유주의에게 또 다시 양보하는 것이 아닌가? 처음에는 이러한 논문제목을 사용하면 나의 평판에 문제가 생기지 않을까 걱정도 했다. 앞으로 나의 일, 직업, 승진 또는 새로운 곳에서 일터를 찾는데 방해가 되진 않을까? 하지만 이런 걱정을 하는것 자체가 신자유주의로부터 자기 스스로를 억제 하는 것 같았다. 빌어먹을.

고백하건데, 나는 신자유주의를 격없이 적절하게 비판할 수 있는 방법은 없다고 생각했다. 또한, 다양성 (variegation), 혼종성 (hybridity), 변이성 (mutation)과 같은 복잡한 지리학적 이론들로만 신자유주의를 비판해야 한다고 생각했고, 이는 나의 논조를 약화시킬 뿐이었다. 사실, 위에서 언급한 이론과 학설들을 연구한바 있지만[3], 이런 식의 프레이밍은 나의 논점과 항상 모순이 되고 있었다. 다시 말하면, 우리는 지극히 평범하면서 격없는 방법으로 신자유주의에 대한 정치적 비판을 해야만 한다. 따라서 본 논문의 제목을 '빌어먹을 신자유주의'로 정했다. 내가 하고 싶은 말의 전부다. 물론, 나의 논점을 좀 더 구체화하고, 그 미묘한 감정들을 표현하기 위해 사용한 '빌어먹을'에 대한 수많은 생각을 (아마도 내 인생에서 가장 많이) 했다. 이 얼마나 아름다운 표현법인가! '빌어먹을'은 명사, 동사, 형용사로 쓰일 수 있으며, 아마도 [영어에서] 가장 많이 쓰이는 감탄사일 것이다. 우린 이 단어를 분노, 경멸, 성가심, 무관심, 조바심, 또는 놀람을 표현할 때 쓰기도 한다. 우린 무언가를 '빌어먹을' 상태로 만들 수도 있고, '빌어먹을 놈'이 되기도 하고, '빌어먹을…' 하며 무관심 해질 수 있고, 또는 '에잇 빌어먹을' 하며 다른 사람에게 분노를 표현하기도 한다. 지금쯤 독자들을 '그래서 어쩌라고? 누가 상관이나 해?' 라고 생각할 수도 있다. 뭐, 아직 난 상관한다. 독자들이여, 만약 당신 또한 신자유주의를 끝장내고 싶다면 관심을 갖길 바란다. '빌어먹을'이란 단어가 가져다 주는 힘은 우리가 신자유주의에게 던지는 잠재적인 도전장과 같다. 그 도전장의 힘과 능력을 이해하기 위해서는 '빌어먹을 신자유주의'란 구절의 미요함을 자세히 뜯어 보아야 한다. 그러나, 그 미묘함? 따위는 우선 버리자. Kieran Healy[4] 란 학자가 말했듯이, 미묘함은

표현하면 표현할 수록 "이론이 가져오는 학술적
흥미, 경험에서의 생성, 그리고 응용성을 방해하기
마련이다." 논설을 미묘하게 표현하려는 페티시즘은
버리고, 빨리 어떤식으로든 신자유주의를 비판하는
토론을 해보도록 하겠다.

　　본 논문의 첫번째 의견은 바로 당신이 예상한대로다.
'빌어먹을 신자유주의'란 말을 던짐으로써 우리의
열망과 분노를 표현할 수 있다. 그 유독한 악의 얼굴에
대고 우리의 원망과 원통을 외치고 싶은 욕구를
표출할 수 있는 계기가 될 수 있다. 한 가지 방법은
신자유주의를 향해 항의 또는 비판하는 학술논문과
책을 쓰는 것이다. 논문과 책이 우리의 저항력을
키우는데 중요한 전략이라고 생각한다. 하지만, 이
방법만으로는 어렵다는 것 또한 잘 알고 있다. 다만
이런 전문적이고 공식적인 방법을 통해 좀 더 많은
주요 관계자들이 우리의 목소리를 들어줄 것이라,
어리석지만, 믿어본다[5]. 또 물어본다. 우리 이제
신자유주의를 그만두어야 하는 것 아닌가? '빌어먹을
신자유주의'를 배제의 관점에서 바라봐야 하는 것은
아닌가? J.K. Gibson-Graham[6]의 학술개념처럼, 그냥
여기서 신자유주의는 끝이 났다고 생각하고 무시해야
한다. 그러면, 기존의 학자들은 신자유주의를 더 이상
그들의 주요 연구이론으로 사용하지 않게 될 것이다.
물론 신자유주의의 존재 자체를 완전히 부정하는 것은
아니다. 다만, 신자유주의가 아닌 다른 주제로 글을
쓰게 만드는 것이다. 이렇게 학자들이 신자유주의를
비판적으로 인지하는 것 자체로 성공이다. 글로
표현한다는 것 만으로 신자유주의에서 모두가
벗어나기에는 터무니없이 부족하다. Mark Purcell[7]이
주장하듯, "우리는 신자유주의란 개념을 외면하고
우리 스스로를 바라보아야 하며, 스스로 이 상황을

해결해야 한다 – 힘들겠지만 그만큼 행복해질 것이다.”
물론 글로써 부정하고, 항의하고, 비평하는 것은
필요한 행동이지만, 어떻게 하면 좀 더 적극적으로
우리가 기존에 할 수 없었던 틀에서 신자유주의를
망하게 할지 고민해봐야 한다.

신자유주의의 개념을 넘어선 직접적인 행동을
수행하려면 예시적 정치 (prefigurative politics)[8]란
개념을 연구해 볼 필요가 있다. ‘예시적 정치’란 미래의
사회를 반영한 정치적 센트리즘 (centrism), 계급조직,
권위를 보기 전에, 그것들을 포함한 형태를 부여하는
사람들의 습관과 버릇을 강조시켜 분석해야 한다는
개념이다[9]. ‘예시화’ 시킨다는것과 직접적인 행동은
‘더 이상 말할 필요도 없어’ 라는 배제적 관점을
벗어나, ‘어차피 말할 필요도 없었다’ 라고 인지하며,
우리 스스로가 변한점을 직접 찾아야 한다는것을
요점으로 두고있다. 그럼에도 불구하고 신자유주의란
개념은 현재 많은 정치적 논설과 명령들을 비판하는데
쓰여왔다[10]. 비평가 David Harvey[11]는 극히 소수의
국가들만이 신자유주의를 비평하는 질문에 응답할 수
있다고 주장했으며, 그 이론 안에서도 그는 비계층적
단체는 제외한 채 수평적 정치만이 존재한다고
말한다. 이런 염세주의를 논의하면서도 그는 예시적
정치의 뜻을 미래반영적 개념이 아닌 현재의 끝이란
개념으로 오해하고 있다[12]. 정확히 말하자면, 예시적
정치의 개념엔 지금까지도 끊임없는 불신이 침범해
있으며, 우리가 실행시키고자 하는 참된 예시화는
성공하기 어렵다는 것이다. 예시적 정치는 사회를
반사적이며 주의깊게 파고들지만, 늘 생산, 발명,
창조만이 공동사회의 욕구를 만족시켜 준다고
주장한다. 명시적으로 예시적 정치는 신자유주의에
반대되는 개념이다. 끝없이 이념 운동과 그 이념에

맞는 실천을 현 사회에서 병행하는 것이다. 예시적 정치란, 하층사회 선구자들이 만드는 초월적 유토피아 '무공간'이 아닌, 동등한 급진주의자들이 나누는 주흥과 기쁨을 포용하며, 이 '오래된 둥지'안에서 지금 당장 매일매일 재확인 하며 부단히 새로운 세상을 만들어 나가자는 뜻을 표현한다[13].

　　신자유주의에 대해서 존중할 만한 것이 단 하나도 없으며, 창조라는 것을 예시적 정치의 개념으로 본다면, 내가 하고싶은 말은 간단히 '빌어먹을' 이다. 우리의 정치적 상상력을 장악 시켜버린 빌어먹을 신자유주의. 그것이 낳은 폭력과 경멸들이여 망해라. 부당함을 장점이라고 찬양하는 빌어먹을 것들. 자연환경을 파괴한 모든 것들. 끝없는 성장을 예찬하는 집단들이여 모두 꺼져라. 몽 펠르랭 소사이어티, 그리고 그것을 만들고 홍보하는 모든 연구기관들아 망해라. 우리에게 이 모든 아이디어들을 심어준 빌어먹을Friedrich Hayek (프리드리히 하이에크) 그리고 Milton Friedman (밀턴 프리드먼). 대처 (Thatchers)들아, 레이건 (Reagans)들아, 그리고 이 자기밖에 모르는 비겁한 남의 등골이나 빼먹는 탐욕 많은 정치인들아, 모두 꺼져라. 우리의 화장실과 바닥을 닦아줄 만큼은 되지만, 그들을 공동사회에서 제외시키려는 이 무서운 혼란적 사상 – 꺼져버려라. 점점 더 커져만 가는 운율학 그러나 정말 중요한 것은 셀 수 없다는 것을 깨닳지 못하는 빌어먹을 시대의 흐름. 공동사회에게 필요한 것보다 본인의 이득부터 챙기는 빌어먹을 욕망. 신자유주의를 대표하는 모든 것들은 꺼지고, 이걸 타고 달린 트로이의 목마도 망해라! 너무 긴 시간동안 우리는 '다른 대안은 없다'고 들어왔고, '올라가는 기운이 모든 배를 태워 나를 것이다' 라고 배웠고, 다윈설의 신봉자가 되지 않으려 노력했으며 '강한자만이 살아남는다'

라고 인식해왔다. 우린 '공유지의 비극'을 현실이라 믿었다; 다만 현실적으로 생각하면 '자본주의 비극'의 끝없는 전쟁과 같다[14]. 개럿 하딘(Garrett Hardin)[15]의 취약점은 사실 방목하고 있는 소떼를 언제나 개인의 소유라고 생각했었던 것이다. 만약 우리가 공유지를 개인의 소유가 없는곳이라고 재전제한다면 어떤 일이 생길까?[16]? 공유법을 조직의 특권이며 특혜라고 미리 대안해 왔다면 어떤 일들이 벌어졌을까?[17]? 우리가 경쟁과 장점이라는 그 쓴 약을 목으로 넘기며 신자유주의 처방전으로 우리 몸을 치료 하는 것이 아닌, 협력과 상호협동이 가져다주는 진정한 치료에 에너지를 쏟았다면 어땠을까?[18]?

  Jamie Peck[19]이란 학자는 신자유주의를 어느 한 '급진주의 정치적인 슬로건' 이라고 말했었지만, 이젠 이 정도 가지고는 비판이라 할 수도 없는 시점에 도달했다. 우린 이미 너무도 긴 시간동안 무엇이 우리의 적인지 확인하였고 그것을 글로써 항의해왔다. 2008년 경제난, 그후의 예술인 학습 공동체운동이 우리의 적을 패배 시켰다고 확신했었지만, 그는 지속적으로 좀비처럼 숨을 헐떡이며 되살아 나고 있다[20]. Japhy Wilson[21]은 이것을 '신자유주의 고딕'의 힘이라고 말하고 있으며, 난 이 공포영화 같은 상황에서 우리가 빠져나오려면 현재 정치적 사항을 법규화시켜야 한다고 생각한다[22]. '빌어먹을 신자유주의'가 정치적 새로운 만트라가 된다면 어떨까? 우리의 행동을 가능하게 하는 구절이 아닌, 우리가 매일 살고 있는 이 공간과 시간들을 교정시킬 수 있는? 우리가 매번 이 구절을 말 할때면 어느 한 입법 기관이 우리가 말로만 하는 것을 벗어나, 의견과 실상이 결합된 아름다운 재설정을 요구하는 것이란 걸 알아 차려준다면? 우리는 신자유주의를 배제 시키기 위한 여러가지의 연장된 접근성을 찾아야 한다. 우린 이것을 전적으로 무시하고 잊을 수 없으며, 설득력있는 공연을 하고 설득을 공연한다는 것에서 벗어나 좀더 적극적으로 부딪쳐 싸워야 한다. 어디 한 번 급진주의적 정치적 슬로건을 전진 시켜보자. 우리의 경멸을 헤쉬테그 (#fuckneoliberalism)로 표현해보자! 하지만 그저 표현만으론 부족하다. 우리의 결심을 바로 제정하고, 이 모든 것은 우리가 매일 느끼고 경험하는 작은 것들에 내제되어 있다는 것을 알아차려야 한다[23]. 우리가 직접 나서서 사회를 다시 만들어야 하며, 진행을 연기시켜서는 안된다.

우린 스스로 정치적 사상과 배열만을 호소하며 우리를 속이고 힘 없게 만들어왔다. 우리의 맹목적인 신념은 누군가 하늘에서 우리를 구해줄거라 끝없이 기다리게 만들었다. 시스템 자체가 타락하였음을 시간과 그동안 거쳐간 수많은 정치적 후보인들이 증명하였다. 지금 우리가 있는 신자유주의 시대는 힘있는 정치인들의 문제만이 아니다. 현재 시스템을 믿고 있는 우리의 믿음 자체가 문제점을 생기게 한다. 우리 스스로가 제도의 상황을 '악의 평범성' (the Lucifer effect) 으로 만들고 가능하게 한다[24]. '악의 평범성'은 정치인들이 아무리 권력을 남용하더라도 그들은 자본주위시스템을 구축하기위해 본인들이 맡은 업무를 수행한다고 믿게 만들었다[25]. 하지만 우린 복종 할 필요 없다. 우린 그 규칙에 신세를 진 적도 없다. 우리의 직접적인 행동과 대안의 실천으로 우린 이 지독한 학대의 순환에서 빠져나올 수 있다. 정치적 시스템이 자본주위로 규정되고, 정의되어 있는 상태는 우리의 사회의 본질과 앎을 대리할 수 없으며, 집단적인 개척이 필요하다. 우리의 정치를 입법화 시켜야 하며, 한사람의 괴로움은 모두의 수난임을 인정해야 한다[26]. 우린 모두 갱신된 헌신으로 다른사람의 삶을 들여다

보아야 하며, 상호협동과 비 계층적 업무를 실행하면서 민주주의 어원록적인 개념부터 힘에서 민간 으로 바꾸어 나가야 한다. 궁극적으로 신자유주의는 아주 더러운 사상이며 저속한 결과를 불러냈다. 그것은 공격적인 언어와 행동으로 답변해야만 한다. 우리가 만들어내는 공동 협력과 돌봄은 신자유주의가 견딜 수 없을 것이다. 우리가 찬양하는 모든 것은 그의 증오의 대상이다. 우리의 '빌어먹을 신 자유주의'라는 울부 짖음은 그냥 말이 아닌, 우리의 헌신적 재정으로 만들자. 크게 말해라, 나와 함께 말해라, 이 말을 들어줄 모든이에게 말해라, 그리고 무엇보다 가장 중요한건 이 말이 그 빌어먹을 단어를 우리의 힘으로 바꿀수 있다고 밝게 울러퍼지는 소리가 되게끔 하자. 빌어먹을 신자유주의!

CHAPTER 15

नेपाली – Nepali

थुक्क ! नबउदारबाद

Translated by बिनोद न्यौपाने – Binod Neupane

Translator's Commentary

When I read "Fuck Neoliberalism," I was impressed by its theme, spirit, and strategic analysis of globalization. In August 2018, I wrote a book of my own titled *Federalism in Nepal and Political Economic Flow*. My book was based on the concept of neoliberalism. In the book, I linked neoliberalism to the obstruction of the development discourse and to the social, economic, and political fragmentation in a developing country like Nepal. Professor Springer approached me to have his paper translated into Nepali. I saw the value of translating this paper for Nepalese readers who would not understand the articles related to globalization or "Fuck Neoliberalism" in the English language.

While translating, there were times I had difficulty finding phrases in Nepali similar to the English phrases, as we had no corresponding words in Nepali. In such situations, I tried to maintain the core theme, strength, and flow of expression found in the source.

Neoliberalism has swept across Nepal like a vast tidal wave of institutional reform, forcing the political parties, leaders, and NGOs toward federalism. It has brought discursive adjustment and changed the prior institutional frameworks and the power structures. It also has brought social fragmentation along the lines of castes and other social agglomerations. This small least-developed country is suffering from privatization, financialization, crises created and managed by India, and the restoration of power in a multiparty system. So we suffer eternal political instability, corruption, inequality, and dismal economic growth. I found the article "Fuck Neoliberalism" an excellent way to study in the context of Nepalese political and economic flow.

Last but not the least, as a student of modern political systems, I also feel like saying "fuck the Mont Pelerin society and all the think tanks," and "fuck Friedrich Hayek and Milton Friedman" who gave us inequality and developed the discourse model of capitalism and the resulting social fragmentation of Nepalese society.

थुक्क ! नबउदारबाद

फक नबउदारबाद, यो नर्क लोक जावोस ! यो मेरो भुत्ते सन्देश हो ! मैले मेरो कुरो यही सक्दा पनि केही फरक पर्दैन, तपाईंले बुझी सक्नु भयो होला मेरो स्थिति बिलकुलै प्रस्ट छ, यहाँ म के भन्न खोजिरहेको छु ! नबउदारबाद बारे चर्चा गर्न म सँग केही पनि सकारात्मक कुरो छैन ! वास्तविक सत्य बोल्दा, यसबारे सोच्दा पनि मलाई ज्वरो आउँछ ! ओहो ! यसले गर्दा धेरै राजनीतिक-आर्थिक विषय वस्तु यस विश्वमा कलिकली सम्म आउन्जेल भई नै सक्यो ! समय सँगसँगै ; यस लेखलाई मैले "नबउदारबाद भुलौं" लेख्नु पर्दथ्यो ! मैले धेरै वर्ष देखि यस विषयमा लेखिरहेको छु[1]; अब म एक बिन्दुमा आएर उभिएको / टेकिएको छु जहाँ यस बिचारमा प्रतिबिद्ध भएर यसलाई जीवित राख्न धेरै ऊर्जा (शक्ती) खर्च गर्न सकौँदैन !

अगाडी आउने भविष्यको हाम्रो प्रतिबिम्ब हेर्दा, मैले यसको पहिचान गर्दा राजनीतिक युद्ध्याभ्यास धेरै छ ! शुतुरमुर्ग जस्तो बालुवामा टाउको घुसारेर हाम्रो यो साझा संसारमा नबउदारबादले गर्ने विनाशकारी साथै गम्भीर परिणामलाई हल्का रूपले हेर्यौं भने मानवीय जीवनमा धेरै नराम्रो स्थिति हुनेछ ! वास्तविक, नबउदारबादको बढिरहेको शक्तिलाई नकार्न मुस्किल छ, साथै मलाई ज्ञान छ; रणनीतिक रूपले नकार्नु सही बाटो/ तरिका होइन[2] ! त्यसैले,

यो नबउदारबाद मेरो सटिक बिचारमा भड्खालो परोस् अर्थात् "वेल फक इट देन" !

मैले यस बिचारको लेखलाई शालीन शीर्षक छानेको भए; नबउदारबादको अपराधलाई सम्भावति कमजोर ब्यन्जति गरेको ठहर्थ्यो त्यसैले यो शीर्षक छानियो ! ठिकै छ, यसलाई पछि हेरौला ! यसैमा कोही कसैले गाली गरिरहेको छ भने; हामी समाजलाई लिएर बहुत चिन्तति बनेर बोलिरहेका छौं, जबकि हाम्रो सामु चिन्तन गर्ने उ भन्दा घृणति चीज नबउदारबाद उभएको छ ! मैले सोचे, अब मैले नियम उलंघन गर्नु नै छ ! म दिक्क भैइसकेको थिएँ ! नबउदारबाद द्वारा गरिरहेको अपमान साथै शोषण प्रस्ट हेरिरहेको थिएँ ! त्यसैले यो राम्रो कुरो होइन, अब हामी सबैले नबउदारबादको उलंघन र विरोध गर्नु पर्दछ !

मैले मेरो लेखको शीर्षक छान्न नम्रता लिएको भए पनि यसको शक्ति हेर्दा नवउदारबाद प्रति उदारता मानिँदैन थियो ! वास्तवकि सुरुमा म केही चिन्तति भएको थिएँ, यो शीर्षकले मेरो प्रतिष्ठा तल झारी त दिँदैन ? यसले मेरो अगाडिको बाटो पदोन्नति हुने, राम्रो जागिरको प्रस्ताव, मेरा शैक्षिक गतिविधिहरू वा अन्य छेत्रमा जाने साथै उन्नति र प्रगतिको बाटो त रोकिदिँदैन !

यस्तो सोच्दा, नबउदारबादको अगाडी मेरो हार भएको जस्तो लाग्यो तर केही छैन; नबउदारबाद भड्खालो परोस्/ यसको सत्यानाश होस् ! मलाई महसुस भयो, बिचार पलायो ! म मान्दछु, नबउदारबा-दको बिचार र विमर्शको प्रतिवाद गर्न गहकिलो वैचारिक उत्तर छैन ! त्यसैले सोझै मानिसहरू यसलाई किन नकारिदिँदैन !

खाली, हामी शैक्षिक जगतमा रङ्गी बिरंगी देखिनि, चाप्लुसी गर्ने साथै सामाजिक अवधारणा कमजोर पार्ने/ बखिन्डन गराउने अनि आफैलाई कमजोर पार्ने भौगोलिक सिदान्तको रङ्गी बिरङ्गी, वर्ण शङ्कर र उत्परविर्तन उपयोग गरेर शान्त भएर बस्दछौं जसले नबउदारबादको शक्तिमा कुनै फरक नै पार्दैन ! मेरो लेखनमा पनि; मेरो योगदान यस्तै सैदान्तिक कुराहरूको उपयोगमा आधारति छ ३ ! वास्तवकितामा म, यस्ता विचारहरूको विरोधमा केही गर्न चाहन्थ्ये किनकि मेरा दैनिक सोच बिचारमा, सामान्य जीवनमा, अपरिवर्त-नीय विषय बस्तुहरूमा, नैरास्यताहरुमा मलाई लाग्छ, इन्कारको राजनीति अवस्थति हुनुपर्छ। यी सबै कारणहरूले गर्दा मैले यस लेखको शीर्षक "थुक्क नबउदारबाद (Fuck Neoliberalism)" राखिदिएँ किनकि यसको लागि यो नै सही पद हो जसले मैले दिन

खोजेको बिचार र दृष्टि व्यक्त गर्दछ ! मेरा तर्कमा यो नबउ-
दारबादलाई नांगेझार पार्ने शब्द थुक्क (Fuck) रोजें, जुन शब्द
बारे यति जोड गरेर अन्य कुनै शब्द बारे मैले जीवन मै सोचेको
थिइनँ ! क्या ! गज्जबको रङ्गी बिरङ्गी अविश्वसनीय शब्द छ यो;
अङ्ग्रेजीमा विस्मय बोधक यो शब्द संज्ञा, क्रिया, र विशेषणको
रूपमा प्रयोग गर्दछौ ! यो थुक्क/ थुइक्क (Fuck) शब्दलाई हामी
क्रोध, अव्यवहार, कष्टप्रद, अपरिचितता, आश्चर्य, अपमानित,
उदाशिनता वा भ्रामक कुराहरूलाई व्याख्या गर्नको लागी लिन्छौ
किनभने यसले धेरै जसो जिब्रोबाट मात्र भूमिका खेल्छ वा
फुत्कन्छि !

जस्तै: 'थुक्क ! बकवास बन्द गर'; छ्या... ! थुक्क के
गरेको; हावा कुरो नगर (फक समथिङ अप, फक समथिङ ओभर,
फक अराउण्ड, नट गभि अ फक) र निश्चिति रहेको एक निश्चिति
भौगोलिक विन्दुको शब्दको रूपमा सन्दर्भ जोडेर थुक्क ! वा जा
(बकवास तीर जान) आफैं ! भनी पनि निर्देशति (गो फक योर सेल्फ)
गर्न यो शब्दले सकिन्छ । यो बिन्दुमा आएर सोचिरहँदा, ठिक छ
! तर कसले दिन्छ फक ? राम्रो ! छोडीदिउ ! वास्तविक, साँच्चिकै
तपाईं नबउदारबादलाई मसान घाट पुर्‍याउन इच्छुक हुनुहुन्छ भने
तपाईंले केही गर्नै पर्छ !

नबउदारबाद शब्दको साथ आउन सक्ने शक्तिशाली
क्षमताहरूले नै नबउदारबादलाई एक सम्भावति चुनौतीहरूसँगै
देखाउँछ ! थुक्क नबउदारबाद (फक नबउदारबाद)का जराहरू खनेर
उसका क्षमताहरू खोतल–खातल पारी अध्ययन र अनुसन्धान गरी
त्यहाँ पुगेपछि हामी यसलाई बुझ्न र मशान घाट पुर्‍याउने औजारहरू
प्राप्त गर्न सक्छौं अर्थात् "फक नबउदारबाद" वाक्यांश बुझ्दछौं
! यसै समयको राजनीतिक- आर्थिक बहावलाई 'थुक्क गतिछाडा'
भन्न सक्छौं !

क्यूरिण हिली का अनुसार सामान्यतया विकासको अबरोधक यो
सिद्धान्त बौद्धिक रूपले चाखलाग्दो [4] ! त्यसैले, यससँग सम्मोहित
नभई, यसलाई अति सूक्ष्म अन्तर कुन्तर स्थानान्तरण हुन नदिँदै
छिटी थुक्क / थुइक्क नबउदारबादमा मैले सोचेअनुसार कार्य गरौं !

यसमा पहिलो तात्पर्य प्रस्ट छ, थुक्क/ थुइक्क नबउदारबाद
(फक नियोलिबरेलिज्म) भनेर यस उदारवादी यन्त्र प्रति रोष
प्रकट गरिरहेका छौं ! यो हाम्रो रिस, क्रोधको सङ्केत, हाम्रो
असन्तुष्टलाई चिन्ता गर्ने हाम्रो इच्छा आएर उभिएको छ जहाँ

तल्लो स्तरको, दुर्भावनापूर्ण स्थितिको मुखमा थुक्ने सङ्केत हो ! यो नबउदारबाद, यसको दुस्प्रभाब, बखिन्डनकारिता विरुद्ध धेरै विरोध प्रदर्शन गरेर, धेरै सङ्ख्यामा लेख/समालोचना लेखेर साथै पुस्तकहरू लेखेर यसको प्रभाव विरुद्ध आफ्ना अभिबिक्ति ल्याउन सक्छौँ ! यसले उत्तरार्द्ध रूपान्तर गरन उपदेश दिन्छ साथै पहिलि देखि विकृत आकांक्षाको बाटो बदलिदिनि तयार हुन्छ ! म यो नै प्रतिरोध गर्ने सटिक पद्धति ठिक हो र सिद्ध हुनेवाला हो भनिरहेको छैन ! मलाई विश्वास छ यो सबै उपायहरूले नबउदारबादको सामर्थ्यलाई बाँध्ने, नबउदारबादको ज्वार भाटाको प्रतिरोध गर्ने वाला छैन साथै सबै हाम्रो पक्षमा छैन !

यस मुद्दामा जनताको विशाल रक्षात्मक प्रतिरोध दर्ता गराउन शक्तिशाली सरोकारवालाहरूलाई संवादमा सहभागी गराइनु पर्छ ! यसमा हामीले यो सोच्नु गलत हुन्छ कि उनीहरू यो प्रतिरोधी आवाज सुन्न साथै सहभागी गराउने कुरोमा अगुवाइ गर्छन् [5] ! के हामीले कुरो गर्दा हुँदैन ?

अब हामी थुक्क नबउदारबाद(फक नबउदारबाद)को दोस्रो बुँदामा आउँछौ, जुन नबउदारबादको अस्वीकार धारणामा (जुन हामीलाई लाग्दछ) आधारित छ ! जे. के ग्रबिसन ग्राहम [6] द्वारा विकसित गरेको यो तरिका नबउदारबादलाई निर्मूल गरन धेरै उपयोगी लाग्छ ! यस तरिका अन्तर्गत नबउदारबाद बारे सिधा सिधा बहस, छलफल वा कुरा गरन छोडिदिनु ! विशेष गरी विद्वान, अध्येता र सोधार्थीहरूले अध्ययनको प्राथमिकितामा नबउदारबादलाई नराखी यसको अध्ययन बन्द गरनु पर्छ !

हुनसक्छ; यसलाई हामी पुरै भुल्न नसकौँला वा उपेक्षा गरन नसकौँला; मलाई पनि यो समस्या हो लाग्दछ तर अन्य विषयवस्तु भन्दा यसलाई कम महत्त्व दिनि सक्छौँ ! पुनःएक पटक यो हाम्रो सम्पर्कको महत्त्वपूर्ण बिन्दु बनेको छ जुन हामी नबउदारबादको दुनियाँ भन्दा माथि छौँ तर यहाँ पनि म पूर्णतया यो विश्वस्त छैन कि यो पर्याप्त छ ! जस्तो मारक पर्सेल को तर्क छ; "हामीले नबउ-दारबादको दिशा उल्टाउनु मात्रै छैन, दिशा हाम्रो पनि उल्टाउनु पर्ने छ, सुरु गरन गाह्रो छ तर हाम्रा कठिन मुद्दाहरू हामी आफैँ प्रबन्धन/व्यवस्थापन गरी समाधान गरन सक्छौँ त्यसैले आनन्ददायी सुरुवात हुन [7] ! यहाँ निषिध, प्रतिरोध, विरोध, आलोचनाको जरुरी छ तर सचेत भएर सोच्न जरुरी छ कि यो पत्रु नबउदारबादको पहुँचबाट अन्य चजिहरूलाई कसरी टाढा राख्ने !

अब तेस्रो साथै महत्त्वपूर्ण बुँदामा; मलाई लाग्दछ, हामीले थुक्क नबउदारबाद ("फक नबउदारबाद") विचार गर्ने समयमा ध्यान केन्द्रित गर्न पर्छ त्यो भनेको: पूर्व निर्धारित राजनीति भित्र बसेर नबउदारबाद माथि सिधै कारबाही [8] हो ! यसको लागि पूर्व निर्धारित रूपमा केन्द्रित राजनीतिको साथै केन्द्रियता, अनुक्रम र आधिकारितालाई अस्वीकार गर्न जरुरी हुन्छ ! यसको लागि समानान्तर सम्बद्ध, सङ्गठनको रूपहरूलाई ध्यान दिनु पर्दछ, जसले भविष्यको समाजको मागलाई प्रतिबिम्बित गर्ने प्रयास गर्दछ [9] ! यसरी, संवाद - स्थापन बेगर, पूर्व निर्धारण साथै सोझै कारबाहीले केही हुन सक्दैन ! ध्यान राख्नु पर्दछ; हामीले जे गर्नु छ, आफै गर्नु पर्दछ !

यद्दपि, त्यहाँ महत्त्वपूर्ण ध्यान नव उदारवादले कब्जा गर्न सक्छयम गर्ने बाटाहरू साथै सबै तरिका का राजनीतिक बहस र आदेशहरूलाई सही ठहर्याइयो [10] ! डेविड हार्बे [11] जस्ता आलोचकका कुराहरू मान्दा स्वयम् राज्य नबउदारबादको प्रश्न समाधान गर्न सक्दछ ! जहाँ विशेष गरी, गैर श्रेणीबद्द सङ्गठन साथै तेर्सो (होरिजेन्टल) कुदिरहेको राजनीतिलाई सबैभन्दा पहिले खारेजी गर्न पर्छ जुन, कुदिरहेको रेलगाडीमा ग्रसिको जस्तै नबउदारवादी भविष्यको जरुरत बनिरहेको छ ! अर्थात ग्रसिको आर्थिक अवस्थाले चित्रण गर्दछ !

बस्तुत: अहिले आफ्नो अतालिएको अवस्थामा उनीहरू पूर्व निर्धारित राजनीतिलाई गलत सम्झिएर बसेका छन् ! जबकि यो बाटो साधन हो जुन भविष्यको लागी अत्यावश्यक बाटो तर अन्त्य बिन्दु होइन [12] ! अन्य शब्दहरूमा भन्दा, वहाँ पहिले देखि नै पूर्व राजनीतिलाई लिएर लगातार सतर्कता अपनाइएको छ जहाँ वास्तविक प्रीफिगरेसनको वास्तविक अभ्यास गर्न नसकियोस ! यो एक प्रभावी साथै सर्घै कान ठाडा पार्ने स्थिति हो अनि सँगै उत्पादन, आविष्कार र नवीनताका साथै समुदायको इच्छा शक्तिलाई सन्तुष्टि दिने निर्माण तीरको दिशा पनि मानिन्छ !

यो दृष्टिकोणबाट हेर्दा, प्रस्ट पुर्वनिर्धारित राजनीति नबउदारबाद विरोधी हो ! ती साधनहरू, बाटोलाई आफ्नो सम्झिएर हामी तिनीहरू माथि कब्जा गरिरहेका छौं तर हाम्रो बाटो अन्तहिन छ ! यसलाई प्रकल्पित गर्न एकता र सबै सँगै होड्न जरुरी छ जहाँ प्रफुल्लता र आनन्द अनुभूति आउँछ त्यो अगुवा बनेर पाईदैन साथै न त कट्टर सर्वहारा वर्गको झुटो आदर्श – राज्य वा भाबबहिन शून्य

राज्य बनाउने वाचा/ प्रतिज्ञा गर्दा नै हुन्छ ! हो; यो यथार्थको कठोर साथै पुरानो भूमिमा नयाँ र वास्तविक संसार निर्माणमा छ ! जसको लागी कडा मेहनत साथै एक चोटि फेरी बचनको पक्का हुन आवश्यकता छ [13] !

नबउदारबादमा त्यस्तो केही छैन जसलाई हामी महत्त्व दउँ, यसैले निर्माणको पूर्वराजनीतिको सन्दर्भमा मेरो सरल सोझै भन्नु नै "थुक्क ! नबउदारबाद !" ! हाम्रो राजनीतिक कल्पनालोकमा पनि यो (नबउदारबाद) नकचरोको घुसपैठ भैसकेको छ ! यसैको कारणले हिंसा बढेको छ, थुक्क हिंसा, असमानता एक सद्गुण बनेको छ, पर्यावरणलाई चौपट पारेको छ, सञ्चयको अन्तहीन प्रवृत्ति र वृद्धि र विकासलाई छद्म रूपलाई बढाई चढाई गरेको छ !

थुक्क ! माउन्ट पेरेलिन समाज र थिनिक ट्याङ्क जसले यसलाई सहारा दिएको छ र बढाई चढाई गरिरहेका छन् ! थुक्क, फ्रेडेरिक ह्यायेक र मिल्टन फ्रयायड म्यान यनिले उनको विचारको ऋण हामीलाई बोकाएका छन् ! तिमीहरूलाई पनि थुक्क, थ्याचर, रेगन जो लोभमा अन्धा, डरपोक, आत्म केन्द्रित राजनीतिज्ञ ! भड्खालो परोस्, तिनीहरूको जसले जानी बुझी बुझी, बुझ पचाएर यसको डर देखाएर आफ्नो व्यापारमा लागिरहेका छन् !

उनीहरूको आँखामा अन्य व्यक्तिको सामर्थ्य र क्षमता चर्पी सफा गर्ने र भुईँ पुछ्ने देखि छैन ! यस्ता मान्छेहरू कसैलाई पनि आफ्नो समाजको सम्मानित नागरिक मान्दैनन् ! थुक्क, तिनीहरू तीव्र गतिमा मापन तीर मोडिन्छन्, अन्यको कदर गर्दैनन् बेइमानी सम्झन्छन्; अन्य सँग इमान हुन्छ भन्ने सम्झँदैनन् ! धिक्कार छ, तिम्रो नाफा कमाउने इच्छालाई जहाँ समाजको हितको उपेक्षा गरिरहेका छौ ! सधिा, सरल भन्दा प्रत्येक चजिलाई धिक्कार छ, जुन नबउदारबादले गर्छ ! यो धिक्कार त्यो ट्रोजन हर्षलाई पनि जसमा नबउदारबाद बुई चढेको छ !

धेरै समय अघि देखि, हामीलाई सम्झाई रहेको छ के यसको विकल्प अन्य व्यवस्था छैन ! यो उही प्रकारको स्थिति हो जस्तै: समुन्द्रमा उठेको ज्वारभाटाले सबै डुङ्गाहरूलाई चपेटामा पार्छ साथै हामी एक डरछेरुवा डार्बनियिन संसारमा रहन्छौ जहाँ एक – अर्काको विरोधी छौ " सर्भाइवल अफ फटिस्ट" ! सबैका सबै योग्यतम उत्तरजबिताको सिदान्तको विरोधी भएका छौ ! यहाँ सङ्घर्षको सिद्धान्तले काम गरिरहेको छ ! हामी पुरै "कामन्सको त्रासदि"को विचारमा डुबेका छौ जबकि सत्यतामा यो यस्तो चाल हो जुन

पुजीबादीको त्रासदी साथै उनीहरू द्वारा युद्ध स्तरमा गरिरहेको
अन्तहीन लुट अगाडी आउँछ [14] !

गैरेन हार्डीन लाई चस्स बझ्निे यही थियो, उनले खुला चौरमा
चरिरका पशुहरू कसरी व्यक्तिको स्वामित्वमा पुगे कैले सोच्न [15] !
यहाँ के हुन सक्छ जब हामी सक्कली कामन्स र निजी स्वामित्वको
पूर्व निर्धारित नभएको कामन्सको बिचमा झुक्किएर अघि बढ्यौं
भने [16] ? यहाँ हामीले विकल्पहरूको पूर्व प्रारूपहरुमा ध्यान केन्द्रित
गर्न सुरु गर्यौं भने जुन पहिलो महत्त्वपूर्ण सङ्गठनका रूपहरू
अभ्यासहरूबाट सिद्ध भैसकेका छन् [17] ?

के हुन सक्छ, जब हामी प्रतियोगिता साथै योग्यताको दवाईको
कडा गोली खान छोडी आफ्नो ऊर्जा वा शक्ति निबउदारवादी डाक्टरी
पुर्जीले दिएको औषधि खान छोड्यौं भने, तर एक आपसी सहयोग र
सहायता गर्दै गहिरो उपचारात्मक विधि प्रयोग गर्यौं भने [18] ? एक
चोटि, जेमी पेक [19] ले नबउदारबादको "एक कट्टरपन्थी राजनीतिक
नारा" घोषणा गरेका थिए तर अहिले हामी यो आलोचनाको क्षेत्रबाट
नै बाहिर भयौं ! हामीले धेरै वर्ष पहिले नै शत्रु चिनिसकेको थियो
तर त्यतखिर हामीले लेखन साथै प्रतिरोधको शक्ति मात्रै जानेको
थियो ! अब हामी यसलाई खत्तम गर्न निश्चित भइसकेका छौं ! सन्
२००८ को वित्तीय सङ्कट साथै कब्जा आन्दोलनको परिणामको
कारणले स्या...स्या.. फ्या ..फ्या गर्दै हाफ रहेको छ साथै आफ्नो
खराब हालत कुनै तरिकाले शक्तिशाली ढङ्गबाट ल्याउनको लागी
सङ्घर्ष गरिरहेको छ [20] !

जेफ्फ विल्सन ले यसको बढ्दो शक्तिको [21] भनेका छन्, र म
यकिन गरेर भन्न सक्छु यो हरर सो लाई रोक्नको लागि हाम्रो
आफ्नो राजनीतिलाई कानुनी दायरा भित्र ल्याउनु पर्छ [22] ! के यो,
थुक्क ! नबउदारबाद !! हाम्रो राजनीतिमा घुस्रियेर हाम्रो राजनिति
बदल्ने मन्त्र बने के हुन्छ ? एक वाक्यांश जीवन्त राख्नु पर्दछ
जसले हामीलाई क्रियाशील हुन र उर्जावान बन्न प्रेरणा दिओस
साथै हाम्रो भूमि र क्षण लाई सुधारोस जहाँ हामी बाचिरहेका छौं
? के प्रत्येक चोटि हामी यो वाक्यांशको प्रयोग गर्छौं, हामीलाई
निस्क्रिय संस्थाको सम्झना आउँदैन जुन शब्दजालमा उल्झिरहेको
साथै सिदान्तको सङ्कलन तथा व्यवस्थाको पुरानै स्वरूपको
समरक्छयन गर्न चाख र अभ्यासमा लिप्त भएर लागेको हुन्छ ?
हामीहरूले नबउदारबादलाई अस्वीकार गर्न बहुविधिको प्रयोग गर्न
पर्छ ! जब, हामी नबउदारबादलाई पूर्ण रूपले नकारन सक्दैनौं साथै

भुल्न सक्दैनौ; अन्तत: हामीले यसको विरोध यसरी नै गरनु पर्छ जहाँ यसको प्रदर्शनको शाब्दिक प्रतिवाद भन्दा अगाडी जावोस ! कुनै पनि हालतमा हामीले यस विरुद्ध उग्र राजनीतिक नारा प्रबल बनाउनु पर्दछ ! ह्यशट्याग (#fuckneoliberalism) हामीले प्रयोग गरेर हामी रिसाएको भाइरल बनाउन सक्छौ ! बुझनु पर्दछ, हामीले रिस प्रकट गर्नु भन्दा अरू बढी अन्य धेरै कार्य गरनु पर्दछ !

हाम्रो समस्या समाधानको साथै आफ्ना अभिलाषाहरू यसै समयमा दरोसँग उठाउनु पर्छ ! हामीले दुनियाँलाई यो महसुस गराउनु पर्छ कि यो विरोधको लहर रोकिने वाला छैन ! हामी स्वेच्छाले यो व्यवस्था प्रति मोहित भयौ साथै घरी घरी वर्तमान राजनीतिक संरचनासँग प्रतिनिधित्वको माग गर्दै आफैलाई कमजोर बनायौ ! हामीले लामो समयसम्म आकाशबाट एक थोपा पाउने निरर्थक प्रतिक्षा गर्यौ ! यस व्यवस्थाले आफै प्रमाणित गरेको छ कि यो भ्रष्ट छ ! यही व्यवस्थाको कारण आउने वाला हाम्रा महान् उम्मेदवार पनि असफल साबित हुन्छन् ! यस नबउदारवादी संरचनामा हाम्रा समस्याहरूको कारण समस्या ग्रस्त व्यक्ति सत्तामा थियो भनेर होइन, हाम्रो यस व्यवस्था प्रतिको अन्धविश्वास नै मूल समस्या हो !

हामीले एक यस्तो संस्थाको अवस्था/संस्थागत समस्याह-रूलाई जन्म दिएका छौ साथै बढाएका छौ जसले "दि ल्युसिफिर इफेक्ट (the Lucifer effect)" लाई खुलेर आफ्नो प्रभाव देखाउने अवसर दियो [24] ! "दि बेनालीटि अफ इभिल (the Banality of Evil)" पुस्तकमा लेख्दै, यस समस्याको कुरुपता यो हो कि यसमा काम गर्ने राजनीतिज्ञ आफ्नो नोकरी यस व्यवस्था भित्र सत्ताको उलटफेर हुँदा आफ्नो पालो वा अवसर सत्तामा बस्ने आउँछ भनेर तयार गरिएको हुन्छ जसले पुजिबादलाई समर्थन गररिहन्छ [25] ! तर, हामी उनको आज्ञाको पालन गर्दैनौ ! हामी यस व्यवस्था प्रति आभारी छैनौ ! हाम्रो सिधै कारबाही साथै सङ्गठनात्मक संरचना बदलेर हामी यस व्यवस्थाको दोष साथै शोषणको बृहत् चक्र भत्काउन सक्छौ !

जब राजनीतिक पद्धति/ व्यवस्थाको हलो अड्कियो/ उल्झरियो साथै उदारवाद अनुरूप परिभाषित भएर नियमित भयो तब हामीले सोचे अनुसार/महसुस गरिएका आवश्यकता अनुसार नहुनुको साथै दुनियाँको प्रतिनिधित्व गर्न सक्दैन ! त्यसैले: अब हामीले तय गरेको जीवन पथको जिम्मेदारी उठाउनु पर्छ साथै एक

समग्र संस्थाको निर्माणको माग जोडदार रूपले गर्न पर्छ ! हामीले आफूलाई राजनीतिक रूपमा सक्रिय हुन आरम्भ गर्न पर्छ साथै यी सम्बन्धहरू प्रति समर्थन जनाउनु पर्छ जसले यी रेखांकित गरेका छन्; एउटाको पिडा, दुख साथै अपमान सबैको शोषण हो [26] ! हामी सम्भावनाहरूले भरिएको यस दुनियाँमा एक आपसी दोहोरो सहयोग र प्रतिबद्धताका साथ बस्न सुरु गर्न सक्छौ जसमा आपसी सहयोग, फेलो सिप, पारस्परिक आदान प्रदान तथा अश्रेणीबद्ध सङ्गठन हुन्छ ! यस्तो व्यवस्था जसमा मानिसहरूको शक्तिमा आधारित लोकतन्त्रको मूल भावना चलोस् !

मुख्यतः: नबउदारबाद एक बकवास विचार हो जसले छाडापन परिणाम साथै मूर्खतापूर्ण मान्यताहरू ल्याउँछ ! वास्तविक यसलाई दिने जवाफमा, समानखालको प्रतिरोधात्मक/ आक्रामक भाषा साथै आन्दोलनको सामना गर्न योग्य छ ! हाम्रो समुदाय, हाम्रो सङ्गठन साथै एक आपसी चिन्ता गर्नु यसलाई घिनलाग्दो लाग्छ ! हामी जेमा खुसी मनाउँछौ त्यसलाई यो घृणा गर्छ !

अन्ततः हामी सबै भन्न सक्छौ: "थुक्क नबउदारबाद (fuck neoliberalism)" ! आउनोस् ; यसलाई चिच्याएर/ जोडले कराएर भनौ ! म सगसगै भनौ ! जहाँ सम्म पुग्छ, सबैले भनौ !

वास्तविक, यो सबैको एक नै मतलब छ यो शक्तिको पुरातन स्वरूप बदल्न एक पुरा जोड लगाइएको आव्हान हो; यहाँ, यो विभेदकारी दुनियाँलाई बदल्न सकियोस !

थुक्क ! नबउदारबाद (Fuck Neoliberalism) !!!

Jebać Neoliberalizm

Translated by Filip Brzeźniak

Translator's Commentary

I have to start by stating the fact that Simon's text works differently for everyone that reads it. At least that is something that I gathered from what my friends told me. For me, it's very much connected with academia. In fact, I found this text at a special time in my life, as a sort of pinnacle of a whole year of activities. Near the end of 2017, I organized a few meetings of a Marxist discussion group at my university, where we talked about the contradictions of academia—it is an instrument of capitalist and neoliberal discipline, but at the same time it is an object of constant brutal neoliberal attacks. A few months passed, and we had an occupation on our hands, a real student strike in all the universities across Poland. Obviously, not as spectacular or as large as those that one reads about in the British or American press, however, factoring in the programmed apathy of Polish students and a feeling of hopelessness among doctoral students, it was definitely something new. The government wanted to push through a number of reforms that curbed the autonomy of universities (that is if one is not a fan of the Schmittian type of autonomy that belongs to the sovereign), transferred control from the local academic communities (however hierarchical and feudal they may be—let's not have any illusions about that) to the central government, and, in the final analysis, proposed a neo-liberal, business management style for higher education institutions, beautifully named "cooperation with business." What a fantastic configuration! Clearly something that we are getting accustomed to after the recent elections and power struggles worldwide—a union of neo-liberalism and authoritarianism, in short, an intensified version of the neoliberalism that was already in place. Unfortunately, the protests were not enough. The reforms passed, but not in their original form. And now we had a community, a potential network for upcoming struggles.

The occupation and translating "Fuck Neoliberalism" together made me realize how much of a tension there is between studying and studies, between freely doing science and formally being disciplined into learning. Not a new idea in itself; plenty of books and pamphlets have been already written by anarchists about schooling and higher education, and plenty of experiments have taken place similar to those taking place right now. Everything I had read up to this point was now experienced knowledge, experienced and observed while some of my friends from the occupations were failing their university courses (the protests coincided with the exams). But their inquiries into the lives of other academics, professors included, made for great research and for a different kind of knowledge and science. "Fuck Neoliberalism" reminded me how much fun doing science can be, and, obviously, it's not only about the content—just playing with words, scientific conventions, researching, the references, the whole publication process when you're doing it with friendly people. For me, it was also a great example of how play works against power and how it can work in academia, as well as elsewhere. When the translation was published, there was an explosion of positive reaction—support, laughter, and agreement. How happy I was when I read that there are seminars on the text—one during a forum about the present state and future of work in Polish capitalism, the other being a reading assignment and a discussion during an official course on political philosophy for the students of law at my very own university. Thank you, Simon, and thank you to all of the translators. The fight goes on, and we will win!

Jebać Neoliberalizm

Jebać neoliberalizm. Mówię to wprost. Pewnie mógłbym w tym miejscu zakończyć swój wywód i to by w zupełności wystarczyło. Moje stanowisko jest jasne i powinniście już wyczuć sedno tego, co chcę powiedzieć. Nie mam nic pozytywnego do dodania w dyskusji o neoliberalizmie i jeżeli mam być szczery, to mdli mnie, gdy tylko muszę o nim myśleć. Po prostu mam tego dosyć. Przez jakiś czas nosiłem się z myślą zatytułowania tego artykułu „Zapomnieć neoliberalizm", jako że w pewnym sensie dokładnie to chciałem uczynić. Przez lata zajmowałem się tym tematem[1] i doszedłem do momentu, w którym nie chciałem już wkładać więcej energii w to przedsięwzięcie z obawy, że kontynuowanie namysłu nad tą ideą przysłuży się utrzymaniu jej panowania. Po dalszej refleksji zdałem sobie jednak sprawę z tego, że schowanie głowy w piasek i zbiorowe ignorowanie zjawiska o tak destrukcyjnych i destabilizujących skutkach dla współdzielonego przez nas świata jest potencjalnie dosyć niebezpiecznym manewrem politycznym. Ciężko jest zaprzeczyć istnieniu władzy neoliberalizmu i nie jestem przekonany, że strategia jej ignorowania jest właściwym podejściem[2]. „Jebać go w takim razie"—pomyślałem. I choć spokojniejszy i łagodniejszy tytuł dla tego artykułu mógłby stonować wynikającą z niego potencjalnie obraźliwość, to zdecydowałem się przy nim pozostać. Dlaczego mielibyśmy bardziej przejmować się użyciem wulgaryzmu niż okropnym dyskursem samego neoliberalizmu? Zdecydowałem, że chcę dokonać transgresji, chcę wkurzyć i zgorszyć właśnie dlatego, że powinniśmy być zgorszeni neoliberalizmem, to on jest całkowicie wkurzający i dlatego *trzeba* dążyć ostatecznie do jego przekroczenia. Czy uładzenie tytułu nie byłoby kolejnym ustępstwem wobec władzy neoliberalizmu? Z początku martwiłem się, jak taki tytuł może wpłynąć na moją reputację. Czy nie przekreśli on przyszłych awansów oraz ofert pracy, gdybym zechciał skorzystać z mobilności przysługującej akademikowi—zarówno tej związanej ze statusem społecznym, jak i geograficznej? Odczuwałem to jako osobistą porażkę polegającą na poddaniu się neo- liberalnemu dyscyplinowaniu. Jebać to.

Czułem się również tak, jakbym przyznawał, że nie istnieje żadna potoczna odpowiedź, która byłaby odpo- wiednią kontrą wobec dyskursu neoliberalnego. Tak jak- byśmy w celu osłabienia jego gmachu mogli posługiwać się jedynie akademickim językiem złożonych, geogra- ficznych teorii na temat wielorakości, hybrydyczności i mutacji. Wydawało się to osłabiające i choć sam przyczy- niłem się do artykulacji niektórych z tych teorii[3], to często mam poczucie, że tak określone ramy są szkodliwe z punktu widzenia argumentu, który naprawdę chcę przed- stawić. Uważam, że polityka odmowy musi ulokować się właśnie w tym, co codzienne, przeciętne, najzwyklejsze i prozaiczne. Tym samym zdecydowałem się na tytuł „jebać neoliberalizm", bo myślę, że oddaje istotę tego, co właści- wie chcę powiedzieć. Argument, który chcę zaprezento- wać jest jednak odrobinę bardziej zniuansowany niż owa motywacja, z tego względu ostatnimi czasy myślałem nad słowem „jebać" („*fuck*") więcej niż w jakimkolwiek innym okresie swojego życia. Cóż za fantastycznie wielobarwne słowo! Funkcjonuje jako rzeczownik lub czasownik, a w formie przymiotnika używane jest prawdopodobnie jako najczęstszy wykrzyknik w języku angielskim. Może wyrazić gniew, pogardę, irytację, obojętność, zaskoczenie, niecierpliwość albo być nic nieznaczącą formą emfazy— tylko dlatego, że samo nawija się na język. Możesz „coś zjebać lub rozjebać", „kogoś jebać lub ujebać", „mieć na coś wyjebane" i z pewnością jest pewien geograficzny sens tego słowa, gdy tylko ktoś każe ci „pójść się jebać". W tym momencie możesz nawet zadawać sobie pytanie „ja jebię, kogo to obchodzi?". Cóż, mnie i jeżeli jesteś zainteresowany skończeniem z neoliberalizmem, to powinno to obchodzić i ciebie. Ogromne możliwości, które daje nam to słowo, tworzą potencjalne wyzwanie dla neoliberalizmu. By dokopać się do nich i je odkryć, musimy docenić niuanse tego, co może kryć za sobą fraza „jebać neoliberalizm". Jednocześnie jednak jebać niuanse. Jak ostatnio argumentował Kieran Healy[4] niuans „z reguły blokuje rozwój teorii, która jest intelektualnie interesująca, generuje materiał empiryczny lub jest skuteczna praktycznie". Więc bez fetyszyzowania niuansów spróbujmy szybko przejść przez to, co uważam za nasz priorytet w rozjebywaniu neoliberalizmu.

Pierwsze znaczenie jest prawdopodobnie najbardziej oczywiste. Przez stwierdzenie „jebać neoliberalizm" możemy wyrazić naszą wściekłość przeciwko neoliberalnej maszynie. To oznaka naszego gniewu, naszego pragnienia wykrzyczenia resentymentu, wyplucia z powrotem jadu prosto w twarz cholerstwa, które nam wszystkim pokazano. Może się to zamanifestować poprzez większą liczbę protestów przeciwko neoliberalizmowi albo więcej artykułów i książek, które krytykowałyby jego wpływ. Ta ostatnia opcja przemawia do już przekonanych, ta pierwsza liczy na to, że ci spaczeni przez neoliberalizm zmienią swoje podejście. Nie twierdzę, że te metody nie są ważną taktyką w naszym oporze, ale jestem również całkiem pewny, że nigdy nie będą wystarczające, by przechylić szalę zwycięstwa na naszą korzyść. W wielkich publicznych gestach buntu staramy się wciągnąć do dyskusji potężnych aktorów, mylnie sądząc, że mogą oni w ogóle słuchać i zaczną przyjmować ludową odmowę[5]. Czy to nie my powinniśmy raczej mówić? Tu pojawia się drugie znaczenie słów „jebać neoliberalizm", które odnajdujemy w pojęciu odmowy. Polegałoby na opowiedzeniu się za końcem neoliberalizmu (jakim go znaliśmy) w stylu prezentowanym przez J.K. Gibson-Graham[6], czyli po prostu zaprzestaniu mówienia o nim. Akademicy w szczególności winni zaprzestać traktowania go jako priorytetowego celu swych badań. Może nie całkowicie o nim zapomnieć, czy w ogóle zignorować neoliberalizm, co byłoby—jak już zauważyłem—problematyczne, ale zabrać się do pisania o innych rzeczach. Powtórzę to jeszcze raz—to kluczowy, niezwykle ważny punkt, który pozwala kontaktować się osobom próbującym pracować poza neoliberalnym światopoglądem. I w tym nie jestem jednak całkowicie przekonany czy to wystarczy. Jak argumentuje Mark Purcell[7]: „Musimy odwrócić się od neoliberalizmu i zwrócić ku nam samym, rozpocząć trudną, ale i radosną pracę zajmowania się własnymi sprawami dla samych siebie". Podczas gdy negacja, protest i krytyka są niezbędne, musimy również zastanowić się nad aktywnym rozjebywaniem neoliberalizmu poprzez robienie rzeczy wykraczających poza jego zasięg.

Akcja bezpośrednia poza neoliberalizmem odnosi się do polityki prefiguratywnej[8], która jest trzecim i najważniejszym znaczeniem, nad którym powinniśmy się moim zdaniem skupiać, gdy przywołujemy ideę „jebania neoliberalizmu". Prefigurować znaczy odrzucać centryzm, hierarchię i autorytet, które otrzymujemy w zestawie z polityką reprezentatywną. Odrzucać poprzez podkreślanie ucieleśnionych praktyk realizujących horyzontalne relacje i formy organizacji, które już teraz odzwierciedlają przyszłe społeczeństwo, do którego zmierzamy[9]. Poza

„skończeniem z paplaniną" prefiguracja i akcja bezpośrednia przekonują, że nigdy nie było potrzeby dyskutowania
co do tego, że cokolwiek chcemy zrobić. Możemy zrobić
to sami. Zwrócono bowiem uwagę na to, jakimi sposobami neoliberalizm jest w stanie pochwycić i zawłasz-
czyć wszelkie polityczne dyskursy i imperatywy[10]. Dla
krytyków takich jak David Harvey[11] tylko kolejna dawka
państwa jest w stanie rozwiązać problem neoliberalizmu.
Autor ten jednocześnie z łatwością odrzuca niehierar-
chiczną organizację i horyzontalną politykę, traktując je
jako wodę na młyn neoliberalnej przyszłości. Jednak w
swym pesymizmie Harvey zupełnie błędnie rozumie politykę prefiguratywną, która nie jest środkiem do celu, ale
jedynie do przyszłych środków[12]. Innymi słowy, w politykę
prefiguratywną wbudowana jest stała i ciągła czujność
jako zabezpieczenie przed przechwyceniem rzeczywistej
praktyki prefiguracji. Praktyka ta jest refleksyjna i uważna,
ale przede wszystkim zawsze ze wzrokiem zwróconym
ku produkcji, wynalazczości i twórczości rozumianymi
jako spełnienie pragnień wspólnoty. W ten sposób polityka prefiguratywna jest wyraźnie antyneoliberalna. Jest
przejęciem środków jako naszych środków, środków bez
celu. Prefigurować to cieszyć się towarzyskością i rado-
ścią, które przychodzą wraz z byciem razem pośród rady-
kalnie równych, nie przedstawicieli awangardy i proleta-
riatu na drodze ku transcendentnej pustej obietnicy utopii
albo „nie-miejsca", ale jako ugruntowanej immanencji tu i
teraz, rzeczywistego tworzenia nowego świata „w skoru-
pie starego", nieustannej ciężkiej pracy oraz odnajdywa-
nia wymaganego przez nią potwierdzenia[13].

W neoliberalizmie nie ma nic, co zasługuje na nasz
szacunek i tym samym nie ma nic, co byłoby w zgodzie z
prefiguratywną polityką tworzenia. Moje przesłanie brzmi
w tym kontekście po prostu: „jebać go". Jebać to, jak ogra-
nicza nasze wyobraźnie polityczne. Jebać przemoc, którą

rodzi. Jebać nierówności, które podnosi on do rangi cnoty. Jebać to, jak pustoszy środowisko. Jebać niekończący się cykl akumulacji i kult wzrostu. Jebać stowarzyszenie Mont Pelerin i wszystkie think-tanki, które wciąż go wspomagają i lansują. Jebać Friedricha Hayeka i Miltona Friedmana za obarczanie nas swoimi ideami. Jebać Tchatcherki, Reaganów, wszystkich tchórzliwych, zainteresowanych własnym dobrem polityków, którzy dążą tylko do zaspokojenia swojej zachłanności. Jebać oparte na sianym przez niego strachu wykluczanie, które postrzega „innych" jako godnych czyszczenia naszych toalet i mycia podłóg, ale nie jako członków naszych społeczności. Jebać coraz dalej idący ruch ku parametryzacji i niedocenianie tego, że nie wszystko, co się liczy, da się policzyć. Jebać absolutnie wszystko, za czym opowiada się neoliberalizm i jebać konia trojańskiego, na którym wjechał! Zbyt długo wmawiano nam, że „nie ma alternatywy", że „wznosząca fala podnosi wszystkie łodzie", że żyjemy w świecie darwinowskiego koszmaru walki wszystkich ze wszystkimi, „przetrwania najsilniejszych". Bez zastrzeżeń połknęliśmy (aż po wędkę) haczyk „tragedii dóbr wspólnych", podczas gdy w rzeczywistości jest to podstęp, który odzwierciedla „tragedię kapitalizmu" wraz z jej niekończącymi się grabieżczymi wojnami[14]. Pięta Achillesowa artykułu Garretta Hardina[15] brała się stąd, że jego autor nigdy nie zatrzymał się, aby pomyśleć o tym, że to bydło z pastwisk było już na starcie własnością prywatną. Co możemy osiągnąć, gdy ponownie potraktujemy rzeczywiste dobra wspólne jako *dobra wspólne* niezakładające własności prywatnej[16]? Co możemy osiągnąć, gdy zaczniemy ściślej przyglądać się prefiguracji alternatyw, które już się dzieją i wybierzemy te doświadczenia jako najważniejsze formy organizacji[17]? Co może się zdarzyć, gdy zamiast połykania gorzkiej pigułki konkurencji i merytokracji skupimy naszą energię nie na medykalizacji nas samych podług neoliberalnych zaleceń, lecz na głębszym uzdrowieniu, które przychodzi wraz z kooperacją i pomocą wzajemną[18]?

Jamie Peck[19] nazwał kiedyś słowo „neoliberalizm" radykalnym sloganem politycznym, ale tkwienie w domenie krytyki to dzisiaj za mało. Wiele lat minęło odkąd pierwszy raz wskazaliśmy wroga i od tego czasu dobrze go poznaliśmy poprzez nasze protesty i teksty. Ale nawet gdy jesteśmy pewni jego porażki, jak podczas kryzysu finansowego z 2008 roku i następującego po nim ruchu Occupy, to on wciąż łapie oddech i powraca do życia w silniejszej, przypominającej zombie formie[20]. Japhy Wilson[21] nazywa tę trwającą władzę „neoliberalnym gotykiem" i jestem przekonany, że by przekroczyć ten horror show, musimy przesunąć naszą politykę w sferę działania[22]. Co gdyby „jebać neoliberalizm" stało się mantrą dla nowego rodzaju polityki? Mobilizującą frazą, która nie zwracałaby się tylko do działania, ale również do odzyskania naszego życia w przestrzeniach i chwilach, w których aktywnie je przeżywamy? Co jeżeli za każdym razem podczas użycia tej frazy zdawalibyśmy sobie sprawę, że oznacza ona wezwanie do aktu samostanowienia, który wychodziłby poza zwykłe słowa, łącząc teorię i praktykę w piękną praxis prefiguracji? W naszym odrzuceniu neoliberalizmu musimy przyjąć wielowymiarową postawę. Choć nie możemy całkowicie go zignorować czy o nim zapomnieć, to możemy aktywnie działać przeciwko niemu, drogami, które idą dalej niż działanie retoryczne i retoryka działania. Wystąpmy z nowym radykalnym sloganem politycznym, używając do tego wszystkich dostępnych nam środków. Użyjmy hashtagu (#fuckneoliberalism, #jebaćneoliberalizm) i rozsiejmy po Internecie naszą pogardę. Musimy jednak zrobić więcej, niż tylko wyrazić nasz gniew. Musimy wcielić w życie nadzieję jako immanencję naszego ucieleśnionego doświadczenia *tu* i *teraz*[23]. Musimy odnowić świat sami; to proces, którego nie można odkładać na później.

Z własnej woli łudziliśmy się i osłabialiśmy samych siebie poprzez ciągłe odwoływanie się do *status quo* politycznej reprezentacji. Nasza ślepa wiara prowadzi do nieskończonego wyczekiwania, aż zbawca spadnie nam z nieba. System udowodnił, że jest na wskroś skorumpowany i z czasem wszyscy nasi wspaniali kandydaci polityczni okazują się porażką. W czasach neoliberalizmu nie jest to jednak wyłącznie kwestia problematycznych jednostek u władzy. To raczej nasza własna wiara w sam system stanowi sedno problemu. Tworzymy warunki instytucjonalne, w których swobodnie zaczyna występować „efekt Lucyfera"[24]. „Banalność zła" polega na tym, że ci politycy po prostu wykonują swoją pracę w systemie, który wynagradza zwyrodnienie władzy, ponieważ wszystko jest zaprojektowane tak, by służyć prawom kapitalizmu[25]. Ale my nie musimy być posłuszni. Nie jesteśmy nic dłużni temu porządkowi. Poprzez akcję bezpośrednią i organizację alternatyw możemy postawić w stan oskarżenia całą strukturę i przerwać błędne koło nadużyć. Kiedy cały polityczny system wywodzi się z kapitalizmu i jest przez niego zdefiniowany oraz uwarunkowany, to nigdy nie może reprezentować naszych sposobów poznania i bycia w świecie. Musimy zatem objąć kontrolę nad tymi sposobami życia i odzyskać naszą zbiorową sprawczość. Musimy zacząć być aktywne w naszej polityce i zacząć doceniać bardziej relacyjny sens solidarności, w którym zawiera się to, iż podporządkowanie oraz cierpienie jednego wskazuje jednocześnie na opresję wszystkich[26]. Możemy rozpocząć życie z myślą o innych możliwych światach poprzez odnowione zaangażowanie w praktyki pomocy wzajemnej, wspólnotowości, wzajemności i niehierarchicznych form organizacji, które odnawiają demokrację w jej etymologicznym sensie *władzy w rękach ludzi*. Koniec końców neoliberalizm jest wybitnie obrzydliwą ideą, której towarzyszy cała gama prostackich założeń i

wulgarnych skutków. Zasługuje na to, aby w odpowie-
dzi na to spotkać się z równie obraźliwym językiem i
działaniem. Nasza wspólnota, nasza kooperacja i nasza
wzajemna troska są dla neoliberalizmu czymś odrażają-
cym. Nienawidzi on tego, co my celebrujemy. Gdy więc
mówimy „jebać neoliberalizm", niech znaczy to więcej niż
tylko słowa, niech będzie materializacją naszego wzajem-
nego zaangażowania. Powiedzcie to głośno, powiedzcie to
ze mną i powiedzcie to każdemu, kto posłucha, ale przede
wszystkim wyrażajcie to jako wezwanie do działania i jako
ucieleśnienie naszej prefiguratywnej siły, by zmienić ten
jebany świat. *Jebać neoliberalizm!*

Foda-se o neoliberalismo

Translated by Eduardo Tomazine

Translator's Commentary

When Simon asked me to translate "Fuck Neoliberalism" into Portuguese, he told me I had the option to remain anonymous. I initially considered anonymity absolutely unnecessary in this case, but readily acknowledge that my lack of concern about the consequences of translating such a manifesto is related to the fact that academic careers in Brazil are generally pursued at public universities, which (still. . .) provide a high degree of stability and intellectual freedom to their professors. I think it is a simple but interesting example of the relationship between institutional conditions and personal autonomy for intellectual work.

Foda-se o neoliberalismo

Foda-se o neoliberalismo. Essa é minha mensagem contundente. Eu poderia terminar por aqui minha controvérsia e isso não teria a menor importância. Minha posição é clara e você provavelmente já captou o fundamental do que tenho a dizer. Não tenho mais nada de positivo a acrescentar à discussão sobre o neoliberalismo e, para ser bem honesto, estou me sentindo mal por ter que pensar sobre esse assunto. Para mim já deu. Durante algum tempo, cheguei a considerar dar outro título a esse artigo, algo como "Esqueça o neoliberalismo", pois, de certo modo, era exatamente isso o que eu queria fazer. Venho escrevendo sobre esse assunto há muitos anos[1] e cheguei a um ponto em que simplesmente não queria mais gastar nenhuma energia nessa empreitada, por receio de que continuar trabalhando com essa ideia serviria apenas para perpetuar a sua força. Numa outra reflexão eu também reconheço que, enquanto manobra política, é potencialmente perigoso simplesmente enterrarmos nossas cabeças na areia e coletivamente ignorar um fenômeno que tem tido efeitos tão devastadores e debilitadores sobre o nosso mundo compartilhado. Há um crescente poder no neoliberalismo que não pode ser negado e tampouco estou convencido de que a estratégia de ignorá-lo seja efetivamente a maneira correta de encarar o problema[2]. Daí eu pensei "bom, então que se foda", e embora um nome mais discreto e polido para esse artigo pudesse atenuar a potencial ofensa causada pelo título que escolhi, voltei atrás logo em seguida e decidi mantê-lo. Ora, por que razão deveríamos nos preocupar mais com malcriações do que com o discurso em si mesmo sórdido do neoliberalismo? Decidi que eu queria transgredir, incomodar, insultar, justamente porque nós *somos obrigados* a ser insultados pelo neoliberalismo; ele *é* completamente perturbador, e por isso nós deveríamos buscar transgredi-lo custe o que custar. Afinal, pegar leve no título não significaria fazer mais uma concessão ao poder do neoliberalismo? Fiquei preocupado, a princípio, com as consequências de um título como esse para a minha reputação. Isso não atrapalharia futuras promoções ou ofertas de trabalho se eu quiser manter minha mobilidade enquanto acadêmico, tanto para subir na carreira quanto para lecionar em outras universidades? Isso me soou como conceder uma derrota pessoal à disciplina neoliberal. Que se foda.

Parecia também como se eu estivesse admitindo não existirem respostas coloquiais que pudessem ser dadas de maneira apropriada para fazer frente ao discurso do neoliberalismo. Como se pudéssemos tão somente responder de uma forma acadêmica, empregando complexas teorias geográficas de diversificação, hibridismo e mutação para solapar o seu edifício intelectual. Isso me pareceu desempoderamento, e embora eu mesmo tenha contribuído para articular algumas dessas teorias[3], sinto frequentemente que esta forma de abordagem vai na contramão do tipo de argumentação que eu de fato quero fazer. Pois é justamente no cotidiano, no ordinário, no comum e no mundano onde eu penso que uma política de recusa deve estar localizada. E por isso eu mantive o *"Foda-se o neoliberalismo"*, pois acho que isso converge com aquilo que eu realmente quero dizer. O argumento que desejo apresentar é ligeiramente mais nuançado que isso, o que me levou a pensar mais detidamente sobre o termo "foda-se" do que eu provavelmente já fiz em qualquer outro momento da minha vida. Mas que palavra fantasticamente colorida! A palavra *"Fuck"* funciona como substantivo ou como verbo, e como adjetivo ela talvez seja o ponto de exclamação mais usado na língua inglesa. Ela pode ser empregue para expressar raiva, desprezo, pesar, indiferença, surpresa, impaciência, ou ainda como ênfase sem um sentido preciso, pois ela simplesmente escorrega da língua. Você pode "foder com alguma coisa", "botar pra foder", "foder com alguém", "estar pouco se fodendo", e há também um ponto de referência decididamente geográfico para a palavra, na medida em que você pode ser instruído a "ir se foder".* Neste ponto da argumentação você deve estar pensando "tudo bem, mas quem se importa?" (*who gives a fuck?*). Bem, eu me importo, e se você pretende acabar com o neoliberalismo, então não

---

* No original, em inglês: *"Fuck something up," "fuck someone over," "fuck around," "not give a fuck"* e *"go fuck yourself."*

deveria estar se fodendo para isso. As poderosas capacidades que a palavra traz representam um desafio potencial para o neoliberalismo. Para aprofundar e desatar essas habilidades é preciso prestar atenção às nuances do significado que poderiam estar contidas na frase "foda-se o neoliberalismo". Por outro lado, foda-se a nuance. Como sustentado recentemente por Kieran Healy[4], a nuance "normalmente obstrui o desenvolvimento de uma teoria intelectualmente interessante, empiricamente profícua ou bem-sucedida na prática." Portanto, sem fetichizar as nuances, passemos logo para a análise daquilo que eu acho que deveríamos priorizar ao foder com o neoliberalismo.

O primeiro sentido é provavelmente o mais óbvio. Ao dizer "foda-se o neoliberalismo", podemos expressar nossa revolta contra a máquina neoliberal. É uma demonstração da nossa raiva, o desejo de gritar nosso ressentimento, de vomitar o veneno na cara da maldade que tem sido apresentada a todos nós. Isso pode ser feito mobilizando mais protestos contra o neoliberalismo ou escrevendo mais artigos e livros que critiquem a sua influência. No entanto, este último recurso equivale a pregar para os convertidos, e o primeiro espera que os já pervertidos estarão dispostos a mudar suas atitudes. Não nego que esses métodos sejam táticas importantes para a nossa resistência, mas eu também tenho plena convicção de que eles jamais serão de fato suficientes para fazer virar a maré contra o neoliberalismo e a nosso favor. Ao realizar grandes demonstrações de rebeldia, procuramos dialogar com atores poderosos, acreditando equivocadamente que eles podem escutar e começar a acomodar as vozes populares de recusa[5]. Não deveríamos, ao invés disso, dar esse assunto por encerrado? É aqui que aparece o segundo sentido de "foda-se o neoliberalismo", sentido que se encontra na noção de rejeição. Isto significaria reivindicar o fim do neoliberalismo (como o conhecíamos) da maneira como proposta por J.K. Gibson-Graham[6], simplesmente parando de falar sobre ele. Os acadêmicos, em particular, deixariam de priorizar este assunto em seus estudos. Talvez sem esquecê-lo de todo ou ignorar completamente o neoliberalismo, postura que eu já identifiquei como problemática, mas, ao invés disso, passaríamos a dedicar nossos escritos a outros assuntos. Mais uma vez, este é um ponto de contato crucial para nós, tão logo comecemos a trabalhar para além da visão de mundo neoliberal, embora eu tampouco esteja inteiramente convencido de que isto seja suficiente. Segundo Mark Purcell[7], "Precisamos dar as costas ao neoliberalismo e nos voltar para nós mesmos, para iniciar o árduo—mas também prazeroso—trabalho de administrar os nossos assuntos por nossa própria conta". Mesmo que a negação, o protesto e a crítica sejam necessários, é preciso pensar também a respeito de foder com o neoliberalismo fazendo as coisas por fora do seu alcance.

A ação direta para além do neoliberalismo dialoga com uma política prefigurativa[8], que é o terceiro e mais importante sentido daquilo que eu acho que deveríamos focalizar quando evocamos a ideia de "foda-se o neoliberalismo". Prefigurar é rejeitar o centrismo, a hierarquia e a autoridade que vêm a reboque da política representativa, enfatizando as práticas que encarnam relações horizontais e formas de organização que se esforçam para refletir a sociedade futura que se está procurando[9]. Para além de "encerrar o assunto", a prefiguração e a ação direta sustentam nunca ter existido um diálogo a ser estabelecido, reconhecendo que independentemente do que queiramos fazer, só podemos fazê-lo nós mesmos. Apesar disso, tem-se dado muita importância sobre os modos como o neoliberalismo é capaz de capturar e se apropriar de todas as formas de discurso político e reivindicações[10]. Para críticos como David Harvey[11], somente uma nova dose de

Estado pode resolver a questão neoliberal, apressando-se em rechaçar as formas de organização não-hierárquicas e as políticas horizontais, pois elas supostamente pavimentariam o caminho para um certeiro futuro neoliberal. Com esse pessimismo, Harvey interpreta de forma completamente equivocada as políticas prefigurativas, que são meios não para um fim, mas apenas para meios futuros[12]. Em outras palavras, já existe uma vigilância constante e continuada no âmbito das políticas prefigurativas, de maneira que a atual prática prefigurativa não pode ser cooptada. Ela é reflexiva e vigilante, mas sempre com uma orientação para a produção, invenção e criação enquanto satisfação do desejo de comunidade. Nesse sentido, as políticas prefigurativas são explicitamente antineoliberais. Elas se apropriam dos meios enquanto *nossos* meios, um meio sem fim. Prefigurar é abraçar a convivialidade e a alegria que advêm do fato de estarmos juntos em igualdade radical, não como vanguardas e proletariado em direção à promessa transcendental e vazia da utopia, ou "*não-lugar*", mas na imanência alicerçada na construção, aqui e agora, do novo mundo "na carapaça do velho" e no incessante trabalho duro e confirmação que essa tarefa exige[13].

Não há nada sobre o neoliberalismo que mereça o nosso respeito, e então, coerentemente com uma política prefigurativa de criação, minha mensagem é pura e simplesmente "foda-se". Que se foda a atração que ele exerce sobre os nossos imaginários políticos. Foda-se a violência que ele engendra. Foda-se a desigualdade que ele exalta como uma virtude. Foda-se o modo como ele tem devastado o meio ambiente. Foda-se o ciclo interminável de acumulação e o culto ao crescimento. Foda-se a Sociedade Mont Pelerin e todos os *think tanks* que continuam a apoiá-lo e promovê-lo. Que se fodam Friedrich Hayek e Milton Friedman por nos fazerem "pagar o almoço" dos ricos com suas ideias. Que se fodam as Thatchers, os Reagans e todos os políticos covardes e egoístas que buscam apenas seu próprio favorecimento. Foda-se a medonha exclusão que enxerga os "outros" como dignos para limpar os nossos banheiros e enxugar nosso chão, mas não para serem membros de nossas comunidades. Foda-se o movimento cada vez mais intenso em direção à estatística e ao fracasso em compreender que nem tudo o que conta pode ser contado. Foda-se o desejo de lucro acima das necessidades da comunidade. Foda-se tudo o que o neoliberalismo representa e foda-se o cavalo de Tróia que ele representa! Por muito tempo nos disseram que "não há alternativa", que "quando a maré sobe, levanta todos os barcos", que vivemos num pesadelo de mundo darwiniano de todos contra todos, em que apenas "os mais aptos sobrevivem". Fomos fisgados pela ideia da "tragédia dos comuns", quando na verdade isto é um estratagema que reflete a "tragédia do capitalismo" e sua infindável guerra de pilhagem[14]. O calcanhar de Aquiles de Garrett Hardin[15] reside no fato dele nunca ter parado para pensar sobre como o pasto do gado já havia sido privadamente apropriado. Mas o que pode acontecer se reunirmos os comuns enquanto *comuns*, sem a pressuposição da apropriação privada[16]? O que pode acontecer quando começarmos a prestar mais atenção na prefiguração de alternativas que já estão em curso e privilegiar essas experiências como sendo as formas de organização mais relevantes[17]? O que pode acontecer se, em vez de tomarmos as pílulas amargas da competição e do mérito, concentrássemos nossas energias não em nos prescrever os remédios neoliberais, mas na cura mais profunda que advém da cooperação e do apoio mútuo[18]?

Jamie Peck[19] certa vez chamou o neoliberalismo de "slogan político radical", mas isto já não é mais suficiente para esposar o domínio da crítica. Muitos anos transcorreram desde que identificamos pela primeira vez o inimigo, e a partir de então passamos a conhecê-lo melhor em função de nossos escritos e protestos. Mas mesmo quando estamos convencidos da sua derrota, como durante o rescaldo da crise financeira de 2008 e o subsequente movimento Occupy, o neoliberalismo segue respirando e se recompõe sob uma forma zumbi ainda mais poderosa[20]. Japhy Wilson[21] classifica esse processo em curso como o "gótico neoliberal", e estou convencido de que, para superar seu show de horrores, temos que voltar nossa política para o domínio do *enativo*[22]. E se acaso o "foda-se o neoliberalismo" se tornasse um mantra para um novo tipo de política? Um lema que não chamasse apenas à ação, mas à afirmação das nossas vidas nos espaços e momentos nos quais vivemos ativamente? E se todas as vezes que usássemos essa frase, reconhecêssemos que ela significa um apelo à ação enativa, que vai para além de meras palavras, combinando teoria e prática na bela práxis prefigurativa? Devemos adotar uma abordagem plural em nossa rejeição ao neoliberalismo. Enquanto não pudermos ignorá-lo ou esquecê-lo completamente, podemos trabalhar ativamente contra ele empregando expedientes que vão para além da performance da retórica e da retórica da performance. Sigamos adiante com um novo *slogam* político, valendo-nos de todos os meios disponíveis. Use um *hashtag* (*#fuckneoliberalism*) e faça com que o nosso desprezo viralize. Mas temos que fazer mais do que expressar nossa indignação. Temos que agir (*enact*) com determinação e entender que nossa esperança é imanente às nossas experiências incorporadas no *aqui* e *agora*[23]. Precisamos refazer o mundo com as nossas próprias mãos, um processo que não pode ser adiado.

Temos intencionalmente nos desiludido e desempoderado ao mantermos nossas esperanças no arranjo político representativo que está aí. Nossa fé cega nos faz esperar o tempo todo por um salvador que virá do céu. Mas o sistema demonstrou ser completamente corrupto, com nossos grandes candidatos provando ser, um após o outro, uma frustração. Nesses tempos de neoliberalismo a questão não se limita meramente a indivíduos problemáticos ocuparem o poder. Ao contrário, o cerne do problema está na nossa crença no sistema em si. Produzimos e legitimamos as condições institucionais para que o "efeito Lúcifer"—em que as pessoas boas se tornam más em circunstâncias dadas—aconteça[24]. É a "banalidade do mal"[25], que faz com que esses políticos apenas executem os seus trabalhos em um sistema que recompensa a perversão do poder, pois ele é moldado em seus mínimos detalhes para servir às leis do capitalismo. Mas não devemos obediência a ele. Não estamos em dívida para com esta ordem. Por meio da ação direta e da organização de alternativas, podemos condenar toda a estrutura e romper com o ciclo vicioso de abusos. Quando o sistema político é definido, condicionado, atado e produzido pelo capitalismo, ele jamais pode representar nossas formas de conhecer e de estar no mundo, e por isso precisamos assumir a responsabilidade desses modos de vida e afirmar nossa ação coletiva. Precisamos começar a ser enativos em nossas políticas e a assumir um sentido mais relacional de solidariedade, capaz de reconhecer que a submissão e o sofrimento de um é, na realidade, um sinal da opressão de todos[26]. Podemos começar a viver em outros mundos possíveis através de um engajamento renovado pela prática do apoio mútuo, camaradagem, reciprocidade e formas não-hierárquicas de organização que façam renascer a democracia no seu sentido etimológico de *poder* para o *povo*. O neoliberalismo é, em última instância, uma ideia particularmente idiota, impregnada de conclusões vulgares e pressuposições grosseiras. Em resposta, ele merece ser confrontado com linguagem e ação igualmente ofensivas. Nossa comunidade, nossa cooperação e cuidado uns com os outros são repugnantes ao neoliberalismo. Ele odeia aquilo que celebramos. Portanto, quando dissermos "foda-se o neoliberalismo", que isso represente mais do que palavras. Façamos com que seja uma enação (colocar em cena, ação no lugar de palavras) do nosso compromisso uns para com os outros. Diga alto, diga comigo, e diga para qualquer um que escute; mas que isso represente, acima de tudo, um rufar de tambores convocando para a ação e a encarnação do nosso poder prefigurativo para mudar esse mundo fodido. *Foda-se o neoliberalismo!*

Nasrať na neoliberalizmus

Translated by Patrik Gažo

Translator's Commentary

In general, it is really interesting and enriching (for me as a PhD student) to cooperate on this project. It could be the political risk. However, it is only a small part of the risky political and academic actions that I have taken part in, so I am okay with it. I also took it as an opportunity to learn something new as a reader, editor, and translator. Slovakia (and the Czech Republic) is a post-"socialist" country, so it is always a bit tricky to criticize the neoliberal or capitalist approach that this country adopted after the 1989 Velvet Revolution. If you disagree with the current state of affairs, you are instantly marked as a proponent of the old totalitarian State Socialist regime and/or as a proponent of Russia. We still live with a Cold War logic to some extent. In Slovakia, we don't have "real" left parties in the government, even though for the last decade the governing party has been a social democratic party called SMER.* In reality, it is made up of little more than corrupt nationalists and servants of global capital who resemble every other politician. Today, everyone hates them, and so the public hates "the left," because they think this is what leftists are. We are still far from

---

* Smer—sociálna demokracia (Direction—Social Democracy), governed 2012–2020, losing the February 29, 2020 election.

engaging the general public in debates about neoliberal-ism and its impact.

I am not sure that this is not simply an opportunity to skip or avoid debates about neoliberalism and forget it before it even enters into general discourse. The word *neoliberalism* is often used out of fear of talking about capitalism itself. This could (and in many cases does) weaken the criticism of capitalism. By talking about neo-liberalism, we confirm for liberals the idea that there is a "bad" capitalism (neoliberalism) and a "good" capital-ism (Nordic model, welfare state, etc.). When we talk about neoliberalism, it is easy to miss the point that the problem is the logic of accumulation of capital and not fewer or more state interventions. I think that the radical left should stick with the term *capitalism*. However, I am not convinced that is possible in my cultural context.

In the original text, Simon works with the word "fuck," which in English comes in several verbal forms and is unaltered despite its intended meaning. In Slovak, however, this is not possible, and, therefore, if we want to create a similar effect, we have to change the word-forming basis in a number of ways, for example, by means of prefixes and suffixes. In practice, it would seem that while the word "fuck" in English can act as a noun, verb, or conjugation, we would have to create several variations for the word in Slovak. We have several options for translation of the word "fuck," so I used the word "srať," which means something like "shit." It is not the most vulgar word that could be used, but it still delivers the original meaning. It was hard to translate a few parts of this essay. I got help from a friend of mine who is a professional translator. I just hope that this translation will help those at universities in Slovakia and Czechia who are not particularly fluent in English.

It is definitely true that some of the translator's voice is in the final text!

Nasrať na neoliberalizmus

Nasrať na neoliberalizmus. To je moje priamočiare posolstvo. Tu by som pravdepodobne mohol ukončiť diskusiu a bolo by to úplne jedno. Moja pozícia je jasná a pravdepodobne už chápete podstatu toho, čo chcem povedať. Neexistuje nič pozitívne, čo by som dodal k diskusii o neoliberalizme, a aby som bol načisto úprimný, už som dosť chorý z toho, že nad tým musím neustále premýšľať. Jednoducho mám už toho dosť. Chvíľu som zvažoval nazvať tento článok „Zabudnite na neoliberalizmus" („Forget Neoliberalism"), pretože istým spôsobom je to presne to, čo som chcel urobiť. Písal som o tejto téme veľa rokov[1] a prišiel som do bodu, keď som jednoducho už nechcel vložiť viac energie do tohto úsilia. Obával som sa, že už moje samotné zaoberanie sa touto tematikou potvrdí daný koncept. Po ďalšom premýšľaní však tiež uznávam, že ako politický manéver je potenciálne dosť nebezpečné jednoducho strčiť hlavu do piesku a kolektívne ignorovať fenomén, ktorý mal také ničivé a oslabujúce účinky na náš spoločný svet. Pretrvávajúcu moc neoliberalizmu len ťažko poprieť a nie som presvedčený, že stratégia ignorácie je v skutočnosti tým správnym prístupom[2]. A tak som si pomyslel: „Dobre teda, srať na to." A hoci slušnejší a jemnejší názov tohto článku by mohol zmierniť možné rozhorčenie, rozhodol som sa prehodnotiť svoje rozhodnutie. Prečo by sme sa mali viac obávať používania nadávok, ako skutočne odporného diskurzu samotného neoliberalizmu? Rozhodol som sa, že chcem prekročiť medze, rozrušiť a uraziť práve preto, lebo by sme mali byť neoliberalizmom urazení. Pretože *je* maximálne znepokojujúci, a tak by sme sa *mali* pokúsiť konečne ho prekonať. Nebolo by zjemnenie názvu ďalším ústupkom sile neoliberalizmu? Spočiatku som sa obával, čo by mohol takýto názov znamenať pre moju povesť. Bolo by to prekážkou pre moje budúce povýšenie alebo pracovné ponuky, ak by som si chcel udržať svoju mobilitu ako akademik, či už smerom nahor alebo na nové miesto? Pociťoval som to ako priznanie osobnej porážky voči neoliberálnej disciplíne. Srať na to.

Mal som tiež pocit akoby som pripúšťal, že v bežnej reči neexistuje žiadna odpoveď, ktorá by mohla byť vhodnou reakciou na diskusiu ohľadom neoliberalizmu. Akoby sme ho mohli oslabiť len tým, že naň budeme reagovať v akademickom formáte za použitia komplexných geografických teórií variácie, hybridizácie a mutácie. Demotivovalo ma to, a hoci som sám prispel k formulácii niektorých z týchto teórií[3], často mám pocit, že takéto rámcovanie je v skutočnosti v rozpore s tým, čo chcem povedať. Myslím si, že politika odmietnutia by mala byť prítomná v každodennom, bežnom, nenápadnom a obyčajnom svete. A tak som sa rozhodol pre názov „Nasrať na neoliberalizmus" („Fuck Neoliberalism"), pretože si myslím, že vyjadruje podstatu toho, čo chcem vlastne povedať. To, čo chcem vyjadriť, je však o niečo rozmanitejšie, čo ma viedlo k premýšľaniu o variáciách slova „nasrať" („fuck") v rozmere ako nikdy predtým v mojom živote. Aké úžasne rozmanité podoby môžeme vyčarovať zo základu tohto slova! Môžeme z neho vytvoriť podstatné mená aj ďalšie slovesá, veľmi často ho používame vo forme zvolania.[*] Dokážeme ním vyjadriť hnev, pohŕdanie, mrzutosť, ľahostajnosť, prekvapenie či netrpezlivosť, alebo ho použijeme len na zdôraznenie povedaného, bez konkrétneho

---

[*] Pozn. prekl.: Autor v texte originálu pracuje so slovom „fuck", ktoré sa v angličtine vyskytuje vo viacerých slovných druhoch v nezmenenej podobe. V slovenčine však takýto jav neexistuje, a preto ak chceme vytvoriť podobný efekt, musíme slovotvorný základ „srať" obmieňať viacerými spôsobmi, napríklad pomocou predpôn a prípon. V praxi by to vyzeralo tak, že kým slovo „fuck" v angličtine môže vystupovať ako podstatné meno, sloveso či zvolanie, v slovenčine by sme museli pre dané slovo vytvoriť viaceré variácie—napríklad „sračka" (podstatné meno), „osrať" (sloveso) či „Nasrať!" (zvolanie).

významu jednoducho preto, lebo nám svojvoľne vykĺzne z úst. Môžete „niečo posrať" („fuck something up"), „niekoho osrať" („fuck someone over"), „zasierať sa" („fuck around"), „srať na niečo" („not give a fuck"), a dokonca v tejto súvislosti existuje aj jednoznačný geografický bod, keď vám povedia, aby ste sa „išli posrať" („go fuck yourself"). V tejto chvíli ste si možno dokonca pomysleli: „Dobre, a koho to má srať?" („Who gives a fuck?") No, mňa to serie, a ak je vo vašom záujme skoncovať s neoliberalizmom, malo by aj vás. Silné významy, ktoré sa spájajú s týmto slovom, môžu pre neoliberalizmus predstavovať potenciálnu hrozbu. Aby sme porozumeli takýmto možnostiam a rozvinuli ich, potrebujeme chápať rôzne významové odtiene toho, čo by mohla znamenať fráza „nasrať na neoliberalizmus". No ale na druhej strane, nasrať na skryté významy! Ako nedávno vyhlásil Kieran Healy[4], „zvyčajne bránia vývoju intelektuálne zaujímavých, empiricky plodných alebo prakticky úspešných teórií". Takže poďme rýchlo a bez ďalšieho fetišizovania k tomu, čo by podľa mňa malo byť prioritou pri rozosieraní neoliberalizmu.

Prvý význam je možno ten najjednoznačnejší. Tým, že povieme „nasrať na neoliberalizmus", môžeme vyjadriť svoju zúrivosť voči neoliberálnej mašinérii. Je to znamenie nášho hnevu, našej túžby vykričať rozhorčenie, vypľuť jed späť do tváre odpornej nenávisti, ktorú voči nám všetkým prejavila. Môžeme to urobiť formou organizovania väčšieho počtu protestov proti neoliberalizmu alebo formou písania ďalších článkov a kníh kritizujúcich jeho vplyv. Pri prvom spôsobe apelujeme na tých zasvätených, pri druhom dúfame, že tí skazení budú ochotní sa zmeniť. Nepochybujem, že tieto metódy sú dôležitými taktikami nášho odporu, ale som si tiež celkom istý, že v skutočnosti nebudú nikdy stačiť na to, aby obrátili situáciu proti neoliberalizmu a v náš prospech. Pri veľkých verejných gestách vzdorovania sa snažíme do diskusie zapojiť silných aktérov, pričom mylne veríme, že by mohli počúvať a začať sa prispôsobovať odmietavému hlasu ľudu[5]. Nemali by sme však namiesto toho skončiť s diskusiami? Tu nachádzame druhý význam frázy „nasrať na neoliberalizmus", a to v zmysle jeho odmietnutia. Znamenalo by to hlásať koniec neoliberalizmu (ako sme ho doteraz poznali) spôsobom, ktorý priblížili autorky J.K. Gibson-Graham[6]. Podľa nich by sme o neoliberalizme jednoducho mali prestať hovoriť. Predovšetkým akademici by naň mali prestať klásť dôraz vo svojich výskumoch. Možno nie úplne naň zabudnúť alebo ho kompletne ignorovať (čo som už označil za problematické), ale namiesto toho písať o iných veciach. Aj toto je pre nás dôležitým východiskovým bodom k tomu, aby sme sa zbavili neoliberálneho pohľadu na svet. No ani v tomto prípade nie som úplne presvedčený, že to stačí. Ako tvrdí Mark Purcell[7]: „Potrebujeme sa odvrátiť od neoliberalizmu smerom k sebe samým, vydať sa na ťažkú, no zároveň radostnú cestu spravovania našich vlastných záležitostí." Zatiaľ čo odmietanie, protest a kritika neoliberalizmu sú nevyhnutné, musíme tiež premýšľať o tom, ako ho aktívne rozosierať tým, že budeme robiť veci mimo jeho dosah.

Priama akcia nad rámec neoliberalizmu apeluje na prefiguratívnu politiku[8]. Toto je tretím a najdôležitejším významom toho, na čo by sme sa mali zamerať, keď sa budeme odvolávať na myšlienku „nasrať na neoliberalizmus". Prefiguratívne akcie znamenajú odmietanie centrizmu, hierarchie a autority reprezentatívnej politiky. Namiesto toho by sme sa mali zamerať na ucelený postup, vďaka ktorému vytvoríme horizontálne vzťahy a organizačné formy odrážajúce budúcu podobu spoločnosti[9]. Okrem „skoncovania s diskusiou" sa však prefigurácia a priama akcia potýkajú s faktom, že vlastne ani nikdy nebolo o čom hovoriť. Hlásajú, že čokoľvek chceme urobiť, dokážeme to sami. Jednako sa ale značná pozornosť venovala aj spôsobom, akými neoliberalizmus dokáže zachytiť a privlastniť si všetky formy politického diskurzu a imperatívov[10]. Podľa kritikov ako David Harvey[11], neoliberálnu otázku môže vyriešiť iba ďalšia dávka štátnej moci. Rázne odmieta najmä nehierarchickú organizáciu a horizontálnu politiku, keďže tieto údajne nepochybne smerujú len k neoliberálnej budúcnosti. Pre svoj pesimizmus ale vôbec nepochopil prefiguratívnu politiku, ktorá nemá byť prostriedkom vedúcim k ukončeniu tohto problému, ale prostriedkom vedúcim k ďalším prostriedkom[12]. Inými slovami, stála a nepretržitá ostražitosť je súčasťou prefiguratívnej politiky, takže skutočnú prax prefigurácie nemožno pretvoriť. Je reflexívna a pozorná, ale vždy so zreteľom na výrobu, vynaliezavosť a tvorbu, aby uspokojila túžby verejnosti. V dôsledku toho je prefiguratívna politika výlučne anti-neoliberálna. Ide o dosahovanie cieľov určitými prostriedkami—*našimi* prostriedkami— bez obmedzení. Prefiguratívna akcia znamená otvoriť sa priateľstvu a radosti, ktoré prichádzajú vtedy, keď sa stretávame ako radikálni a rovnocenní ľudia. Nie ako predvoj a proletariát na ceste k transcendentálne prázdnemu sľubu utópie alebo „neexistujúcemu miestu", ale ako zakotvenie princípu *tu* a *teraz*. Ako skutočné vytvorenie nového sveta „v plášti starého" spolu s neustálou ťažkou prácou a potrebným opätovným uisťovaním sa o správnosti našich činov[13].

Nič, čo sa týka neoliberalizmu, si nezaslúži našu úctu. A čo sa týka prefiguratívnej politiky a jej vytvárania, moje posolstvo je jednoduché: „vysrať sa na to". Nasrať na vplyv, ktorý má na našu politickú predstavivosť. Nasrať na násilie, ktoré plodí. Nasrať na nerovnosť, ktorú velebí ako cnosť. Nasrať na devastáciu, ktorú spôsobuje životnému prostrediu. Nasrať na nekonečný cyklus akumulácie a kultivácie rastu. Nasrať na Montpelerinskú spoločnosť a všetky think tanky, ktoré ho nepretržite podporujú a propagujú. Nasrať na Friedricha Hayeka a Miltona Friedmana za to, že nám nanútili svoje názory. Nasrať na Thatcherové, Reaganov a všetkých zbabelých a egoistických politikov, čo si z chamtivosti navzájom kryjú zadky. Nasrať na zastrašovanie a vylučovanie „ostatných" zo spoločnosti pod zámienkou, že sú hodní len umývania záchodov a čistenia podláh, no nie sú hodní byť plnohodnotnými členmi našich komunít. Nasrať na neustále rastúcu potrebu zavádzania metrík. Nasrať na to, že sa nám nedarí vážiť si fakt, že nie všetko, čo sa ráta, sa dá zrátať. Nasrať na túžbu po zisku na úkor potrieb komunity. Nasrať absolútne na všetko, za čím neoliberalizmus stojí, a nasrať na trójskeho koňa, na ktorom pricválal! Príliš dlho nám tvrdili, že „neexistuje žiadna alternatíva", že „príliv zdvihne všetky lode", že žijeme v darvinovskej nočnej more, vo svete, kde sú všetci proti všetkým a kde prežijú len tí najschopnejší. Myšlienku „tragédie občiny" sme zhltli aj s navijakom, no v skutočnosti je to len podvod odrážajúci „tragédiu kapitalizmu" a jeho nekonečné rabovanie[14]. Achillovou pätou Garretta Hardina[15] bolo, že sa nikdy nezamyslel nad tým, že pasúci sa dobytok bol už v súkromnom vlastníctve. Čo sa môže stať, ak znovu ustanovíme skutočné občiny ako *občiny* bez predpokladu súkromného vlastníctva[16]? Čo sa môže stať, keď začneme venovať väčšiu pozornosť prefigurácii už existujúcich alternatív a uprednostníme tieto skúsenosti pri výbere najdôležitejších foriem organizácie[17]? Čo sa môže stať, keď namiesto prehltania horkých tabletiek súťaživosti a zdanlivých hodnôt, sústredíme našu energiu na to, aby sme si nepredpisovali neoliberálne lieky, ale namiesto toho sa sústredili na naše skutočné uzdraven' vyplývajúce zo vzájomnej spolupráce a pomoci[18]?

Jamie Peck[19] kedysi nazval neoliberalizmus „rad nym politickým sloganom". To však už nie je dostato' dôvodom, aby pretrvával v oblasti kritiky. Od prvé' poznania nášho nepriateľa uplynulo mnoho rok' sme ho za ten čas dobre spoznali prostredníctv' písania a protestov. Ale aj keď sme si istí jeho porážkou (tak, ako sme si boli istí následkami finančnej krízy v roku 2008 a následným hnutím nazývaným „Occupy movement"), vieme, že naďalej lapá po dychu a prebúdza sa k životu v mocnejšej podobe—ako zombie[20]. Japhy Wilson[21] nazýva túto pretrvávajúcu moc „neoliberálnou gotikou" a ja som si istý, že na prekonanie tejto hororovej show musíme posunúť naše politické pôsobenie na iný level[22]. Čo keby sa fráza „nasrať na neoliberalizmus" stala mantrou pre nový druh politiky? Silným sloganom, ktorý by vyzýval nielen k činom, ale aj k rekultivácii našich životov na skutočných miestach a v reálnych okamihoch? Čo keby sme si zakaždým, keď použijeme túto frázu, pripomenuli, že je to výzva k aktivite presahujúca slová a spájajúca teóriu a prax s úžasným praktizovaním prefigurácie? Naše odmietanie neoliberalizmu si vyžaduje mnohostranný prístup. Hoci ho nemôžeme úplne ignorovať alebo naň zabudnúť, môžeme proti nemu aktívne bojovať spôsobom presahujúcim rečnícke predstavenie či rečnenie v predstavení. V každom prípade ale posuňme ďalej nový radikálny politický slogan. Použite hashtag (#fuckneoliberalism) a šírte internetom naše opovrhovanie! Musíme však urobiť viac, než len vyjadriť svoje rozhorčenie. Musíme šíriť povedomie a dúfať v podstatu našich ozajstných zážitkov *tu* a *teraz*[23]. Potrebujeme tento svet pretvoriť a musíme s tým začať hneď.

Prostredníctvom nášho neustáleho apelovania na existujúci systém politickej reprezentácie sme sa vedome nechali oklamať a pripraviť sa o moc. Naša slepá viera nás neustále necháva čakať, kým spasiteľ spadne z neba. Ukázalo sa, že systém je totálne skorumpovaný, a že čas, a len čas, ukáže, že náš ďalší politický kandidát je len opätovným zlyhaním. V tejto fáze neoliberalizmu ale nejde len o to, že pri moci sú bezvýznamné, no problematické indivíduá. Základom problému je práve naša silná viera v

samotný systém. To my vytvárame a umožňujeme inštitucionálne podmienky pre rozvoj „Luciferovho efektu"[24].
„Správa o banalite zla" značí, že títo politici si len robia svoju prácu v systéme, ktorý odmeňuje za perverznosti moci, pretože všetko je koncipované tak, aby to slúžilo zákonom kapitalizmu[25]. My však nemusíme poslúchať. Tieto nariadenia pre nás nie sú záväzné. Prostredníctvom priamej akcie a organizovania alternatívnych aktivít môžeme obviniť celý systém a narušiť tento začarovaný kruh zneužívania. Politický systém definovaný, podmieňovaný, zamotaný a odvodený od kapitalizmu nikdy nemôže reprezentovať naše spôsoby poznania sveta a našu existenciu. Preto musíme vziať svoje životy do vlastných rúk a získať späť našu kolektívnu moc. Musíme začať s aktívnou politikou, využiť našu silnejšiu vzájomnú solidaritu a uvedomiť si, že zotročenie a utrpenie jednotlivca je v skutočnosti príznakom utláčania všetkých[26]. Keď znovu nájdeme odhodlanie a spojíme sa, zameriame sa na vzájomnú pomoc a podporu a nehierarchické formy organizácie spoločnosti, keď obnovíme demokraciu v pôvodom zmysle slova—ako *moc* pre ľudí, môžeme sa ocitnúť v novom svete. Koniec koncov, neoliberalizmus je len mimoriadne odporný výmysel prichádzajúci s celým radom hlúpych predpokladov a vulgárnych výsledkov. Preto si zaslúži stretnúť sa s rovnako urážlivým vyjadrovaním a počínaním. Naša komunita, naša spolupráca a starosť o druhých sú neoliberalizmu proti srsti. Nenávidí to, čo my oslavujeme. Takže keď povieme „nasrať na neoliberalizmus", nech to znamená viac ako len slová, nech je to prejavom našej vzájomnej oddanosti. Povedzte to nahlas, povedzte to spolu so mnou a povedzte to každému, kto bude ochotný počúvať. No predovšetkým to vnímajte ako naliehavú výzvu k aktivite a ako stelesnenie našej prefiguratívnej sily, ktorou spoločne zmeníme tento zasraný svet. *Nasrať na neoliberalizmus!*

¡A la Mierda el Neoliberalismo!

Translated by xaranta baksh

Translator's Commentary

For me, translations are important, because they're how i connect to other people, ideas, cultures, feelings, and other parts of myself that i may not have yet met. If i think about my world and all the works and pieces that i have had the privilege of loving or being impacted by (in both positive and negative ways), i'd say that translation/translated works have exposed me to the possibility and reality of other worlds and experiences, which in some strange way helps me to find and feel a sense of community and hope in a place that sometimes leaves me feeling lonely and questioning whether we will ever get it right.

¡A la Mierda el Neoliberalismo!

A la mierda el neoliberalismo. Esto es mi mensaje principal. Podría terminar mi argumento ahora y no importaría nada. Mi posición está claro y es probable que ya entiendas lo que quiero decir. No tengo nada positivo para agregar al debate sobre el neoliberalismo, y si les fuera sincero, estoy cansado de tener que pensar sobre ello. Simplemente estoy harto. Por un tiempo pensaba titular este documento 'Al olvido el neoliberalismo', ya que de algunas maneras, olvidar el neoliberalismo fue exactamente lo que quería hacer. He escrito sobre este tema por muchos años[1] y llegué a un punto en que ya no quería dedicarle más tiempo a este proyecto por miedo de que si yo continuara trabajando en ello, funcionaría para seguir apoyando su posición en el mundo. Tras reflexionar, me di cuenta de que como una maniobra política, es posible que sea peligroso simplemente ignorar un fenómeno que ha tenido consecuencias tan debilitantes y devastadoras sobre nuestro mundo colectivo. Es difícil negar que el neoliberalismo no sigue teniendo un poder fuerte y por eso, no estoy convencido de que un estrategia de ignorancia sea la mejor medida[2]. Por eso mis pensamientos exactos fueron 'pues a la mierda con ello' y mientras ponerle un título más agradable a este trabajo podría suavizar la posible reacción que quizás enfrentaré con el título que he escogido, posteriormente reconsideré. ¿Por qué deberíamos preocuparnos más por el uso de groserías en vez del el actual discurso despreciable del neoliberalismo en sí mismo? Decidí que quería superar, molestar, y ofender, precisamente porque *deberíamos* estar ofendidos por la existencia del neoliberalismo ya que *es* una gran molestia, y por lo tanto *deberíamos* comprometernos a superarlo. ¿Si hubiera suavizado el título, no habría sido otra concesión al poder del neoliberalismo? Al principio pensé mucho sobre las consecuencias de un título como el de este artículo, en cuanto a mi reputación. ¿Impediría ascensos o ofertas de trabajo en el futuro si quisiera mantener mi puesto como académico, sea ascendente o en un lugar nuevo? Esto sintió como si fuera concediendo una derrota personal a la disciplina neoliberal. A la mierda con eso.

Además me sentí como si fuera admitiendo que no hay una respuesta coloquial que se pueda utilizar para contrarrestar el discurso del neoliberalismo. Como si solo podemos responder de una manera académica, empleando complejas teorías de geografía por ejemplo, *variegation*, hibridismo y la mutualidad para debilitar su existencia. Esto me pareció un poco desalentador, y aunque yo mismo haya contribuido a la articulación de algunas de estas teorías[3] me siento, a menudo, que esta manera de verlo va en contra del tipo de argumento que quiero hacer. Es precisamente en lo cotidiano, lo ordinario, lo común y lo mundano que pienso que hay que localizar la política de "rechazo". Por eso decidí quedar con el título 'A la mierda el neoliberalismo' ya que para mí, comunica la gran parte de lo que quiero decir. El argumento que quiero hacer es un poco más complejo que eso, lo cual me hizo pensar en la frase 'a la mierda' (*fuck*) más que he hecho en cualquier otro momento de mi vida. ¡Qué frase tan diversa! En inglés, *fuck*, puede funcionar como sustantivo o verbo y como adjetivo, es quizás la palabra más empleada como un signo de exclamación. Se puede utilizar para expresar la ira, el desprecio, la molestia, la indiferencia, la sorpresa, la impaciencia, o como un énfasis sin significado porque sale fácilmente de la boca. Se puede 'joder algo', 'joderle a alguien', 'joder', 'no importarle ni un culo', y además hay un punto de referencia decididamente geográfico para la palabra que hasta te pueden mandar a "que te vayas a la mierda". Quizás en este momento estás pensando 'vale, pero a quien le importa todo eso?' Bueno, yo, y si tú también quieres terminar con el neoliberalismo, deberías estar interesado. Las habilidades poderosas que se asocia con la frase 'a la mierda' representan un posible desafío al neoliberalismo. Para profundizar y analizar estas habilidades tenemos que entender los matices que estén presentes en la frase 'a la mierda el neoliberalismo'. Pero al mismo tiempo, a la mierda los matices. Como Kieran Healy[4] recientemente argumentó, "típicamente impiden el desarrollo de la teoría que es intelectualmente interesante, empíricamente generativo o prácticamente exitoso". Así que, sin exagerar el estado del matiz, hablemos rápidamente de lo que pienso que debemos priorizar para que el neoliberalismo se vaya a la mierda.

El primer punto quizás sea lo más obvio. Al decir 'a la mierda el neoliberalismo' podemos expresar nuestra rabia para el sistema neoliberal. Indica nuestra ira, representa nuestro deseo de gritar nuestro rencor y resentimiento, es una oportunidad para volverle a escupir veneno en la cara del neoliberalismo por la nociva maldad que nos ha mostrado a todos. Esto se puede lograr organizando más protestas contra el neoliberalismo, o escribiendo más artículos y libros criticando su influencia. Este último predica a los convertidos, y el anterior espera que los que ya están "pervertidos", estarán dispuestos a cambiar su actitud, sus costumbres, sus comportamientos. No dudo que estos métodos son estrategias importantes para nuestra resistencia, pero al mismo tiempo, estoy seguro de que no serán suficientes para derrotar el neoliberalismo a nuestra favor. Al hacer un gran desafió público, intentamos involucrar los sectores poderosos en una conversación, creyendo por error que nos vayan a escuchar y empezar a acomodar la voz popular del "rechazo"[5]. ¿Al contrario no deberíamos dejar de hablar ya? Les voy a introducir al segundo sentido de 'a la mierda el neoliberalismo', el cual se encuentra en el concepto del "rechazo". Esto, se trataría de abogar por el fin del neoliberalismo (como lo conocíamos) de una manera adelantada por J.K. Gibson-Graham[6] en que simplemente dejamos de hablar sobre ello. Los académicos en particular dejarían de priorizar el neoliberalismo como el énfasis de sus investigaciones. Quizás no será que olvidemos o ignoremos el neoliberalismo en total, lo que ya he identificado como algo problemático, sino que nos dedicaríamos a escribir sobre otros temas. De nuevo, esto es un punto de mucha importancia para poder ver más adelante del punto de vista neoliberal, pero con esto tampoco estoy convencido de que es o será suficiente para superarlo. Como argumenta Mark Purcell[7], "necesitamos dar la espalda al neoliberalismo y volver a nosotros mismos, para empezar el trabajo difícil—pero también gozoso—de gestionar nuestros asuntos para nosotros mismos". Mientras el rechazo, la protesta y la crítica son necesarios, también tenemos que pensar sobre una manera de joderle al neoliberalismo de una forma activa por ser y hacer las cosas fuera de su alcance.

La acción directa por encima del neoliberalismo se identifica con una *política prefigurativa*[8] la cual, es el tercer punto más importante, el que creo que deberíamos concentrarnos cuando invocamos la idea 'a la mierda el neoliberalismo'. *Prefigurar* es rechazar el centrismo, la jerarquía y la autoridad que viene con la política representativa por enfatizar la practica consagrada de promulgar o establecer las relaciones horizontales y los tipos de organizaciones que luchan o se esfuerzan para reflejar la sociedad futura que se busca establecer[9]. Más allá de 'dejar de hablar', la prefiguración y la acción directa, en primer lugar, plantean que no hubo nunca la necesidad de tener una conversación, reconociendo que cualquier cosa que queremos hacer, podemos hacer por nosotros mismos. No obstante, ha habido un gran enfoque en las maneras en que el neoliberalismo es capaz de capturar y apropiar cualquier tipo del discurso e imperativo político[10]. Para críticos como David Harvey[11] solo otra intervención del estado puede solucionar la problemática neoliberal, ya que en particular rechaza fácilmente la organización no-jerárquica y la política horizontal como medidas para abrir y forjar el camino para un asegurado futuro neoliberal. Sin embargo, con su pesimismo, malinterprete el concepto de la política prefigurativa que no se trata de un fin, sino la generación de recursos futuros[12]. En otras palabras, hay una vigilancia constante y continuo ya integrado en la política prefigurativa que la actual práctica de prefiguración no puede ser cooptado. Es reflexiva y atenta pero siempre con un fin hacia la producción, la invención y la creación como la satisfacción del deseo de la comunidad. De este modo, la política prefigurativa es explícitamente contra-neoliberal. Es una toma de los recursos como *lo nuestro*. Prefigurar es abrazar la convivencia y la alegría que viene con el estar juntos como iguales, no como las vanguardias y el proletariado en el camino hacia la promesa transcendental y vacía de una utopía o 'un lugar que no existe' sino, como la inmanencia enraizada en el aquí y el ahora, de construir un nuevo mundo 'en la cáscara del anterior' y el trabajo duro y perpetuo, y la reafirmación que todo esto requiere[13].

No hay nada del neoliberalismo que merece nuestro respeto, así que junto con una política prefigurativa, mi mensaje es simplemente 'a la mierda con ello', 'que se vaya a la mierda'. A la mierda el control que tiene sobre nuestras imaginaciones políticas. A la mierda la violencia que genera. A la mierda la desigualdad que nos presenta como una virtud. A la mierda la manera en que ha destruido el medioambiente. A la mierda el interminable ciclo de acumulación y el culto del crecimiento/desarrollo. A la mierda la sociedad Mont Pelerin y todos los grupos de reflexión que siguen sosteniéndolo y promoviéndolo. A la mierda Friederich Hayek y Milton Friedman por imponernos sus ideas. A la mierda los Thatchers, los Reagans y todos los políticos cobardes y egoístas que solo buscan raspar la espalda de la avaricia. A la mierda la exclusión basada en el miedo que ve 'los otros' como dignos de limpiar nuestros baños y trapear nuestros suelos, pero no como miembros de nuestra comunidad. A la mierda el paso cada vez más intensa hacia la métrica y la falta de reconocer que no todo que cuenta se puede contar. A la mierda el deseo para la ganancia sobre las necesidades de la comunidad. ¡A la mierda todos los principios del neoliberalismo y a la mierda el caballo de Troya sobre lo cual cabalgó! Durante demasiado tiempo nos han dicho que 'no hay otra alternativa', que 'la marea alta levanta todos los barcos', que vivimos en un mundo de una pesadilla darwiniana de todos contra todos, un mundo de 'supervivencia del más apto'. Hemos aceptado totalmente la idea de 'la tragedia de los bienes comunes'; cuando en realidad es una treta que en actualidad refleja 'la tragedia del capitalismo' y la guerra interminable del pillaje[14]. El talón de Aquiles de Garrett Hardin[15] fue que nunca se le ocurrió considerar que el pastoreo de ganado ya fue propiedad privada. ¿Qué pasará cuando se reúnen un actual patrimonio como *patrimonio* sin premisas de propiedad privada[16]? ¿Qué pasará cuando empezamos a prestar más atención a la prefiguración de alternativas que ya está ocurriendo y privilegiando estas experiencias como las formas más importantes de organizar[17]? ¿Qué pasará cuando en vez de tragar las píldoras amargas de la competencia y el mérito, decidimos enfocarnos no en el medicarnos con las prescripciones neoliberales, sino con la curación profunda que viene con la cooperación y la ayuda mutua[18]?

Jamie Peck[19] una vez dijo que el neoliberalismo es 'un extremista lema político', pero ya no es suficiente permanecer en el ámbito de la crítica. Han pasado muchos años desde que identificamos el enemigo y desde aquel entonces, hemos llegado a conocerlo bien por nuestras escrituras y protestas. Sin embargo, aun cuando estamos seguros de su derrota, como después de la crisis financiera de 2008 y el sucesivo 'Occupy Movement', el neoliberalismo continúa jadeando por aire y reanimándose de una manera zombificado más poderosa[20]. Japhy Wilson[21] identifica este poder como el '*neoliberal gothic*', y estoy convencido de que para superar este espectáculo de horror tenemos que guiar nuestra política hacia el dominio del '*enactive*'[22]. ¿Qué tal si la frase 'a la mierda el neoliberalismo' llega a ser un nuevo lema para un nuevo tipo de política? ¿Qué tal si logra ser una frase habilitante que

se identifique no solo con la acción, sino con la recupera-
ción de nuestras vidas en los espacios y momentos en los
cuales los vivimos completamente?¿Qué tal si cada vez
que utilizamos esta frase, reconocemos que representa
una llamada para una participación que va más allá de
las palabras, uniendo la teoría y la práctica para formar
un praxis de prefiguración? Hay que adoptar un enfoque
múltiple en nuestro rechazo del neoliberalismo. Aunque
no podemos ignorarlo u olvidarlo totalmente, podemos
trabajar en contra de ello de una manera activa, en formas
que van más allá del rendimiento de la retórica y la retórica del rendimiento. De todos modos avancemos y desa-
rrollemos un nuevo radical lema político. ¡Publique un
hashtag (#fuckneoliberalism/alamierdaelneoliberalismo)
para que nuestro desprecio sea viral por todas partes!
Pero, tenemos que hacer más que expresar nuestra indig-
nación. Tenemos que promulgar nuestra determinación,
nuestra voluntad y comprender nuestra esperanza como
la inmanencia de nuestras experiencias compartidas en
el aquí y el ahora[23]. Tenemos que rehacer el mundo para
nosotros mismos, un proceso que no se puede aplazar.

Nos hemos engañado y debilitado voluntariamente
por continuar apelar al presente acuerdo político de la
representación. Nuestra fe ciega nos tiene esperando eter-
namente para que algún salvador baje del cielo. El sistema
ha demostrado que es totalmente corrupto, donde cada
vez más el candidato político más prometedor termina
siendo un fracaso. En esta época tan neoliberal, no se
trata de que individuos problemáticos tengan el poder.
Al contrario, nuestra propia creencia en el sistema es lo
que representa el núcleo del problema. Producimos y así
dejamos que las condiciones institucionales para 'el efecto
de lucifer' muestren sus efectos[24]. 'La trivialidad del mal'
es tanto que estos políticos solo están haciendo su trabajo
dentro de un sistema que recompensa las perversiones

del poder porque está diseñado para servir las leyes de capitalismo[25]. Pero no tenemos que obedecer. No estamos en deuda al sistema. Por nuestra acción directa y por la organización de distintas alternativas, podemos acusar el sistema entero y romper el ciclo vicioso del abuso. Cuando el sistema político está definido por, preparado para, sumergido en y derivado del capitalismo, nunca puede representar nuestras maneras de conocer y ser en el mundo, y por eso tenemos que encargarnos de nuestras formas de vidas y recuperar nuestra representación colectiva. Tenemos que empezar a participar en nuestra política y empezar a adoptar un sentido de solidaridad que reconoce que el sometimiento y el sufrimiento del uno, de hecho representa la opresión de todos[26]. Podemos empezar a vivir en otros posibles mundos por un renovado compromiso a las prácticas de la convivencia, la fraternidad, la reciprocidad y formas no-jerárquicas de organización que reúnen la democracia con el sentido etimológico de *dejarle el poder al pueblo*. Últimamente el neoliberalismo es una mala idea que se asocia con un sin número de resultados groseros y asunciones bordas. En respuesta, merece que lo enfrentemos con un lenguaje y una acción que es igualmente ofensiva. Nuestra comunidad, nuestra cooperación y nuestra consideración por el uno al otro, son detestables para el neoliberalismo. El neoliberalismo detesta todo lo que celebramos. Así que, cuando digamos 'a la mierda el neoliberalismo que represente mucho más que palabras, deja que sea una representación de nuestro compromiso a la humanidad. Digámoslo alto y claro, dígalo a cualquier persona que le escuche, pero sobre todo, que lo diga como una llamada de atención y como la encarnación de nuestro poder prefigurativo para cambiar el puto mundo. ¡A la *mierda el neoliberalismo*!

Fuck nyliberalismen

Translated by Gustav Sjöberg

Commentary—Aeron Bergman and Alejandra Salinas
Unfortunately Gustav was unavailable to comment, but the Swedish translation was organized by Aeron Bergman and Alejandra Salinas for inclusion in a Special Issue of the Swedish magazine OEI *entitled* "Art in the Age of Kleptomania." *They offer their thoughts here.*

One of the most insidious and yet admirable aspects of the neoliberal virus is the use of simplified language signaling simple concepts that are easily internalized by a mostly disinterested, easily alarmed, overworked, and opinionated public.

The problem with most criticism of neoliberal thought and policy is that it comes from individuals who understand its duplicitousness and respond with wonkish deliberation to the grey area of truth, statistics, and other ambiguities. While academic work toward truth and justice has great value, publicly palatable messaging is needed to spread ideas through society as counter-memes. It is thus necessary to employ an interdisciplinary array of intellectuals to develop and implement strategies (anti-neoliberal think tanks, in other words). Psychologists, economists, geographers, political strategists, designers, artists, philosophers, biologists, and so on need to determine the best terminologies and mental maps necessary to advance policies that walk back our miserable Age of Kleptomania toward an equitable, ecologically just ecosystem.[*]

However, currently, even purported critics of neoliberalism use its assumptions in the same way that Satanists are still solidly within Christian liturgy and are, therefore, in fact, still Christian. We see this in academics who hustle ruthlessly up the tenure track, while endebting students and functioning as intellectual apologists for education as a social control system.[†] We see this in Nancy Pelosi's (and other "liberals" in congress and so on) cynical endorsement of the corporatist neoliberal attack of a socialist country backed by extreme US military violence: "The United States must respect legitimate democratic processes, and support the right of the people of Venezuela to protest and defend their human rights."[‡] We read about how the founder of BuzzFeed wrote academic papers on Deleuze: "Identity formation is inextricably linked to the urge to consume, and therefore the acceleration of capitalism necessitates an increase in the rate at which individuals assume and shed identities."[§] The problem is that even most intellectuals accept neoliberal premises as though they were natural, because the labor done to normalize its terms has been extraordinarily successful.

[*]   Our term, first used in our book *Telepathy* (Geneva, CH: INCA Press, 2018). We hope it is catchy enough to spread.

[†]   Alex Usher, "Universities and Competition (Neoliberalism Part 3)," Higher Education Strategy Associates, November 22, 2017, accessed September 10, 2020, http://higheredstrategy.com/universities-and-competition-neoliberalism-part-3.

[‡]   Nancy Pelosi, "Pelosi Statement on the Situation in Venezuela," Nancy Pelosi: Speaker of the House, February 8, 2019, accessed September 10, 2020, https://www.speaker.gov/newsroom/2819-2.

[§]   Eugene Wolters, "From Deleuze to Lolcats, the Story of the Buzzfeed Guy," April 8, 2013, accessed September 10, 2020, http://www.critical-theory.com/from-deleuze-to-lolcats-the-story-of-the-buzzfeed-guy.

Friedrich Hayek, James Buchanan, and the rest of the Mont Pelerin Society understood that hardcore, perverted policy needs a public relations spin to sound agreeable and be publically normalized. One example of many is the brilliantly evil "Right to Work" slogan used for union busting. Neoliberal policy spinners invented the term so the average disconnected citizen would unquestionably believe when their state becomes a "Right to Work" state that the legislation simply corrects an unnatural course toward a more natural one. A thousand duplicitous terms such as this have normalized neoliberalism nearly everywhere on earth.

One way to respond could be clever, easy to visualize respin. "Right to Walk" states would be those that do not penalize or forbid workers to walk off a job that doesn't pay enough or to quit a company that will not negotiate with its workers or their unions. This could also be rechristened a "Right to Paycheck" or simply an "Anti-Slavery" law, but the actual slogan used should probably be workshopped and then tried out in focus groups. (Because it is difficult as fuck to understand how most people interpret their neoliberal hellscape.) Terms and slogans need to be developed to rebuild every single aspect of society for people and consequently save the biosphere.

So when we first read Simon Springer's wonderful text "Fuck Neoliberalism," we felt his rejection enacted with an almost bodily force. This rejection is as inane and catchy as neoliberal slogans themselves. Springer's physical and wholly natural response to a disgusting invented reality is simple—and necessary. This term is the root for the thousands of terms and phrases that need to grow outward from "intellectuals" into the public world, transforming well-adjusted assumptions of neoliberal economic "realism" into the steaming pile of extremist excrement they are. All further terms need to be developed with the core message "Fuck Neoliberalism!"

Fuck nyliberalismen

Fuck nyliberalismen. Det är mitt raka budskap. Jag skulle troligen kunna avsluta min diskussion vid denna punkt utan att det spelade någon egentlig roll. Min position är tydlig och du förstår säkert redan kärnan i det jag vill förmedla. Jag har inget positivt att tillägga till diskussionen om nyliberalismen, och för att vara fullständigt uppriktig är jag riktigt less på att behöva tänka på den. Jag har helt enkelt fått nog. Till en början övervägde jag att ge denna text titeln "Glöm nyliberalismen" i stället, och i vissa avseenden är det precis det jag ville göra. Jag har skrivit om ämnet under många år[1] för att sedan komma till en punkt där jag kort sagt inte ville lägga någon mer energi på detta åtagande av rädsla för att det fortsatta arbetet kring denna idé tjänade funktionen att vidmakthålla dess herravälde. Vid närmare eftertanke inser jag också att det som politisk manöver är potentiellt farligt att kort och gott gräva ned huvudet i sanden och kollektivt blunda för ett fenomen som har haft sådana förödande och försvagande effekter på vår gemensamma värld. Nyliberalismen har en fortsatt kraft som är svår att förneka och jag är inte övertygad om att en skygglappsstrategi verkligen är rätt angreppssätt[2]. Så jag tänkte bokstavligen, *well, fuck it then,* och även om ett mer stillsamt och tillmötesgående namn hade tonat ned den potentiella anstöt som titeln jag valt skulle kunna väcka, kom jag sedan att ändra mig. Varför ska vi oroa oss mer över bruket av vulgärt språk än över själva nyliberalismens verkligt vidriga diskurs? Jag kom fram till att jag ville överskrida, uppröra och förolämpa, just eftersom vi *borde* vara förolämpade av nyliberalismen, den är alltigenom upprörande, och därför *bör* vi ytterst sett försöka överskrida den. Skulle inte en mjukare titel

innebära ännu en eftergift till nyliberalismens makt? Till
en början oroade jag mig för vad en sådan titel skulle
innebära för mitt rykte. Skulle den stå i vägen för framtida
befordran eller jobberbjudanden, om jag nu vill behålla
min rörlighet som akademiker, antingen uppåt eller till
en ny plats? Detta kändes som att tillstå ett personligt
nederlag för nyliberal disciplinering. *Fuck that.*

Det kändes också som om jag erkände att det inte
finns något vardagligt svar som vore adekvat för att mot-
verka nyliberalismens diskurs. Som om vi endast kan
svara i ett akademiskt format med hjälp av komplexa geo-
grafiska teorier om diversifiering, hybriditet och mutation
för att försvaga dess struktur. Detta framstod som demo-
raliserande, och även om jag själv bidragit till att artiku-
lera vissa av dessa teorier[3] har jag ofta känslan av att detta
slags kontextualisering går emot den typ av argument
som jag egentligen vill framföra. Det är just precis i det
vardagliga, ordinära, vanliga och triviala som jag tror att
en vägrans politik måste situeras. Så jag beslutade mig
för *Fuck nyliberalismen* eftersom jag finner att det svarar
bäst mot vad jag verkligen vill säga. Det argument jag
vill föra fram är en smula mer nyanserat, vilket fick mig
att tänka mer på termen *fuck* än jag troligtvis gjort någon
gång tidigare i mitt liv. Vilket fantastiskt färgstarkt ord!
Det fungerar som substantiv eller verb, och som adjektiv
är det kanske det engelska språkets mest använda utrop-
stecken. Det kan användas för att uttrycka vrede, förakt,
irritation, likgiltighet, förvåning, otålighet, och till och
med som meningslös emfas bara för att det slinker ur
en så lätt. Man kan *fuck something up* [fucka upp något],
fuck someone over [rövknulla någon], *fuck around* [svamla,
knulla runt], *not give a fuck* [ge blanka fan], och ordet har
en avgjort geografisk referenspunkt i den mån du kan
bli anvisad att *go fuck yourself* [dra åt helvete]. Vid denna
punkt kanske du till och med tänker, *okay, but who gives a*

fuck [vem fan bryr sig]? Jag gör det, och det borde du också om du är intresserad av att få ett slut på nyliberalismen. De kraftfulla förmågor som följer med ordet erbjuder en potentiell utmaning för nyliberalismen. För att lyfta fram och analysera dessa färdigheter måste vi uppskatta nyanserna i vad satsen *fuck nyliberalismen* kan avse. Men å andra sidan, fuck nyanser. Som Kieran Healy[4] nyligen har argumenterat, "hindrar den typiskt utvecklingen av teori som är intellektuellt intressant, empiriskt generativ eller praktiskt framgångsrik". Låt oss därför, utan att fetischera nyansen, göra en snabb genomgång av vad jag anser att vi bör prioritera för att fucka upp nyliberalismen.

Den första betydelsen är kanske den mest uppenbara. Genom att säga "fuck nyliberalismen" kan vi uttrycka vårt raseri mot den nyliberala maskinen. Det är en indikation på vår vrede, vårt begär efter att skrika ut vår upprördhet, att spy tillbaka galla i ansiktet på den skadliga illvilja som har visats upp för oss alla. Detta kan ske genom att mobilisera fler protester mot nyliberalismen eller genom att skriva fler artiklar och böcker som kritiserar dess inflytande. Det senare är en predikan för dem som redan är omvända, det förra ett hopp om att de som redan har perverterats kommer att visa sig villiga att ändra sitt beteende. Jag förnekar inte att dessa metoder utgör viktiga taktiker i vårt motstånd, men jag är också rätt säker på att de aldrig kommer att vara tillräckliga för att vända vinden mot nyliberalismen och till vår fördel. Genom att göra stora offentliga gester i protest försöker vi inleda en dialog med mäktiga aktörer, i den förfelade tron att de kanske kommer att lyssna och börja ta till sig vägrans folkliga röst[5]. Borde vi inte i stället ha snackat klart? Här finns den andra betydelsen av "fuck nyliberalismen", nämligen i idén om vägran. Detta vore att förfäkta slutet för nyliberalismen (i sin hittillsvarande form) på ett sätt som framförts av J. K. Gibson-Graham[6], där vi helt enkelt upphör att tala om den. Framför allt skulle akademiker upphöra att prioritera den som fokus för sina undersökningar. Kanske inte glömma den helt och hållet eller fullständigt blunda för den, vilket jag redan har identifierat som problematiskt, men i stället bör vi ta oss an vårt skrivande om andra saker. Åter en gång är detta en kontaktpunkt av avgörande betydelse när vi arbetar bortom den nyliberala världsåskådningen, men inte heller här är jag helt övertygad om att det räcker. Som Mark Purcell[7] argumenterar: "Vi måste vända oss från nyliberalismen och mot oss själva." Även om negation, protest och kritik är nödvändiga, måste vi också vinnlägga oss om att aktivt fucka upp nyliberalismen genom att göra sådant som ligger utom dess räckhåll.

Direkt aktion bortom nyliberalismen adresserar en prefigurativ politik[8], vilket är den tredje och viktigaste betydelsen av vad jag tycker att vi borde fokusera när vi åberopar idén "fuck nyliberalismen". Att prefigurera innebär att vägra den centrism, hierarki och auktoritet som medföljer den representativa politiken genom att lägga emfas på den förkroppsligade praktiken att iscensätta horisontella relationer och organisationsformer vilka strävar efter att återspegla det eftersträvade framtida samhället[9]. Prefigurering och direkt aktion går bortom att ha "snackat klart" och hävdar i stället att det hur som helst aldrig fanns något tänkbart samtal, då de inser att vad vi än vill göra kan vi bara göra det själva. Inte desto mindre har avsevärd uppmärksamhet riktats mot de sätt på vilka nyliberalismen är förmögen att fånga upp och appropriera alla former av politiska diskurser och imperativ[10]. För kritiker som David Harvey[11] är det endast ännu en dos av staten som kan lösa den nyliberala frågan, och han är särskilt snabb att avfärda icke-hierarkiska organisationer och horisontell politik som sätt att smörja maskineriet för en viss nyliberal framtid. Men i sin pessimism missförstår han fullständigt prefigurativ politik, som inte är ett medel till ett ändamål utan endast till framtida medel[12]. Å andra sidan finns det en konstant och kontinuerlig vaksamhet som redan är inbyggd i den prefigurativa politiken, så att prefigureringens faktiska praktik inte kan koopteras. Den är reflexiv och uppmärksam men har alltid produktion, invention och skapelse i sikte, som en tillfredsställelse av den samhälleliga gemenskapens begär. På detta sätt är prefigurativ politik explicit anti-nyliberal. Den innebär att fatta tag i medlen som *våra* medel, som medel utan ändamål. Att prefigurera innebär att omfamna den festliga samvaro och glädje som kommer av att vara tillsammans som radikala jämlikar, inte som avantgarde och proletariat på väg mot det transcendentala tomma löftet i en utopi eller ett "*ingenstans*", utan som den grundade immanensen i ett *här* och *nu* som faktiskt bygger en ny värld "i den gamlas skal" och det ständiga hårda arbete och återbekräftande som detta innebär[13].

Det finns ingenting med nyliberalismen som förtjänar vår respekt, så i samstämmighet med en skapandets prefigurativa politik är mitt budskap helt enkelt: *fuck it.* Fuck makten den har över vår politiska fantasi. Fuck våldet den alstrar. Fuck ojämlikheten som den upphöjer till dygd. Fuck sättet på vilket den har ödelagt naturen. Fuck den ändlösa cykeln av ackumulation och kulten av tillväxt. Fuck Mont Pelerin-sällskapet och alla *think tanks* som fortsätter att understödja och befrämja det. Fuck Friedrich Hayek och Milton Friedman för att de har belastat oss med sina idéer. Fuck Thatcher, Reagan och alla fega egoistiska politiker som endast är ute efter att klia girighetens rygg. Fuck den exkludering som sprider rädsla och ser "andra" som värda att städa våra toaletter och tvätta våra golv, men inte som medborgare i vårt samhälle. Fuck den oupphörligt stegrade rörelsen mot metrisk data och misslyckandet att inse att inte allt som räknas kan räknas.

Fuck begäret efter profit framför samhällets behov. Fuck absolut allt som nyliberalismen står för, och fuck den trojanska häst som den red in på! Alldeles för länge har man berättat för oss att det "inte finns något alternativ", att "*a rising tide lifts all boats*", att vi lever i en darwinistisk mardrömsvärld av alla mot alla och "den starkes överlevnad". Vi har svalt idén om "allmänningarnas tragedi" till sista droppen, medan den i grund och botten är en fint som i själva verket återspeglar "kapitalismens tragedi" och dess ändlösa plundringskrig[14]. Garrett Hardins[15] akilleshäl var att han aldrig stannade upp och reflekterade över att betande boskap redan var privat egendom. Vad skulle kunna ske när vi åter sammankallar en verklig allmänning som en *allmänning* utan förutfattade meningar om privat ägande[16]? Vad skulle kunna ske när vi riktar en noggrannare uppmärksamhet mot prefigureringen av alternativ som redan äger rum och ger företräde åt dessa erfarenheter som de viktigaste organisationsformerna[17]? Vad skulle kunna ske när vi, i stället för att svälja konkurrensens och meritens bittra piller, riktade vår energi inte mot självmedicinering med nyliberala ordinationer, utan mot den djupare kurering som följer med samarbete och ömsesidig hjälp[18]?

Jamie Peck[19] kallade vid ett tillfälle nyliberalismen en "radikal politisk slogan", men det räcker inte längre att dväljas inom kritikens sfär. Det har gått många år sedan vi först identifierade fienden och sedan dess har vi lärt känna den väl genom våra texter och protester. Men även när vi är säkra på dess nederlag, som i kölvattnet av finanskrisen 2008 och den åtföljande Occupyrörelsen, fortsätter den att kippa efter andan och återupplivar sig själv i en än mäktigare zombifierad form[20]. Japhy Wilson[21] kallar denna pågående makt "nyliberal gotik", och jag är övertygad om att vi för att ta oss förbi denna *horror show* måste flytta in vår politik i iscensättningens sfär[22]. Tänk om "fuck

nyliberalismen" skulle bli ett mantra för en ny typ av
politik? En möjliggörande sats som inte bara adresserade
aktion utan också återtagandet av våra liv i de rum och
ögonblick i vilka vi aktivt lever dem? Tänk om vi, varje
gång vi använder denna sats, insåg att den innebär ett
upprop till en iscensättande agens som gick bortom blotta
ord genom att kombinera teori och praktik i prefigureringens vackra praxis? Vi måste anta ett mångfacetterat
angreppssätt i vår vägran av nyliberalismen. Även om vi
inte helt och hållet kan blunda för eller glömma den, kan
vi aktivt motarbeta den på sätt som sträcker sig bortom
retorikens prestation och prestationens retorik. Låt oss
för all del föra fram en ny radikal politisk slogan. Använd
en hashtag (#fucknyliberalismen) och ge vårt förakt viral
spridning! Men vi måste göra mer än att uttrycka vår upprördhet. Vi måste iscensätta vårt beslut och förverkliga
vårt hopp som vår förkroppsligade erfarenhets immanens
i ett *här* och *nu*[23]. Vi måste själva göra om världen, en
process som inte kan skjutas upp.

Vi har avsiktligt lurat och omyndigförklarat oss
själva genom att fortsätta att åberopa det existerande
politiska representationssättet. Vår blinda tro får oss att
ändlöst vänta på en frälsare som trillar ned från himlen.
Systemet har visat sig vara alltigenom korrupt, medan
vår nästa stora politiska kandidat gång på gång visar sig
som ett misslyckande. I detta nyliberala ögonblick rör
det sig inte blott och bart om att problematiska indivi-
der har makten. I stället är det själva vår tro på systemet
i sig som sammanfattar problemets kärnpunkt. Vi pro-
ducerar och möjliggör de institutionella betingelserna
för att "Lucifereffekten" ska få fritt spelrum[24]. "Ondskans
banalitet" är av det slag att dessa politiker bara gör sitt
jobb i ett system som belönar perverteringar av makten
eftersom alltsammans är utformat för att tjäna kapitalismens lagar[25]. Men vi behöver inte lyda. Vi är inte bundna

till denna ordning. Genom vår direkta aktion och organiserandet av alternativ kan vi åtala hela strukturen och bryta dess onda cirkel av exploatering. När det politiska systemet definieras och betingas av och är intrasslat i och härstammar från kapitalismen, kan det aldrig representera våra sätt att få kunskap och vara i världen, och därför måste vi ta kontroll över dessa livsvägar och återta vår kollektiva agens. Vi måste börja vara iscensättande i vår politik och omfamna en mer relationell betydelse av solidaritet som erkänner att den enas underkastelse och lidande i själva verket är ett tecken på förtrycket av alla[26]. Vi kan börja leva in i andra möjliga världar genom ett förnyat engagemang i praktiker som ömsesidig hjälp, kamratskap, reciprocitet och icke-hierarkiska organisationsformer som åter kallar samman demokrati i den etymologiska bemärkelsen av *makt* till *folket*. I sista hand är nyliberalismen en osedvanligt motbjudande idé som åtföljs av en hel uppsjö av vulgära resultat och krassa antaganden. Som svar förtjänar den att bemötas med ett lika anstötligt språk och agerande. Vår samhälleliga gemenskap, vårt samarbete och vår omsorg för varandra är alltsammans föraktligt för nyliberalismen. Den hatar det som vi firar. Så när vi säger "fuck nyliberalismen", låt oss då få det att betyda mer än bara ord, låt det bli en iscensättning av vårt engagemang i varandra. Säg det högt, säg det med mig, och säg det till vem som helst som vill lyssna, men mena det framför allt som ett stridsrop till handling och som ett förkroppsligande av vår prefigurativa förmåga att förändra hela fucking världen. *Fuck nyliberalismen!*

Neoliberalizmi Siktir Et!

Translated by Gürçim Yılmaz and
Nezihe Başak Ergin

Translator's Commentary—Gürçim Yılmaz

When Simon Springer asked me to translate one of his articles, which would simultaneously be published in many languages, to be honest, "Fuck Neoliberalism" was not the title I expected. On the other hand, is there a better way to express this? Profanity constructs lateral paths within the dominant language, hollows out holes and forms mounds on it. It refuses to fight the battle whose rules are defined by power; it is a guerilla.

On the other hand, I had some concerns when I began my translation. Profanity originates in a specific cultural context; in the case of Turkish, it mainly evolved among the mobsters of the past in Istanbul (*Kulhanbeyi*). This mobster culture was considerably macho, and its jargon conveyed into today's language inherited this patriarchal culture. Thus, a direct translation of "fuck you/it" into Turkish sounds awfully sexist. Yes, we would like to fuck neoliberalism, but this should not be in the way we say "fuck you."

Yet there is another approach to using "fuck you/it" in Turkish—a more indirect way that contains a certain level of weariness and a deliberate disregard. Whereas the verb "sik-mek" means to actively (sexually) fuck somebody/something (and thus incorporates the sexual act as a means of punishment), the "siktir et," which can be

directly translated as to "fuck somebody/something off"
bears the meaning of expelling something actively and
physically, disregarding and eliminating it from your life
and your mind.

Being part of this collection is invaluable for me.
Thank you, Simon Springer, for letting me translate this
article and Nezihe Başak Ergin for the detailed proofread-
ing. Profanity and humour are perhaps the most challenging parts of a language to translate. This book enables us
to see that there is a way to say "fuck you" to neoliberalism in every language, as different as each may be. How
inspiring!

Translator's Commentary—Nezihe Başak Ergin

My work was a editorial and conceptual revision of
Gürçim Yılmaz's meticulous Turkish translation of "Fuck
Neoliberalism." Thinking about the prospective contribution in—or denial of—the discussions on "neoliberalism," given that I was not sure that I could use this
concept, I was quite excited about the "academic" and
political impacts and challenges of the article. First of all,
the article revisits and invites us to reflect upon the trap
of "neoliberalism" under the rubric of *academic* discussion,
which mainly and merely serves to hide, rather than strug-
gling with, our common enemy, namely "CAPITALISM."
Second, the article was a contribution to the discussions
in Turkey, for or against and beyond the academy, as a
claim for our *commons* using a common language. I would
also like to mention some difficulties with possible translations of some hopeful concepts, such as *prefiguration*.
Moreover, it is an invitation for self-reflection about the
academy and its "benefits" as well, starting with the article's "format": Is another article possible? I consider "fuck"
as a part of this comprehensive challenge; however, I can
admit that I had some "academic?" and mainly "feminist"

concerns about its use, especially given its non-use and obscene meaning in Turkish. The article is also both a recent and a timeless call, and I am happy that it could be made in another language, Turkish, and also challenge *neoliberalism*—a term I still use! I would like to underline that this translation was initially created as part of an international and collective work of *ACME*, as encouragement to challenge the academic framework of capitalism and change the world, here and now.

Neoliberalizmi Siktir Et!

Neoliberalizmi siktir et. Kabaca mesajım bu. Tartışmamı muhtemelen burada da bitirebilirdim, pek de bir şey fark etmezdi. Duruşum net ve siz de zannımca söylemek istediklerimin özünü kavradınız. Neoliberalizm tartışmasına ekleyecek hiçbir olumlu katkım yok, ve tamamen dürüst olmak gerekirse, hakkında düşünmek zorunda kalmaktan da usandım. Kısacası, gına geldi. Bir süre bu makaleye "Neoliberalizmi Unut" başlığını vermeyi düşündüm, bazı bakımlardan yapmak istediğim şey tam da buydu çünkü. Bu konu hakkında yıllardır yazıyorum[1] ve öyle bir noktaya geldim ki, bu fikir etrafında çalışmanın onun devamlılığına katkıda bulunacağı korkusuyla, bu çabaya daha fazla enerji sarf etmek istemedim. Biraz daha düşününce, başımızı basitçe kuma gömerek paylaştığımız dünya üzerinde bu kadar korkunç ve güçsüzleştirici etkileri olan bir olguyu topluca görmezden gelmenin, bir siyasi manevra olarak oldukça fazla potansiyel tehdit taşıdığını da teslim ediyorum. Neoliberalizmin inkar etmesi zor, devamlılık arz eden bir gücü var ve bir görmezden gelme stratejisinin bunun karşısında doğru yaklaşım olduğuna ikna olmuş değilim[2]. Böylece düşüncelerim kelimesi kelimesine 'Pekala, o halde siktir et' oldu. Ve her ne kadar bu makaleye daha sessiz ve daha kibar bir başlık vermek bunun yol açacağı müstakbel tepkileri azaltacak olsa da, nihayetinde (tekrar düşündüm). Neden neoliberalizmin kendisinin gerçek aşağılık söylemi varken, küfür kullanımı konusunda daha fazla endişe edelim ki? Çizmeyi aşmayı, asap bozmayı ve rencide etmeyi istediğime karar verdim, tam da neoliberalizm tarafından rencide olmamız gerektiği için, sinir bozucu olduğu için. Ve bu yüzden nihayetinde bu konuda çizmeyi aşmaya çalışmamız gerekiyor. Başlığı yumuşatmak, neoliberalizmin gücüne bir taviz daha vermek olmayacak mıydı? Öncelikle bu tür bir başlığın itibarım açısından ne anlama geleceği konusunda endişelendim. Bir akademisyen olarak yükselmek veya yer değiştirmek istersem, gelecek terfileri, iş tekliflerini engelleyecek miydi? Bu da bana neoliberal disipline etme süreçlerine teslim olmak, yenilmek gibi geldi. O halde bunu da siktir et.

Ayrıca neoliberal söylemlere karşı uygun olarak önerilebilecek gündelik dilde bir cevap yokmuş gibi bir itirafta bulunuyormuşum gibi geldi. Sanki yapısını zayıflatma yolunda sadece akademik bir formatta, çeşitlilik, melezlik, mutasyon gibi karmaşık coğrafi teorilerle cevap üretebilirmişiz gibi. Bu da güçsüzleştirici bir şey gibi göründü. Her ne kadar ben de bu teorilerin dile getirilişine bizzat katkıda bulunmuş olsam da[3], çoğu zaman bu tür bir çerçevelemenin, gerçekte geliştirmek istediğim argümanların aleyhine işlediğini düşünmüşümdür. Bir reddetme politikasının tam da gündelik, sıradan, önemsiz ve dünyevi olanda konuşlanması gerektiğini düşünüyorum. Böylelikle "Neoliberalizmi siktir et"te karar kıldım, çünkü esasen söylemek istediklerimin çoğunu ifade ediyor. Ortaya koymak istediğim argüman bundan biraz daha incelikli, bu da "sik" terimi üzerine hayatım boyunca düşündüğümden çok daha fazla düşünmeme vesile oldu. Ne kadar fevkalade renkli bir sözcük! Hem isim hem fiil olabiliyor, sıfat olarak ise İngiliz dilinin herhalde en fazla kullanılan ünlemini teşkil ediyor. Öfke, küçümseme, kızgınlık, kayıtsızlık, şaşkınlık, sabırsızlık ve hatta dilden öylece dökülüverildiği için anlamsız bir vurgu olarak bile kullanılabiliyor. Bir şeyi "sikip atabilir", birisinin "ebesini sikebilir", birisine "siktiri çekebilir", "sikine takmayabilir" ve yine bu sözcüğün coğrafi bir referans noktası olduğu bir başka durum var ki, "siktirip gidebilir"siniz. Hatta bu aşamada "tamam da, kimin sikinde?" diye bile düşünebilirsiniz. Eh, benim sikimde, ve şayet neoliberalizmi bitirmekle ilgiliyseniz sizin de öyle olmalı. Bu sözcüğün beraberinde taşıdığı güçlü olanaklar, neoliberalizme karşı potansiyel bir meydan okuma sunuyor. Bu olanakları kazıyıp çıkarmak ve açmak için "neoliberalizmi siktir et" ifadesinin hangi anlamlara gelebileceği konusundaki nüansları takdir etmek gerekiyor. Beri yandan, nüansı da siktir et. Kieran Healy'nin[4] yakın zamanda tartıştığı üzere, "[nüans] tipik olarak, entelektüel açıdan ilginç, ampirik bakımdan üretken veya pratik olarak başarılı teorinin gelişimini engeller." Böylelikle nüansı da fetişleştirmeden, ne düşündüğümün hızlıca üzerinden geçelim ve neoliberalizmi siktir etmeye öncelik verelim.

İlk anlamı belki de en aşikar olanı. "Neoliberalizmi siktir et" diyerek neoliberal makineye olan öfkemizi dile getirebiliriz. Bu öfkemizin bir göstergesi, kinlenişimizi haykırmak için duyduğumuz arzu, hepimize gösterilen zararlı kötülüğün yüzüne zehrini geri püskürtme eylemi. Bu, neoliberalizme karşı daha fazla protesto harekete geçirmek veya etkilerini eleştiren daha fazla makale veya kitap yazmak şeklinde tezahür edebilir. Bunlardan ikincisi doğru yolu seçmişlere vaaz verir, ilki ise halihazırda yoldan çıkmışların yola gelmesini ümit eder. Bu yöntemlerin direnişimiz içinde önemli taktikler olduğunu inkar etmiyorum, fakat aynı zamanda hiçbir zaman neoliberalizm dalgasını tersine ve bizim lehimize olacak şekilde çevirmeye yetmeyeceklerinden de oldukça eminim. Büyük kamusal direniş jestleri gerçekleştirerek güçlü aktörleri diyaloga çekmeye çalışıyoruz; oysa bu hareketler bu aktörlerin kulak verebilecekleri ve halkın reddediş sesine yer açabilecekleri gibi yanlış bir inanca dayanıyor[5]. Onun yerine artık konuşmayı bırakmış olmamız gerekmiyor mu? Burada "Neoliberalizmi siktir et"in ikinci anlamına geliyoruz, ki bu anlam reddediş olgusunda saklıdır. Bu da, J.K. Gibson-Graham'ın[6] geliştirdiği tarzda, (bildiğimiz şekliyle) neoliberalizmin sonunun gelmesini savunmak için onun hakkında konuşmayı bırakmaktır. Bu yaklaşımda, özellikle akademisyenler çalışmalarının odağı olarak neoliberalizme öncelik vermekten vazgeçerler. Belki neoliberalizmi tümden unutmak veya görmezden gelmek yerine (bunu sorunlu bulduğumu daha önce belirtmiştim), farklı konular hakkındaki yazılarımıza girişmek olabilir. Bir kez daha belirtmek isterim ki, bu neoliberal dünya görüşünün ötesinde çalışan bizler için önemli bir temas noktası, ancak yine burada da bunun yeterli olduğuna tam olarak ikna olmuş değilim. Mark Purcell'in[7] ileri sürdüğü üzere, "Neoliberalizme sırt çevirerek kendimize dönmeliyiz, kendi meselelerimiz, kendimi başımıza ele almanın zor— ama bir o kadar zevkli—yolculuğuna. . ." Olumsuzlama, protesto ve eleştiri gerekli olsa da, neoliberalizmin erişim alanı dışında işler yaparak aktif olarak ağzına sıçmayı düşünmeliyiz.

Neoliberalizmin ötesinde doğrudan eylem, prefigüratif politikalara seslenir[8], ki bu da "neoliberalizmi siktir et" düşüncesini çağırırken odaklanmamız gerektiğini düşündüğüm üçüncü ve en önemli anlama karşılık gelir. Prefigürasyon temsili politikalarla gelen merkeziyetçiliği, hiyerarşiyi ve otoriteyi reddetmek demektir; bunu da arayışında olunan geleceğin toplumunu yansıtma gayretindeki yatay ilişkiler ve örgütlenme biçimlerini hayata geçirmeyi vurgulayarak gerçekleştirmek demektir[9]. Prefigürasyon ve doğrudan eylem, "konuşmayı bırakma"nın ötesinde, zaten en başından beri bir diyalogun mümkün olmayacağını ileri sürer, gerçekleştirmek istediğimiz her ne ise, onu sadece kendimizin gerçekleştirebileceğini teslim eder. Bununla beraber, neoliberalizmin her türlü siyasi söylemi ve tahakkümü ele geçirme ve kendine mal etme biçimlerine önemli ölçüde ilgi gösterilmiştir[10]. David Harvey[11] gibi eleştirmenlere göre neoliberal meseleyi sadece farklı dozda bir devlet çözebilir, ki özellikle hiyerarşik olmayan örgütlenme ve yatay politikaları neoliberal bir geleceğin yollarına rayları döşeyen unsurlar olarak reddetmede aceleci davranmıştır. Bu karamsarlığın içinde prefigüratif politikaları tamamen yanlış anlamaktadır—bu politikalar bir son için değil, fakat yalnızca gelecek için araçlardır[12]. Başka bir deyişle, prefigüratif politikalarda daimi ve sürekli bir uyanıklık hali zaten içkindir, öyle ki gerçek prefigürasyon eylemi asimile edilemez. Bu eylem düşünümsel ve dikkatlidir, fakat bunun yanında her zaman toplum arzusunun tatmini için üretim, icat ve yaratıcılığı göz önünde bulundurur. Bu yönüyle prefigüratif politikalar açıkça neoliberal-karşıtıdır. Araçlarımıza *kendi araçlarımız olarak*, sonu olmayan araçlar olarak el konmasıdır. Prefigürasyon bir arada yaşamayı ve radikal eşitler olarak bir arada olmakla gelen coşkuyu kucaklamaktır—aşkın bir ütopya veya "hiçbir yer" boş vaadine giden yolda öncüler ve proletarya olarak değil, fakat "eskinin kabuğunda", burada ve şimdi yeni bir dünya yaratmanın ayakları yere basan içkinliği olarak ve bunun gerektirdiği sürekli ve meşakkatli çalışma ve yeniden doğrulama ile[13].

Neoliberalizmde saygımızı hak eden hiçbir şey yok, böylece yaratıcılığın prefigüratif politikalarla da uyumlu olarak, mesajım basitçe "siktir et". Siyasi tahayyüllerimize koyduğu sınırları siktir et. Yol açtığı şiddeti siktir et. Bir erdemmiş gibi göklere çıkardığı eşitsizlikleri siktir et. Çevreyi yağmalayışını siktir et. Bitmek bilmeyen biriktirme döngüsünü ve büyüme kültünü siktir et.

Mont Pelerin topluluğunu ve neoliberalizmi destekle-
yen ve yükseltmeye devam eden diğer bütün düşünce
kuruluşlarını siktir et. Bizi fikirlerine maruz bıraktık-
ları için Friedrich Hayek ve Milton Friedman'ı siktir et.
Thatcher'ları, Raegan'ları, sadece kendi çıkarlarını kol-
layan tüm açgözlü, korkak, bencil politikacıları siktir
et. "Öteki"leri sadece tuvaletlerimizi temizlemeye ve
yerlerimizi silmeye layık gören ama toplumumuzun bir
üyesi olarak görmeyen, korku tacirliği yapan ayrımcılığı
siktir et. Ölçübilime doğru giderek yoğunlaşan hareketi
ve her önemli şeyin ölçülebilir olmadığını anlamayışla-
rını siktir et. Toplumun ihtiyaçları üzerinden kar etme
arzusunu siktir et. Neoliberalizmin temsil ettiği her şeyi
siktir et, ve içinde ilerlediği Truva atını da siktir et! Bize
çok uzun zamandır "bir alternatifi olmadığı", "yükse-
len bir dalganın tüm gemileri kaldıracağı", yaşadığımız
dünyanın "güçlü olanın ayakta kalacağı" bir Darwinist
kabus olduğu söyleniyor. "Müştereklerin trajedisi" fikrini
tamamen içselleştirdik; oysa gerçekte bu "kapitalizmin
trajedisi"ni ve sonsuz yağma savaşlarını yansıtan bir
aldatmacadan başka bir şey değil[14]. Garrett Hardin'in[15]
Aşil topuğu, otlayan büyükbaş hayvanların nasıl halihazırda özel mülk olduğu hakkında düşünmekten asla
vazgeçmemesiydi. Peki asıl müşterekleri özel mülkiyet
varsayımları olmayan *müşterekler* olarak yeniden bir araya
getirsek neler olabilir[16]? Halihazırda gerçekleşmekte olan
ve bu deneyimlere en önemli örgütlenme biçimleri olarak
öncelik veren alternatiflerin prefigürasyonuna daha çok
dikkatimizi versek, neler olabilir[17]? Rekabet ve liyakatin
acı ilacını yutmak yerine, enerjimizi neoliberal reçete-
lerle kendimizi uyuşturmaya değil, işbirliği ve karşılıklı
yardımlaşmayla gelen daha derin bir iyileşmeye odakla-
sak neler olabilir[18]?

Jamie Peck[19] bir defasında neoliberalizmi "radikal
bir politik slogan" olarak tanımlamıştı, fakat eleştiri

dünyasında yaşamak artık yeterli değil. Düşmanımızı ilk kez tespit edişimizin üzerinden yıllar geçti, o zamandan bugüne yazılarımız ve protestolarımızla onu iyi tanır hale geldik. Fakat hezimetinden emin olduğumuz zamanlarda bile—2008 finansal krizi ve ardından gelen Occupy hareketiyle olacağını düşündüğümüz gibi—nefes almaya çalışıyor ve daha da güçlü ve zombileşen bir biçimde kendini yeniden canlandırmaya devam ediyor[20]. Japhy Wilson[21] bu süreklilik arz eden gücü "neoliberal gotik" olarak adlandırıyor. Bu korku gösterisinin üstesinden gelebilmek için politikalarımızı hayata geçirici alana kaydırmamız gerektiğine kaniyim[22]. Peki "neoliberalizmi siktiret" yeni türde bir politikanın mantrasına dönüşse ne olur? Sadece eyleme çağıran değil, içinde yaşadığımız zaman ve mekanlar içerisinde hayatlarımızı geri isteyen bir ifade olarak? Bu ifadeyi her kullanışımızda, sadece lafta kalmayan, hayata geçirici bir eylemliliğe çağrıda bulunan, teori ile pratiği prefigürasyonun harikulade praksisinde birleştiren bir anlam taşıdığını teslim etsek ne olur? Neoliberalizmi reddedişimizde çok yönlü bir yönteme başvurmamız gerekiyor. Onu tamamıyla yok sayamıyor veya unutamıyorsak da, retoriğin performansı veya performansın retoriğinin ötesine uzanan yöntemlerle aleyhine çalışabiliriz. Haydi yeni bir radikal politik slogan geliştirelim. #fuckneoliberalism—#neoliberalizmisiktiret hashtag'ini kullanarak hor görümüzü *viral* hale getirin! Fakat kızgınlığımızı dile getirmekten daha fazlasını yapmalıyız. Kararımızı hayata geçirmeli ve umutlarımızı şimdi ve burada bedenleşmiş deneyimlerimizin içkinliği olarak gerçekleştirmeliyiz[23]. Dünyayı kendimiz yeniden yaratmalıyız—ertelenemeyecek bir süreç bu.

Mevcut politik temsillerin düzenine başvurmaya devam ederek, kendi iradamizle kendimizi yanılttık ve güçsüzleştirdik. Kör imanımız yüzünden gökten bir kurtarıcının inmesini bekleyip durduk. Sistem, kendisinin ne kadar yoz olduğunu ispatladı, bel bağladığımız büyük politikacı adaylarımız yeniden ve yeniden fiyaskoya dönüştüler. Bu neoliberal moment içinde mesele sadece sorunlu bireylerin iktidarda olması değildir. Bilakis, sistemin bizatihi kendisinin sorunun özünün bir örneği olduğuna inanıyoruz. "Lucifer etkisi"nin vuku bulması için kurumsal koşulları üretiyor ve olanaklı hale getiriyoruz[24]. "Kötülüğün sıradanlığı" öyle bir şey ki, bu politikacılar, iktidarın suiistimal edilişini ödüllendiren bir sistem dahilinde sadece işlerini yapıyorlar; çünkü tüm bunlar kapitalizmin kanunlarına hizmet edecek şekilde tasarlanmış durumda[25]. Fakat itaat etmek zorunda değiliz. Bu düzene bir şey borçlu değiliz. Doğrudan eylemlerimizle ve alternatifleri örgütlemekle tüm yapıyı itham edebilir ve bu sömürü kısır döngüsünü kırabiliriz. Siyasal sistem kapitalizm tarafından tanımlandığında, koşullandığına, içeriden sarmalandığında ve ondan türediğinde, asla bizim bilme ve dünyada olma biçimlerimizi yansıtamaz; bu yüzden bu yaşam biçimlerinin dizginlerini elimize almalı ve kolektif eylemliliğimizi geri almalıyız. Politikalarımızda hayata geçirici olmaya ve dayanışmanın daha ilişkisel anlamlarını, bir kişinin itaat ettirilmesinin ve acı çekmesinin aslında herkesin baskılanmasının bir işareti olduğu anlamını kucaklamaya başlamalıyız[26]. Demokrasiyi etimolojik anlamıyla, yani *gücü halka* veren anlamıyla yeniden düzenleyen karşılıklı yardımlaşma, yoldaşlık, karşılıklılık ve hiyerarşisiz örgütlenme biçimleri gibi pratiklerle yenileyeceğimiz bir bağlılıkla, başka olanaklı dünyalarda yaşamaya başlayabiliriz. Nihayetinde neoliberalizm, pek çok hoyrat sonuçlarla ve kaba varsayımlarla birlikte gelen, özellikle kokuşmuş bir fikirdir. Karşılık olarak da eşit derecede rencide edici bir dille ve eylemlerle karşılanmayı hak etmektedir. Topluluğumuz, işbirliğimiz ve birbirimize verdiğimiz önem, hepsi neoliberalizm için nefret edilesi şeylerdir. Neoliberalizm bizim kutladığımız şeylerden nefret eder. Bu yüzden "neolibe-ralizmi siktir et" dediğimizde, bu salt sözcüklerden öte, birbirimize olan adanmışlığımızın kabulü olsun. Yüksek sesle söyleyin, benimle birlikte söyleyin, dinleyecek olan herkese söyleyin ve hepsinden önemlisi, eyleme bir açık çağrı ve bu boktan dünyayı değiştirmek için sahip oldu-ğumuz prefigüratif gücümüzün vücut bulmuş sesi olarak söyleyin. *Neoliberalizmi siktir edin!*

Notes

1   Simon Springer, "The Nonillusory Effects of Neoliberalisation: Linking Geographies of Poverty, Inequality, and Violence," *Geoforum* 39, no. 4 (July 2008): 1520–25; Simon Springer, "Renewed Authoritarianism in Southeast Asia: Undermining Democracy through Neoliberal Reform," *Asia Pacific Viewpoint* 50, no. 3 (December 2009): 271–76; Simon Springer, "Articulated Neoliberalism: The Specificity of Patronage, Kleptocracy, and Violence in Cambodia's Neoliberalization,"*Environment and Planning A* 43, no. 11 (November 2011): 2554–70; Simon Springer, "Neoliberalism," in Klaus Dodds, Merje Kuus, and Joanne Sharp, eds., *The Ashgate Research Companion to Critical Geopolitics* (Burlington, VT: Ashgate, 2013), 147–64; Simon Springer, *Violent Neoliberalism: Development, Discourse and Dispossession in Cambodia* (New York: Palgrave MacMillan, 2015); Simon Springer, Kean Birch, and Julie MacLeavy, "An Introduction to Neoliberalism," in Simon Springer, Kean Birch, and Julie MacLeavy, eds., *The Handbook of Neoliberalism* (New York: Routledge, 2016), 1–14.
2   Simon Springer, *The Discourse of Neoliberalism: An Anatomy of a Powerful Idea* (Lanham, MD: Rowman & Littlefield, 2016).
3   Simon Springer, "Neoliberalism and Geography: Expansions, Variegations, Formations," *Geography Compass* 4, no. 8 (August 2010): 1025–38.
4   Kieran Healy, "Fuck Nuance," *Sociological Theory* 35, no. 2 (2017), accessed September 9, 2020, https://kieranhealy.org/files/papers/fuck-nuance.pdf.
5   David Graeber, *Direct Action: An Ethnography* (Oakland: AK Press, 2009).
6   J.K. Gibson-Graham, *The End of Capitalism (as We Knew It): A Feminist Critique of Political Economy* (Minneapolis: University of Minnesota Press, 1996).
7   Mark Purcell, "Our New Arms," in Springer, Birch, and MacLeavy, eds., *The Handbook of Neoliberalism*, 620.
8   Marianne Maeckelbergh, "Doing Is Believing: Prefiguration as Strategic Practice in the Alterglobalization Movement," *Social Movement Studies* 10, no. 1 (January 2011): 1–20.
9   Carl Boggs, "Marxism, Prefigurative Communism, and the Problem of Workers' Control," *Radical America* 11, no. 6 (1977): 99–122.
10 Clive Barnett, "The Consolations of 'Neoliberalism,'" *Geoforum* 36, no. 1 (January 2005): 7–12, accessed September 9, 2020, https://www.researchgate.net/publication/50952798_The_Consolations_of_

Neoliberalism; Kean Birch, *We Have Never Been Neoliberal: A Manifesto for a Doomed Youth* (Alresford, UK: Zero Books, 2015); Nick Lewis, "Progressive Spaces of Neoliberalism?" *Asia Pacific Viewpoint* 50, no. 2 (August 2009): pp. 113–19, accessed September 9, 2020, https://onlinelibrary.wiley.com/doi/full/10.1111/j.1467-8373.2009.01387.x; Aihwa Ong, "Neoliberalism as a Mobile Technology," *Transactions of the Institute of British Geographers* 32, no. 1 (January 2007): pp. 3–8.

11　David Harvey, "'Listen, Anarchist!' A Personal Response to Simon Springer's 'Why a Radical Geography Must Be Anarchist,'" DavidHarvey.org, June 10, 2015, accessed September 9, 2020, http://davidharvey.org/2015/06/listen-anarchist-by-david-harvey.

12　Simon Springer, "Anarchism! What Geography Still Ought to Be," *Antipode* 44, no. 5 (November 2012): 1605–24.

13　Anthony Ince, "In the Shell of the Old: Anarchist Geographies of Territorialisation," *Antipode*, 44, no. 5, (November 2012): 1645–66.

14　Philippe le Billon, *Wars of Plunder: Conflicts, Profits and the Politics of Resources* (New York: Columbia University Press, 2012).

15　Garrett Hardin, "The Tragedy of the Commons," *Science* 162, no. 3859 (1968): 1243–48.

16　Sandra Jeppesen, Anna Kruzynski, Rachel Sarrasin, and Émile Breton, "The Anarchist Commons," *Ephemera* 14, no. 4 (2014): 879–900, accessed September 9, 2020, http://www.mediaactionresearch.org/wp-content/uploads/2015/02/Anarchist-Commons-FINAL.pdf.

17　Richard J. White and Colin C. Williams, "The Pervasive Nature of Heterodox Economic Spaces at a Time of Neoliberal Crisis: Toward a 'Postneoliberal' Anarchist Future," *Antipode* 44, no. 5 (November 2012): 1625–44, accessed September 9, 2020, https://tinyurl.com/y5hka69d.

18　Jamie Heckert, "Listening, Caring, Becoming: Anarchism as an Ethics of Direct Relationships," in Benjamin Franks and Matthew Wilson, eds., *Anarchism and Moral Philosophy* (New York: Palgrave Macmillan, 2010), 186–207.

19　Jamie Peck, "Geography and Public Policy: Constructions of Neoliberalism," *Progress in Human Geography* 28, no. 3 (June 2004): 403, accessed September 9, 2020, https://www.researchgate.net/publication/246313893_Geography_and_Public_Policy_Constructions_of_Neoliberalism.

20　Colin Crouch, *The Strange Non-Death of Neoliberalism* (Malden, MA: Polity Press, 2011); Jamie Peck, "Zombie Neoliberalism and the Ambidextrous State," *Theoretical Criminology* 14, no. 1 (February 2010): 104–10, accessed September 9, 2020, https://www.researchgate.net/publication/240707442_Zombie_neoliberalism_and_the_ambidextrous_state.

21　Japhny Wilson, "Neoliberal Gothic," in Springer, Birch, and MacLeavy eds., *The Handbook of Neoliberalism* (2016), 592–602.

22　Toby Rollo, "Democracy, Agency and Radical Children's Geographies," in Richard J. White, Simon Springer, and Marcelo Lopes de Souza, eds., *The Practice of Freedom: Anarchism, Geography and the Spirit of Revolt*, vol. 3 (Lanham, MD: Rowman & Littlefield, 2016), chapter 10.

23 Simon Springer, *The Anarchist Roots of Geography: Toward Spatial Emancipation* (Minneapolis: University of Minnesota Press, 2016).

24 Philip Zimbardo, *The Lucifer Effect: Understanding How Good People Turn Evil* (New York: Random House, 2007).

25 Hannah Arendt, *Eichmann in Jerusalem: A Report on the Banality of Evil* (New York: Viking Press, 1971).

26 Deric Shannon and J. Rouge, "Refusing to Wait: Anarchism and Intersectionality," Anarkismo, November 11, 2009, accessed September 9, 2020, http://anarkismo.net/article/14923; Simon Springer, "War and Pieces," *Space and Polity* 18, no. 1 (February 2014): 85–96, accessed September 9, 2020, https://www.researchgate.net/publication/235338274_War_and_Pieces.

About the Contributors

Simon Springer

Simon Springer is professor of human geography and director of the Centre for Urban and Regional Studies at the University of Newcastle, Australia. His research explores the social and political exclusions that neoliberalism has engendered, particularly in post-transitional Cambodia, where he emphasizes the geographies of violence and power. He cultivates a cutting-edge theoretical approach to his scholarship by foregrounding both post-structuralist critique and a radical revival of anarchist geographies.

Ed Repka

Ed Repka is regarded as the undisputed king of "thrash" metal art. He specializes in menacing reminders of impending apocalypse and grim visions of the irradiated aftermath. His vibrant abuse of color and shadow combined with darkly satirical characterizations form his distinctive style. His illustrations have adorned the cover art and merchandise of countless bands, including Megadeth, Atheist, Nuclear Assault, Death, Possessed, 3 Inches of Blood, Sanctuary, Municipal Waste, Agent Steel, Massacre, Vio-Lence, Toxic Holocaust, Gruesome, and many more.

Bengali—Kunaljeet Roy

Kunaljeet Roy is currently a doctoral candidate in the Geography Department, West Bengal State University. Besides teaching, Kunajeet has been conducting ongoing research on various issues, including everyday geography, the transformation of urban cultural landscapes, ethnic identity, and overseas Chinese Diaspora, particularly on Kolkata Chinese community, for about a decade. https://wbsubregistration.academia.edu/KunaljeetRoy.

বর্তমানে পশ্চিমবঙ্গ রাষ্ট্রীয় বিশ্ববিদ্যালয়ের ভূগোল বিভাগে গবেষণারত। অধ্যাপনার পাশাপাশি কলকাতার চীনা সম্প্রদায়ের উপর প্রায় এক দশক ধরে একাধিক গবেষণামূলক প্রবন্ধ রচনা করেছেন এবং দৈনন্দিন নগর ভূগোল, সামাজিক ও নৃতাত্ত্বিক নগর বিকাশ, পরিব্রাজন ও পরিযায়ী সংস্কৃতির বিষয়েও গবেষণারত। https://wbsubregistration.academia.edu/KunaljeetRoy.

Farsi—Morteza Gholamzadeh

Morteza Gholamzadeh has written many articles about contemporary urban planning. His publications have been presented at international and national conferences in Iran. His principal research focuses on theories of planning, specifically urban development policy in developing countries. Morteza has more than ten years of professional experience in different aspects of urban and regional planning. He has been working for the Mashhad municipality as an urban planner and consultant.

شهری معاصر به رشته تحریر آورده است.مقالات او در کنفرانس های ملی و بین المللی در ایران چاپ شده است.رشته تحقیقات اصلی او در مورد تئوری های برنامه ریزی و تاکید بر سیاست توسعه شهری در کشورهای در حال توسعه میباشد.همچنین،ایشان دارای ده سال سابقه تخصصی و کاری در حوزه برنامه ریزی شهری و منطقه ای و در حال حاضر بعنوان مشاور شهرسازی در شهرداری مشهد مشغول به فعالیت است.

بیوگرافی:
مرتضی غلامزاده(دانش آموخته دانشگاه شهید بهشتی تهران و
فردوسی مشهد)میباشد.او مقالات متعددی درباره برنامه ریزی

German—Ursula Brandt

Ursula Brandt studied Communication Design and Illustration in Hamburg. She lives in Berlin, where she works as a copyeditor and translator. www.ursulinskaja.wordpress.com.

Ursula Brandt hat in Hamburg Kommunikationsdesign und Illustration studiert. Sie lebt als Lektorin und Übersetzerin in Berlin. www.ursulinskaja.wordpress.com.

Greek—Charalampos Tsavdaroglou

Charalampos Tsavdaroglou is a Marie Curie Fellow—postdoctoral researcher at the University of Amsterdam's (UvA), Department of Human Geography, Planning and International Development (GPIO). Charalampos holds a PhD in Urban and Regional Planning from the School of Architecture, Aristotle University in Thessaloniki (Greece). His research interests include critical urban theory, autonomy of migration, intersectional, decolonial, and affective geographies, the right to the city, common spaces versus spatial enclosures, and urban social movements.

Ο Χαράλαμπος Τσαβδάρολγου είναι Μεταδιδακτορικός Ερευνητής—υπότροφος Marie Curie στο τμήμα Ανθρωπογεωγραφίας, Σχεδιασμού και Διεθνούς Ανάπτυξης του Πανεπιστημίου του Αμστερνταμ. Είναι κάτοχος Διδακτορικού διπλώματος Πολεοδομίας-Χωροταξίας από το τμήμα Αρχιτεκτόνων Μηχανικών του Αριστοτελείου Πανεπιστημίου Θεσσαλονίκης. Τα ερευνητικά του ενδιαφέροντα περιλαμβάνουν την κριτική αστική θεωρία, την αυτονομία της μετανάστευσης, διαθεματικές, αποαποικιακές και συναισθηματικές γεωγραφίες, το δικαίωμα στην πόλη, κοινοί χώροι έναντι χωρικών περιφράξεων και τα κοινωνικά κινήματα πόλης.

Hindi—Jai Kaushal

Dr. Jai Kaushal is a professor and department head at Hindi Assam University. He has published extensively on Hindi language, literature, and translation.

Indonesian—Okty Budiati

Okty Budiati is an experimental raw performance artist, an individual anarchist, and a writer of poetry and memoir. https://nightforestpoetry.wordpress.com/tag/okty-budiati.

Okty Budiati, lahir di Jakarta 13 Oktober 1977, adalah seniman performa untuk experimental raw, seorang individual anarkis, dan penulis puisi serta memoar. https://nightforestpoetry.wordpress.com/tag/okty-budiati.

Italian—Fabrizio Eva

Fabrizio Eva is a political geographer and annual contract professor at the University of Venice—Cà Foscari, Treviso campus, where he teaches a course in political and economic geography. His academic interests include current geopolitical dynamics, cultural ethnonationalisms, political and economic dynamics in China, Japan, and North and South Korea, and the modern "anarchist approach" to geopolitics. http://fabrizio-eva.info.

Japanese—Sayuri Watanabe

Born in Hakushu, Yamanashi, Japan, Sayuri Watanabe completed her bachelor's degree in English at Kansai Gaidai University in 2000. She has worked as a translator since 2002. She currently lives in the countryside, aiming for self-sufficient living with her family.

山梨県白州町生まれ。2000年、関西外国語大学において英語の学士号を取得。2002年より翻訳の仕事に携わって

いる。現在、家族とともに、自給自足の生活を目指して田舎生活を満喫中。

Khmer—Kanha SOK

Kanha SOK was born and raised in Cambodia. "If there is one thing to know about me, it is that I respect people who are respectful to others regardless of their background. Not everything can be chosen, but I believe we can totally choose to respect someone. With respect, we can live a harmonious life." https://linkedin.com/in/kanha-sok-6aa7b3119.

Korean—Jane Yeonjae Lee

Jane Yeonjae Lee is a research associate in the Department of Geography at Kyung Hee University. Her research revolves around transnational skilled migrants, ethnic communities, mobilities, urban environmental politics, and smart urbanism for socially marginalized groups. Her work on migration, mobilities, and cities has been published in *Health and Place, Asian Survey, Journal of Ethnic and Migration Studies, New Zealand Geographer, Transactions of the Institute of British Geographers, Geography Compass, Elgar Handbook on Medical Tourism and Patient Mobility,* and *Contemporary Ethnic Geographies in America.* She is the author of *Transnational Return Migration of 1.5 Generation Korean New Zealanders: A Quest for Home* (Lexington Books, 2018).

Nepali—Binod Neupane

Binod Neupane is a researcher in the field of globalization, federalism, and decentralization who is affiliated with different institutions at Tribhuvan University, Nepal, and with a number of NGOs.

Polish—Filip Brzeźniak

Filip Brzeźniak is a sociologist, philosopher, activist, and student of Inter-Faculty Individual Studies in the Humanities at Jagiellonian University, Kraków, Poland. Among his interests are plebeian political culture, the history of melancholy, the philosophy of Walter Benjamin and Giorgio Agamben, Theweleitian research on fascism and misogyny, and the history of Marxism and anarchism. https://costam.academia.edu/FilipBrze%C5%BAniak.

Filip Brzeźniak—socjolog, filozof, działacz społeczny, student studiów uzupełniających magisterskich w ramach MISH na Uniwersytecie Jagiellońskim. Do zainteresowań badawczych należą między innymi plebejska kultura polityczna, historia melancholii, filozofia Waltera Benjamina i Giorgio Agambena, Theweleitowskie badania nad faszyzmem i mizoginią, dzieje marksizmu i anarchizmu.

Portuguese—Eduardo Tomazine

Eduardo Tomazine holds a PhD in Geography and has studied urban problems and social movements in Brazil and Latin America. More recently, he has sought to understand the connections between the proliferation of paramilitary militias and the social management of barbarity under neoliberalism in the capitalist periphery.

Slovak—Patrik Gažo

Patrik Gažo is a PhD student at the Department of Environmental Studies at Masaryk University. He deals with the relationships and contradictions between the interests of the working class and climate change. He specializes in the so-called green and just transition of industrial production. Specifically, he examines the role of workers in the automotive industry in Slovakia during the socioecological transformation.

Patrik Gažo je doktorand na Katedre environmentálnych štúdií na Masarykovej univerzite. Zaoberá sa kontradikciami a vzťahmi medzi záujmami triedy pracujúcich a klimatickou zmenou. Špecializuje sa na problematiku tzv. zeleného a spravodlivého prechodu priemyselnej výroby a konkrétne skúma úlohu pracujúcich v automobilovom priemysle na Slovensku počas sociálno-ekologickej transformácie.

Spanish—xaranta baksh

xaranta baksh is a freelance photographer from Trinidad and Toabgo. For the past seven years, she has been engaging with various land and waterscapes, people, and objects. She has a dual focus in photojournalism and abstract photography.

xaranta baksh es fotógrafa independiente de Trinidad y Tobago. Por los últimos 7 años ha trabajado con varios objetos, personas y paisajes. Le interesan mucho el fotoperiodismo y la fotografía abstracta.

Swedish—Aeron Bergman and Alejandra Salinas

Aeron Bergman and Alejandra Salinas live in Portland, Oregon, and collaborate as artists, writers, editors, curators, teachers, and parents and currently run an Low Residency MFA in Visual Studies at Pacific Northwest College of Art. www.alejandra-aeron.com. www.incainstitute.org.

Aeron Bergman och Alejandra Salinas bor i Portland, Oregon och samarbetar som konstnärer, författare, redaktörer, kuratorer, lärare, föräldrar, och driver Low Residency MFA i visuella studier vid Pacific Northwest College of Art.

Turkish—Gürçim Yılmaz & Nezihe Başak Ergin

Gürçim Yılmaz is an independent writer, translator, and researcher based in Istanbul. Her fiction and non-fiction writing has been featured in various magazines and on various platforms, nationally and internationally. She is currently working toward a wider interdisciplinary collaborative project with Deniz Uster, alongside her editorial practice. Yılmaz holds a BA in Journalism from Ankara University and an MS in Media and Cultural Studies from Middle Eastern Technical University, Ankara.

Gürçim Yılmaz bağımsız yazar, çevirmen ve araştırmacı olarak İstanbul'da çalışmalarına devam etmektedir. Kurmaca ve kurmaca-dışı metinleri, çeşitli ulusal ve uluslararası mecra ve platformlarda yayımlanmıştır. Editoryal çalışmalarının yanı sıra, sanatçı Deniz Üster ile birlikte interdisipliner işler üretmektedir. Yılmaz, Ankara Üniversitesi'nde Gazetecilik lisans eğitiminin ardından, yüksek lisansını Ortadoğu Teknik Üniversitesi, Medya ve Kültürel Çalışmalar programında tamamlamıştır.

Nezihe Başak Ergin is an assistant professor in the Sociology Department at Giresun University, Turkey. She has published extensively on urban sociology, urbanization, planning, and gender and is a contributor to *IDEALKENT* and *Moment Journal*.

ABOUT PM PRESS

PM Press is an independent, radical publisher of books and media to educate, entertain, and inspire. Founded in 2007 by a small group of people with decades of publishing, media, and organizing experience, PM Press amplifies the voices of radical authors, artists, and activists. Our aim is to deliver bold political ideas and vital stories to all walks of life and arm the dreamers to demand the impossible. We have sold millions of copies of our books, most often one at a time, face to face. We're old enough to know what we're doing and young enough to know what's at stake. Join us to create a better world.

PM Press
PO Box 23912
Oakland, CA 94623
www.pmpress.org

PM Press in Europe
europe@pmpress.org
www.pmpress.org.uk

FRIENDS OF PM PRESS

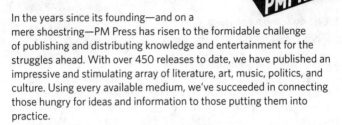

These are indisputably momentous times—the financial system is melting down globally and the Empire is stumbling. Now more than ever there is a vital need for radical ideas.

In the years since its founding—and on a mere shoestring—PM Press has risen to the formidable challenge of publishing and distributing knowledge and entertainment for the struggles ahead. With over 450 releases to date, we have published an impressive and stimulating array of literature, art, music, politics, and culture. Using every available medium, we've succeeded in connecting those hungry for ideas and information to those putting them into practice.

Friends of PM allows you to directly help impact, amplify, and revitalize the discourse and actions of radical writers, filmmakers, and artists. It provides us with a stable foundation from which we can build upon our early successes and provides a much-needed subsidy for the materials that can't necessarily pay their own way. You can help make that happen—and receive every new title automatically delivered to your door once a month—by joining as a Friend of PM Press. And, we'll throw in a free T-shirt when you sign up.

Here are your options:

- **$30 a month** Get all books and pamphlets plus 50% discount on all webstore purchases

- **$40 a month** Get all PM Press releases (including CDs and DVDs) plus 50% discount on all webstore purchases

- **$100 a month** Superstar—Everything plus PM merchandise, free downloads, and 50% discount on all webstore purchases

For those who can't afford $30 or more a month, we have **Sustainer Rates** at $15, $10 and $5. Sustainers get a free PM Press T-shirt and a 50% discount on all purchases from our website.

Your Visa or Mastercard will be billed once a month, until you tell us to stop. Or until our efforts succeed in bringing the revolution around. Or the financial meltdown of Capital makes plastic redundant. Whichever comes first.

Anarchy, Geography, Modernity: Selected Writings of Elisée Reclus

Edited by John P. Clark and
Camille Martin

ISBN: 978-1-60486-429-8
$22.95   304 pages

Anarchy, Geography, Modernity is the first
comprehensive introduction to the thought of Elisée Reclus, the great
anarchist geographer and political theorist. It shows him to be an
extraordinary figure for his age. Not only an anarchist but also a radical
feminist, anti-racist, ecologist, animal rights advocate, cultural radical,
nudist, and vegetarian. Not only a major social thinker but also a
dedicated revolutionary.

The work analyzes Reclus' greatest achievement, a sweeping historical
and theoretical synthesis recounting the story of the earth and
humanity as an epochal struggle between freedom and domination. It
presents his groundbreaking critique of all forms of domination: not
only capitalism, the state, and authoritarian religion, but also patriarchy,
racism, technological domination, and the domination of nature. His
crucial insights on the interrelation between personal and small-
group transformation, broader cultural change, and large-scale social
organization are explored. Reclus' ideas are presented both through
detailed exposition and analysis, and in extensive translations of key
texts, most appearing in English for the first time.

*"For far too long Elisée Reclus has stood in the shadow of Godwin, Proudhon,
Bakunin, Kropotkin, and Emma Goldman. Now John Clark has pulled Reclus
forward to stand shoulder to shoulder with Anarchism's cynosures. Reclus'
light brought into anarchism's compass not only a focus on ecology, but a
struggle against both patriarchy and racism, contributions which can now
be fully appreciated thanks to John Clark's exegesis and [his and Camille
Martin's] translations of works previously unavailable in English. No serious
reader can afford to neglect this book."*
—Dana Ward, Pitzer College

*"Finally! A century after his death, the great French geographer and anarchist
Elisée Reclus has been honored by a vibrant selection of his writings expertly
translated into English."*
—Kent Mathewson, Louisiana State University